MONEY IN STOCKS

ARVIND UPADHYAY

Copyright © Arvind Upadhyay
All Rights Reserved.

This book has been published with all efforts taken to make the material error-free after the consent of the author. However, the author and the publisher do not assume and hereby disclaim any liability to any party for any loss, damage, or disruption caused by errors or omissions, whether such errors or omissions result from negligence, accident, or any other cause.

While every effort has been made to avoid any mistake or omission, this publication is being sold on the condition and understanding that neither the author nor the publishers or printers would be liable in any manner to any person by reason of any mistake or omission in this publication or for any action taken or omitted to be taken or advice rendered or accepted on the basis of this work. For any defect in printing or binding the publishers will be liable only to replace the defective copy by another copy of this work then available.

This book is dedicated to my mother Rajeshwari

After the market debacles of 2000 and 2008, most investors now know that they need to take charge and learn much more about what they're doing when they save and invest their hard-earned money. However, many investors don't know where to turn, whom to trust, or what they must stop doing if they are to achieve dramatically superior investment performance.

You should buy stocks when they're on the way up in price, not on the way down. And when you buy more, you do it only after the stock has risen from your purchase price, not after it has fallen below it. You buy stocks when they're nearer to their highs for the year, not when they've sunk so low that they look cheap. You buy higher-priced stocks rather than the lowest-priced stocks. You learn to always sell stocks quickly when you have a small loss rather than waiting and hoping they'll come back. You pay far less attention to a company's book value, dividends, or PE ratio —which for the last 100 years have had little predictive value in spotting America's most successful companies—and focus instead on more important proven factors such as profit growth, price and volume action, and whether the company is the number one profit leader in its field with a superior product.

You don't subscribe to a bunch of market newsletters or advisory services, and you don't let yourself be influenced by recommendations from analysts, who, after all, are just expressing personal opinions that can frequently be wrong. You also have to acquaint yourself with charts—an invaluable tool most professionals wouldn't do without but amateurs tend to dismiss as complicated or irrelevant. All these vital actions are completely contrary to human nature. In reality, the stock market is human nature and crowd psychology on daily display, plus the age-old law of supply and demand at work. Because these factors have remained the same over time, it is remarkable but true that chart patterns are just the same today as they were 50 years ago or 100 years ago. Few investors know or understand this. It can be to your inspiring advantage.

Contents

Foreword

The money you earn is partly spent and the rest saved for meeting future expenses. Instead of keeping the savings idle you may like to use savings in order to get return on it in the future. This is called Investment. • One needs to invest to 1. earn return on your idle resources 2. generate a specified sum of money for a specific goal in life 3. make a provision for an uncertain future When to Start Investing • The sooner one starts investing the better. By investing early you allow your investments more time to grow, increases your income, by accumulating the principal and the interest or dividend earned on it, year after year. • The three golden rules for all investors are: 1. Invest early 2. Invest regularly 3. Invest for long term and not short term Where to Invest • One may invest in: 1. Physical assets like real estate, gold/ jewellery, commodities etc 2. Financial assets such as fixed deposits with banks, small saving instruments with post offices, insurance/provident/ pension fund etc or securities market related instruments like shares, bonds, debentures etc. Short & Long Term Options for Investment • Short Term: 1. Savings Bank Account 2. Money Market or Liquid Funds 3. Fixed Deposit with Banks • Long Term: 1. Post Office Savings 2. Public Provident Fund 3. Bonds 4. Mutual Funds Before investing in a Market • Before investing, it is always wise to learn the Basics of Stock Market. We have compiled articles and tutorials on the Share Market Basics. Also included here explanation of Stock Market Terms and jargon used by people involved in trading stocks and shares. Whether it is Bombay Stock Exchange (BSE), National Stock Exchange (NSE), London Stock Exchange (LSE) or New York Stock Exchange (NYSE), trading terms or more or less similar Why Trade In Stock Market • 1. You do not need a lot of money to start making money, unlike buying property and paying a monthly mortgage. • 2. It requires very minimal time to trade - unlike building a conventional business • 3. It's 'fast' cash and allows for quick liquidation (You can convert it to cash easily, unlike selling a property or a business). • 4. It's easy to learn how to profit from the stock market. But You need to have your basics clear. Unless you do....you will be wasting your time and loosing money. You need to be crystal clear of each and every aspect of Investments, stock options, Stock Trading, Company, Shares, Dividend & Types of Shares, Debentures, Securities, Mutual Funds, IPO, Futures & Options, What does the Share Market consist of? Exchanges, Indices, SEBI , Analysis of Stocks – How to check on what to buy?, Trading Terms (Limit Order, Stop Loss, Put, Call, Booking Profit & Loss, Short & Long), Trading Options – Brokerage Houses etc. Stock Market System • Primary market • stock market is a secondary market • trade stock for listed corporations • Progressive development of stock market Primary Market • The primary market provides the channel for sale of new securities. Primary market provides opportunity to issuers of securities; Government as well as corporate to raise resources to meet their requirements of investment and/or discharge some obligation. • They may issue the securities at face value, or at a discount/premium and these securities may take a variety of forms such as equity, debt etc. They may issue the securities in domestic market and/or international market Why Companies need to issue shares to Public • Most companies are usually started privately by their promoter(s). However, the promoters' capital and the borrowings from banks and financial institutions may not be sufficient for setting up or running the business over a long term. So companies invite the public to contribute towards the equity and issue shares to individual investors. • The way to invite share capital from the public is through a 'Public Issue'. Simply stated, a public issue is an offer to the public to subscribe to the share capital of a company. Once this is done, the company allots shares to the applicants as per the prescribed rules and regulations laid down by SEBI. Secondary Market • Secondary market refers to a market where securities are traded after being initially offered to the public in the primary market and/or listed on the Stock Exchange. Majority of the trading is done in the secondary market. Secondary market comprises of equity markets and the debt markets • Difference between Primary and Secondary Market is In Primary Market securities are offered to public for subscription for the purpose of raising capital or fund Secondary Market is an equity trading venue in which already existing/pre-issued securities are traded among investors. Equity Investment • When you buy a share of a company you become a shareholder in that company. Shares are also known as Equities. Equities have the potential to increase in value over time. It also provides your portfolio with the growth necessary to reach your long term investment goals. Research studies have proved that the equities have outperformed most other forms of investments in the long term. • Equities are considered the most challenging and the rewarding, when compared to other investment options. • Research studies have proved that investments in some shares with a longer tenure of investment have yielded far superior returns than any other investment. • However, this does not mean all equity investments would guarantee similar high returns. Equities are high risk investments. One needs to study them carefully before investing Types of investors • Speculators • Hedgers • Arbitragers

1

Stock-Picking Secrets

Don't worry if you're a new investor and don't understand these charts at first. After all, every successful investor was a beginner at some point—and this book will show you how to spot key buying opportunities on the charts, as well as critical signals that a stock should be sold. To succeed you need to learn sound, historically proven buy rules plus sell rules. As you study these charts you'll see there are specific chart patterns that are repeated over and over again whether in 1900 or 2000. This will give you a huge advantage once you learn to recognize these patterns that in effect tell you when a stock is under professional accumulation. It is the unique combination of your finding stocks with big increases in sales, earnings and return on equity plus strong chart patterns revealing institutional buying that together will materially improve your stock selection and timing. The best professionals use charts. You too can learn this valuable skill.

2

Who are Investors?

The truth is that WE ARE ALL investors. When we hear the word investors, we may think of a high-fying Wall-Street banker in a blue-pin striped suit. Tat is certainly one type of investor, but so is the business owner, the family trying to save for their kids' college, and the college student trying to scrape up enough quarters to eat dinner. We all need to manage the money we make, and we all hope to end up with as much money as possible. Te question of building wealth in your life will really boil down to two questions? 1) Are you able to save each year? 2) When you save, where do you put the money? Hypothetical Let's assume you're 20 years old and just took a job as a freman, your childhood dream (what kid doesn't want to be a freman, right?). Your salary is meager, but you make the goal to save $1,000 dollars per year and put it in a retirement account. You work and save for the next 50 years until you retire. Does it really matter where I put that money, I mean it's only a thousand bucks a year? Well you have a couple of options, let's evaluate. 1). Te savings Account (otherwise known as the "Under the Mattress" approach). Te easiest and "safest" thing is you could just put the money in cash. Nice and safe! It will never go away and it won't go up and down. Average Annual Return: 0% Amount Accumulated in 50 Years: $50,000 2). Bonds or Real Estate. Most people say that they get most of their retirement funds from investing in their home and watching it increase in value. Or investing in bonds. Both of these options will grow in line with infation, which on average is about 3% per year. Average Annual Return: 3% Amount Accumulated in 50 Years: $116,000.

3). Te Stock Market. Scary, right? It goes up and down. Tere are times when it can decline by 20% in a short period of time, inducing panic and scary headlines. But over time, the stock market grows with how fast corporations grow. In every ten year period, the stock market earns you 8-10% returns. In fact, over the last century, the S&P 500 (the largest 500 companies in the US) have returned 9.8% per year. Average Annual Return: 9.8% Amount Accumulated in 50 Years: $1,359,199 So does it really matter where you put your money? Uh, yeah! It makes all the diference in the world. In fact, the more money that you can put in the stock market early, the more the magnifying efect of "compound interest" or "compounding" can work in your favor. "Compound interest is the eighth wonder of the world" -Albert Einstein Now, I know what you're thinking. If going from 3% to 10% return gets me an extra million dollars, what does getting a 20% return do? Warren Bufett, the legendary investor, for example earned 30% return over a period of 30 years. (called the famous "30/30"). 4). Beating the Market. Tis isn't easy, it isn't for everyone, but let's say you take a few hours per week, and you do your homework, and invest in some exceptional companies through the stock market, and earn an extraordinary 20% return per year. Tis is a very high return (even 12% per year is quite a feat) but let's just assume you're really good at fnding great stocks. Average Annual Return: 20% Amount Accumulated in 50 Years: $109,826,119 (Yes, that's over $100 million dollars) Tat's a huge fortune for a freman saving just $1k per year. So, now you know why you heard your dad's friend bragging that he "beat the market" on his investment portfolio last year. Te diference between 3% and 10% may seem small, but it makes all the diference in the world towards building wealth. Starting Early Compound interest is a powerful efect, and the EARLIER you start investing the more it will work for you. Consider the example above with the freman, but instead of starting to save at 20 years old, instead he starts to save at 40 years old. Instead of retiring with $1.3 million he will retire with only $190k. Look at the results below assuming he invests in the stock market: Started saving $1,000 per year at ? at Age 40 = $190,773 (at age 70) ? at Age 30 = $535,682 (at age 70) ? at Age 20 = $1,359,199 (at age 70) And then, let's say you join Young Investors Society and start investing when you're 15 years old. What does an extra 5 years get you? ? at Age 15 = $2,224,948 (at age 70) Notice that the diference is almost a million dollars diference if you start just 5 years earlier! In summary, the TWO CRITICAL FACTORS of COMPOUND INTEREST are: 5). Earn a High Return (i.e. the stock market) 6). Start Early And remember, we're all investors, whether we like it or not!

All companies have owners. A small company started by a single individual may have only him or her as the single owner. Te large corporations that have stock (shares that are traded by the general public) have many owners. To simplify and organize the buying and selling of these shares by the general public, companies use the stock market. In fact, US government regulations require that a company, once it reaches a certain number of owners, must go public. Tis is to allow its now large number of owners to be able to buy and sell their shares of stock in the company more easily. Just think about it this way. Let's pretend that your sibling or a close friend is starting a small company. He or she is doing really well, but needs more money (capital) to expand. He or she asks you to become a part owner in the business by investing some of your savings. You agree. Would you try to sell your ownership in the company just a few days later? Most likely not! It should be the same thing when you decide to buy a public company's stock. Te only real diference is that your sibling's or friend's company is a private company with just two shareholders, whereas there are many more owners in a public company with shares in the "stock market." "Without a saving faith in the future, no one would ever invest at all. To be an investor, you must be a believer in a better tomorrow" Benjamin Graham

3

BEATING THE MARKET

To start, let me introduce you to Warren Bufett. Mr. Bufett has been the single most successful investor since the late 1950s. Let's set the stage. Te year is 1984. Recently, there had arisen a growing consensus that the stock market was fully efcient, called "Efcient Market Teory." Basically, academics and investors were declaring it impossible for someone to consistently pick stocks that would beat the overall market average, because everything was priced in already. Columbia Business School hosted an epic debate as a contest between Michael Jensen, a professor from the University of Rochester and one of the leading voices of the Efcient Market Teory versus Warren Bufett, famed stock-picker. Jensen went frst. He argued that if you fipped a coin 50 times, there would be someone that happened to get heads 50 times in a row, but that didn't mean that that person had skill. He called picking stocks a "coin fip". Ten Bufett spoke. He said "let's imagine that we had a coin fipping contest. And that of course we could have some lucky winners and losers. But then, let's assume that all the winners had something in common. What if all the winners of the coin-fipping contest came from Omaha, or had an unusual technique. Wouldn't you be curious to fnd out what made this high concentration of winners? Bufett then went through the investment performance of nine successful investors that just so happened to all practice the same methodology and all had the same teachers, Benjamin Graham and David Dodd. He called them "Te Superinvestors of Graham-andDoddsville." Bufett was unequivocally declared the winner afer his masterful speech. No one could doubt the numbers or the logic. Te clear conclusion is that you can be successful in picking stocks, and it requires following the investment principles of Graham and Dodd and Bufett. Bufett references Benjamin Graham and

David L. Dodd. Together Graham and Dodd wrote Security Analysis in 1934. Tis book, still in print afer several editions, has infuenced many great investors since the very first publication. Additionally, Benjamin Graham wrote Te Intelligent Investor in 1949. Mr. Bufett frst read this book in 1950 and considers it, "by far the best book on investing ever written." Benjamin Graham is considered the father of value investing and so we start here. As you read the article make a note of the key concepts that are referenced. Some are repeated several times.

4

THE SEVEN GOLDEN RULES

Being successful at anything requires following a set of rules. Good rules are the accumulation of decades of wisdom summed up into the few components that really matter. Successful football players win because they avoid penalties and because of the way they train. Successful students get A's because of the way they study. Investing in the stock market is no diferent, except that when you succeed in investing you make money - a lot of money. Take Warren Bufett for example; he started out with $10,000 and turned it into a net worth of $60,000,000,000 (Tat's 60 BILLION!) . But he's not alone. Peter Lynch, Bill Ruane, Walter Schloss, Bill Miller, Charlie Munger, Joel Greenblatt, and many others generated similar extraordinary investment returns, consistently, over a long-term time horizon. Each successful fund manager's style was slightly diferent, but if you study them each carefully you'll start to see signifcant patterns. We summed these patterns into Seven Golden Rules. So, without further ado, here are the Seven Golden Rules of Successful Investing so that you can crush it in the stock market. Trying to time the stock market or risking it all to "double your money in a year" is at best speculating, at worst gambling. You may as well just take your money to Vegas and lose it there. Tose who are able to successfully navigate the stock market are not speculators or gamblers, they are investors. Investors know they can beat the market because they think diferently, they think smarter, and they think longer-term. "Time horizon arbitrage" means that if investors learn to think long-term and can see beyond the daily and quarterly noise, they can gain a real upper hand. In 1964, American Express was a great company but the stock was getting hammered due to an insurance scandal.

Te company had to pay millions of dollars in fnes due to accidentally underwriting barrels of vegetable oil that turned out to be water. Tat is exactly the time when Warren Bufett began purchasing the stock. Te best investors look beyond short term distress and keep their eyes on the long-term horizon. "Only buy something that you'd be perfectly happy to hold if the market shut down for 10 years." -Warren Bufett

RULE 2: GOOD COMPANIES MAKE GOOD INVESTMENTS People need to understand that investing is not like placing a bet on whether the Cowboys will cover the spread against the Packers in the big game. Investing is not trying to get the quarterly press release a microsecond before the other person. It is not even about trying to predict which stock that you think will go up the most. Fundamental Investing is buying a tangible piece of a business, or a share of that business. And your investment portfolio (the collection of all the diferent shares you own) is only as good as sum of the companies in that portfolio. If you buy shares of high quality companies at reasonable prices, you'll end up with a high quality portfolio with less risk. It's as simple as that. Good companies are ones that have a unique advantage that others can't copy. Good companies are ones that generate high returns on capital. Good companies don't need to borrow a lot because their business is selffnancing. "It's far better to buy a wonderful company at a fair price than a fair company at a wonderful price" Warren Bufett "It's far better to buy a wonderful company at a fair price than a fair company at a wonderful price" RULE 3: BUY WITH A MARGIN OF SAFETY Nearly every professional investor began his career reading Benjamin Graham's, Te Intelligent Investor. Warren Bufett called it, "by far, the best book on investing ever written." What makes it so special? One of the reasons is because it introduced the important concept "Margin of Safety." In investing, a margin of safety is formed when one buys an investment at less than its value, while using conservative assumptions. Te idea of a margin of safety is that you want to buy a business at a price that is low enough that your assessment could be completely wrong and you wouldn't lose much.

RULE 4: DO YOU OWN HOMEWORK AND OWN WHAT YOU KNOW Tere is no substitute for your own work. Buying a stock because CNBC recommended it, or because your uncle recommended it, or the stock chart looks good is a sure way to lose money. Successful investors know what they own. Tey buy stocks of companies with products they believe in. Successful investors go the extra mile to analyze the fnancials of the company to make sure they're not missing anything. Remember, most of the extraordinary gains made in the stock market come afer a stock is punished or afer it has already risen a lot, but you're not going to have the conviction to stick with it unless you really know the company. "You have to know what you own, and why you own it." -Peter Lynch RULE 5: DON'T FOLLOW THE HERD, STAY CALM AND RATIONAL Te typical buyer's decision is usually heavily infuenced by those around him: buy when others are buying, sell when others are selling. Unfortunately, this is a recipe that is bound to backfre. Te best investors are ones that can fght this urge and remain calm through a storm, and remain on the sidelines through a bubble. Te world's greatest investor Warren Bufett said it best, "Be fearful when others are greedy, and be greedy when others are fearful!"

RULE 6:DON'T PUT ALL YOUR EGGS IN ONE BASKET, BUT DON'T HAVE TOO MANY BASKETS, EITHER Diversifcation is one of the most critical strategies for your portfolio so that if one stock blows up, it won't sink the entire ship. As much as we think we won't make a mistake, we will. Even the masters do and that is why we can't put all our eggs in one basket. Tere's power in diversifcation. However, research suggests that 90% of diversifcation benefts can be obtained in most markets with a portfolio of just over 20 stocks. Te more you diversify beyond that, the less you know about each investment (See Rule #4). Your frst and second best ideas are always better than your 100th best idea, so while diversifying is crucial, make your best ideas count! Warren Bufett "We try to avoid buying a little of this or that when we are only lukewarm about the business or its price. When we are convinced as to attractiveness, we believe in buying worthwhile amounts".

RULE 7: NEVER STOP LEARNING Perhaps the most important rule is learn, learn more, and then keep learning. Te fun thing about investing is that the markets are always diferent and companies are constantly changing. Never stop learning about businesses, never stop learning from other great investors, and never stop learning from your own mistakes. Humility and an eagerness to learn are two traits found in all of the great investors. Even Warren Bufett credits his partner Charlie Munger with teaching him that it's better to buy a great company at a fair price than a fair company at a great price. "Te game of life is the game of everlasting learning. At least it is if you want to win." -Charlie Munger

8TH BONUS RULE WHEN YOU MAKE A LOT MON- EY, FIND MEANINGFUL WAYS TO GIVE IT BACK. Bill & Melinda Gates took their fortune and lifed millions of people out of poverty through their foundation.

Warren Bufett has done the same with his billions. If you make millions or even billions of dollars through the concepts taught by YIS, we hope that you will take it and make the world a better place. And even if you don't make millions, you can fnd important ways to give back to your community. Giving, can be done not only with money, but also with your time, your energy and your talents. At YIS, we believe it's possible to really make our investments count. Tat's why we're investing in you. KEY TAKEAWAYS ? Warren Bufet and many others made it clear that it is very possible to make exceptional returns from the stock market, following a few simple rules. ? Investing is simple, but it is not easy. Te Golden Rules of Investing are widely known but difcult to follow in practice. ? By investing in a stock you are owning a portion of a business.

5
THE VALUE OF A STOCK

I magine in front of you is a box of a dozen doughnuts. How much would you pay for one donut? If all the donuts in the box are the same, is one worth more than the other? What if the world had a shortage of sugar and this was the last box of donuts in the world, with none being able to be made for the next year? Does the scarcity increase the value of the good? How about if you just ate a box of donuts and can't eat any more, does the value you would pay for a donut decrease? Te box of 12 doughnuts represents a company. When you break the company down, everyone has an opportunity to own some of the donuts, or part of the company. But people may pay wildly diferent prices for the same donut. If you want to maximize the value of a box of donuts, what might be the best approach? One method is to convince people that these are the tastiest donuts in the world and they will only be around for a limited time. In a nutshell, this is how the market works. Te stock market is made up of people that get excited about something or sick of something depending on their mood. What is obvious is that occasionally the market goes nuts! Consider watching the following video to see how legendary investor Warren Bufett responds to the question, "What do you do when the market goes down?" How is Warren Bufett using common sense about when things are "on sale?" Do you agree?

WHY DO STOCK PRICES FLUCTUATE SO MUCH? Open any fnancial newspaper like the Wall Street Journal. Turn to the stock quote section, pick any company at random, and look at the high and low stock price from the past year. (or go to yahoo.fnance) Ok, let's see here. We have GM. Tey make cars and trucks. Over the past 52 weeks, their stock traded as low as $28/share and as high as $39/share. Tey have 1.6 billion (bn) shares outstanding, so that means that the market value of GM was as low as $45bn and as high as $62bn. Tat's a diference of $17 billion dollars in value. Now the car business doesn't really change that much. You sell plus or minus 5% more vehicles per year. Chevy Silverado is a Chevy Silverado and they're not fguring out how to replace gasoline for water, or how to fy to the moon. It's basically the same business this year as it was last year. So how in the world could the value fuctuate by $17 billion dollars? And more so, why is this happening with every single company in the stock market? Was last year an exceptional year of price swings? Nope Is there something the market knows that we don't know? No. So, what's the explanation? Well, it can be summed up into four short words: "THE MARKET GOES NUTS!" MR. MARKET Let me tell you a story. It's a story that legendary investor Benjamin Graham told. It is about a business partner of yours, named Mr. Market. Imagine you own a business together. Now, Mr. Market is a good guy, but he sufers from wild mood swings. One day he wakes up, and the sky is blue and he is feeling really, really good. So he ofers to buy out your stake in the business for way more than it is worth. Ten the next day, he wakes up and it's raining, he's feeling desperate, and he is screaming that the world is going to end. He ofers to sell you all of his stock in the company for half of what you paid for it. You take it! Te next day, Mr. Market ofers to pay a price that is neither extraordinarily high nor extraordinary low, so you just do nothing. Now the value of the business didn't really change from day to day – what changed was the erratic moods of Mr. Market. In short, Mr. Market is one moody dude. So does this mean that we shouldn't invest in the stock market, because of these wild swings in the short term? To the contrary! Te fact that we are ofered deals from time to time should make us very, very excited. Our goal is to 1) identify what the company is worth and 2) to wait for Mr. Market to have a bad day and buy it at a large discount. Benjamin Graham called this giving ourselves a "margin of safety." Tis is the equivalent of buying dollars for ffy cents. Ok, you're thinking. Tis is all well and good. Wait for the market to go crazy and buy below the fair value. However, there is one problem: How can we be sure that we can even come close to knowing the value of a company? How can we be sure that our forecasts (a.k.a. wild guesses) are even in the ballpark? Aren't there a ton of smart people and computer programs waiting to scoop up a bargain as soon as it becomes available? Surprisingly, not as many as you think. QUESTION TO CONSIDER: 1. Tink about something that you got a really killer deal on that you bought in the past, how were you able to get that deal? How is this similar to the stock market?

WHAT IS THE VALUE OF A BUSINESS?

We'll only invest in a company when the price we pay today is signifcantly less than the value we will get tomorrow. Example: Teacher picks a student at random. Teacher holds up a $10 bill and asks the student, "What is the value of this bill?" Ten dollars. Teacher holds up ten $1 bills. She asks the same question, "What is the value of these dollar bills?" Ten dollars. Teacher ofers to sell the student the $10 bill for the ten $1 dollar bills. Tis is a wash so maybe he'll take it, maybe he won't. Ten Teacher ofers to sell the $10 for only fve $1 dollar bills. Of course he should take it. Ask the question to the rest of the class at large, "How many of you would buy this?" Do the reverse. Ask to sell the $10 bill for twenty $1 bills? How many would take this? None of them. Te best investors are able to snatch up $10 bills when the market is only asking $5 for them. But how is this possible? It is possible because 1) the value is tricky to calculate and 2) the market is irrational. Remember the Market goes nuts. Is this a good thing or a bad thing for you? It's a very good thing. If all investors based their investment decisions on rational and conservative estimates of intrinsic value, it would be very difcult to make money in the stock market. Fortunately, the participants in the stock market are humans subject to the corroding infuence of emotions. Many investors will give into hype around stocks, or people will hop on a trend, because they have optimistic views that they can beat the system. As young investor geniuses, we will always check emotions at the door and buy stocks based on what they are really worth. But how do we know what the value of the company is? Let's take Apple. What is the value of the world's largest business of consumer electronics? Te value of any business is the present value of all future cash the company will make minus the cash it needs to invest to make this happen. Ok, that's a bit of a mouthful, stay with me. Let's assume that today Apple sells 200 million (mn) products per year at an average price of $1,000 each. So they make $200 billion dollars a year in sales. But to make those 200mn products, they spend $700 per device to design and make them and $100 to buy the equipment. So they're taking home $200 per device, or 40bn dollars. Would you pay $40 to receive $40 next year? No, not unless you think Apple is going to keep making money the following year. Ok, let's assume Apple sells 5% more products every year at the same price of $1,000. Next year they make $44bn, the following year they make $48.4bn and so on. Te value of Apple then becomes everything under the line. Let's assume Apple can keep this trend for the next 40 years. Te total amount of profts going forward, at today's value is about $675 billion dollars. Not bad, eh? Divide that by the number of shares outstanding, and we have the value of the shares at about $111 dollars per share.

Now let's tweak with the numbers. Let's say instead of growing 5% per year, Apple only manages to sell the same amount of devices every year going forward. Te graph becomes fat and the total value of Apple is nearly cut in half to $391mn, or $64/share. At the current share price that means you're going to lose half your money.

Now, let's assume that Apple manages to have very strong growth of 15% per year for a few years, but in year four the company has competitive pressure and profts get cut in half. Ten they get cut in half again and profts remain at this level going forward. Te value of Apple plummets to $220bn or $36/ share. Ouch!

So frst we have the market defnition of what a company's value is and second, we have tips and tricks from other investor geniuses. Te value of what a company is worth really rests on just two questions: 1) How much are profts going to grow and 2) How long are these profts sustainable? Tose are the two things that determine how much value comes back to you in the long run as an owner of the business. 'How long will this last?' is probably the most important question you can ask yourself, in trying to fgure out what a company is worth. Now, even the best investors will tell you they have been dead wrong on the value of companies on many, many occasions. Tey'll also admit to you that for half of the companies on the market, they frankly have no idea what the true value of the company is. Why? Because the future of many companies is too uncertain to predict. If you don't know how long those profts will last, you can't compute what the company is worth. For most companies it is a wild guess how long those profts can last because they don't have any real defenses. Tey don't have an economic moat. Te good news is that there are some exceptional companies with a substantial moat around their castle that we know can't be competed away easily. By investing in these high-quality businesses we can have much more assurance that they will have a good value today as well as tomorrow. Tese are the companies we can feel confdent that we are at least in the right ballpark when calculating their long term value. So when Mr. Market comes to us in one of his bad moods wanting to sell us shares of really great companies at a discount, we say, "Sure! Give me all you got!"

UNDERSTANDING THE TERMINOLGY

Acompany's worth – its total value – is called its market capitalization and it is represented by the company's stock price. Market cap (as it is commonly referred to) is equal to the stock price multiplied by the number of shares outstanding. For example, a stock with a $5 stock price and 10 million shares outstanding/ trading is worth $50 million ($5 x 10 million). If we take this one step further, we can see that a company that has a $10 stock price and one million shares outstanding (market cap = $10 million) is worth less than a company with a $5 stock price and 10 million shares outstanding (market cap = $50 million). Tus, the stock price is a relative and proportional value of a company's worth and only represents percentage changes in market cap at any given point in time. Any percentage changes in a stock price will result in an equal percentage change in a company's value. Tis is the reason why investors are so concerned with stock prices and any changes that may occur since even a $0.10 drop in a $5 stock can result in a $100,000 loss for shareholders with one million shares. QUESTIONS TO CONSIDER: 1. What is the Market Cap of a Company with a stock price of $20/share and 10 million shares outstanding? 2. What is the current Market Cap of Apple? How many shares do they have outstanding and what is the stock price? Te next logical question is: Who sets stock prices and how are they calculated? In simple terms, the stock price of a company is calculated when a company goes on sale to the public, an event called an initial public ofering. Tis is when a company will pay an investment bank a lot of money to use very complex formulas and valuation techniques to derive a company's value by determining how many shares will be ofered to the public and at what price. For example, a company whose value is estimated at $100 million may want to issue 10 million shares at $10 per share or they may want to issue 20 million at $5 a share. As we saw in the example with Apple, a company's value is dependent on how much the company can grow its earnings in the future. When a company sells more items or enters a new market or improves margins, it can grow profts.

THE "GO-TO" WAY TO VALUE A BUSINESS: P/E RATIO One way to determine the value of a business is with the Price-to-Earnings Ratio or P/E Ratio. Te price-earnings ratio can be calculated as: Market Value per Share (Stock Price) / Earnings per Share For example, suppose that a company is currently trading at $43 a share and its earnings over the last 12 months were $1.95 per share. Te P/E ratio for the stock could then be calculated as $43/$1.95, or about 22x. In essence, the price-earnings ratio indicates how many years an investor has to wait at the current earnings to get all their money back. If the P/E ratio is 22x, you are saying at this level of earnings, it will take you 22 years for the company to earn how much you bought the stock for $43. In general, a high P/E suggests that investors are expecting higher earnings growth in the future compared to companies with a lower P/E. A low P/E can indicate either a company may currently be undervalued or the company's profts are expected to decline. Tink of a P/E as the price you pay for a stock. In general, there are a couple of Price / Earnings (P/E) rules of thumb: ? Te average P/E over the past decade is 15x. An average company, should be worth about 15x. ? Really great companies (very high returns with consistent earnings growth) tend to trade about 20-25x P/E. ? Bad companies, ones whose earnings are unpredictable and make low returns, usually trade at below 10x P/E. ? A company should trade at about the P/E as its earnings are expected to grow in the future. Companies growing profts 30% per year may be justifed to trade at 30x P/E. Companies growing 15% per year may trade at 15x P/E. Companies not growing may trade at 5-10x P/E.

As you can see, valuing stocks is like going to a grocery store. You get what you pay for. If you want to buy the best product, you're likely going to have to pay for it.

1. Stocks fuctuate wildly on a yearly basis. Te true value of the business does not actually change much. 2. Te reason behind this is that there is a man named Mr. Market that is just plain NUTS! 3. If someone ofers you a dollar for ffy cents, take it! 4. Te two most important things that determine the value of a company are 1) how much profts are going to grow to and 2) how long that proft level is sustainable. 5. Te P/E ratio is a good starting point to determine the value of a company.

6

WHAT MAKES A GOOD BUSINESS?

Introduction Think fnding a good long-term business is easy? Just take a quick look at history and you'll see that only a handful of companies survive over time. For example, create a list of businesses that have failed or gone bankrupt in the past 20 years. (Examples: Chrysler, Enron, Delta Airlines, Countrywide Mortgages, and Lehman Brothers) Why do you think that some companies succeed while others fail? How can we identify the winners from the losers for investment purposes?

SECTION 1 HOW DO I KNOW IF A COMPANY IS A GOOD BUSINESS? I magine we have two friends who will both open a small business. Our frst friend, Jack, wants to open a chain of candy stores called "Jacks Candy Shop." It will cost him $2,000 to build and each will earn him $1,000 per year in profts. Tat's a whopping 50% return on investment! (ROI) ($1,000/$2,000) In two years, he will have made his $2,000 investment back. In four years, he will have doubled his money- -assuming the stores stayed just as proftable at $1,000/year. Tis is certainly a pretty incredible business. Now, our other friend, Jill, wants to open a chain of specialty pet stores called "Just Rodents." It also costs $2,000 to build per store, but it's a bad business-- (who wants to own a pet rat, right?). And additionally, it only makes $40 per year in profts, or a 2% return on investment. ($40/$2,000) Both stores cost the same to build but one simply makes more than the other. Both owners approach you to potentially invest and buy half of their respective stores for $1,000 each. Do you invest in Jack's Candy shop or Jill's Rodent Shop? Of course, the answer is obvious: you choose the higher return business (50% in this case). A business that earns a high return on capital (or sometimes called return on equity or ROE) is always the best business. Tink of the ROE as the amount that a business gives back to you each year as a shareholder. It's the diference of receiving a $20 bill each year or a $10 bill each year. A 20% ROE (return on equity) is better than a 10% ROE and Jack's 50% return on capital business is phenomenal. But, is a business that earns a high ROE today always worth more than one that earns a lower ROE today? Not necessarily. Take this example: Would you rather receive $20 dollars today and then $10 dollars-a-day for the rest of your life, or $15 dollars today and $15 dollars-aday for the rest of your life? Answer: You'd defnitely want to take $15 for the rest of your life. (Te diference, in case you're curious, is that you'll receive $350k for the $15/day and $233k for the $10/day).

So, Jack's Candy shop earns a fantastic 50% return on equity today. And this is great-- but since everyone knows what the business is earning today, the real question is: can they keep earning those high returns years into the future? What happens when the Ice Cream Shop in town realizes that Jack's Candy Shop is making amazing profts, so they start selling candy in their store as well? What happens when a retail giant like Wal-Mart decides to open their own Candy stores to compete? Does Jack have to lower his prices so that he only makes $200 proft per store, and that 50% ROE becomes 10% over time? Tese are the key questions a savvy investor must ask himself. Tere are a couple of important laws in investing. Much like the law of gravity, Murphy's Law and under the laws of economics, any time a business like a candy shop earns exceptionally high returns, forces will come in to reduce those returns. If Jack's candy shop is earning a 50% return on capital, like a magnet, this is certainly going to attract more people to open candy shops, charge lower prices, advertise more, and eventually those returns will be reduced. Tis is economics 101: If a company earns a return on capital above the average, competition is going to come in and compete it away. High returns on capital attract competitors like bees to honey. And most high returns end up being whittled down to average over time. Unless, however, this company has something unusually powerful that others can't imitate. Warren Bufett called this an "economic moat". Like a medieval castle, some very good companies are protected by a wide moat to keep competitors at bay. Te best companies are the ones that provide high returns on capital, but are also able to protect and grow those returns through a unique protection (moat) that makes it very difcult for those competitors at the gates to come in and take them away. QUESTIONS TO CONSIDER: 1. If Wal-Mart decided that Candy Shops were a great high-return business, would their Candy

Shops be better, the same, or worse than Jack's Candy Shops? What do you think would happen to Jack's return on capital if Wal-Mart is now a direct competitor? 2. What is an economic moat and why is it important for the long term success of a company?

SECTION 2 WHATEVER FLOATS YOUR MOAT Bigger is not necessarily better when it comes to digging an economic moat. It is very easy to assume that a company with a high market share also has a sustainable competitive advantage—how else would it have acquired such a big chunk of the market? —But history shows us that leadership can be feeting in highly competitive markets. Kodak (flm), IBM (PCs), Netscape (Internet browsers), General Motors (automobiles), and Corel (word processing sofware), are only a few of the frms that have discovered this. In defning an economic moat, what should you look for? Tere's a couple types of moats that have been proven to last the test of time. Here's your list: Types of Economic Moats ? Intangible Assets: A company can have intangible assets, like brands, patents, or regulatory licenses that allow it to sell products or services that can't be matched by competitors. ? High Switching Costs: Te products or services that a company sells may be hard for customers to give up, which creates customer switching costs that give the frm pricing power. ? Network Efect: Some lucky companies beneft from network economics, which is a very powerful type of economic moat. It says that the more people you have on your platform or in your distribution system, the better the value for them, which creates a virtuous cycle. ? Low Cost Advantage: Finally, some companies have cost advantages, stemming from process, location, scale, or access to a unique asset, which allow them to ofer goods or services at a lower cost than competitors. Tese four categories cover the vast majority of frms with moats. Now that you know them, you can begin to identify them. Tey are used by the best stock investors to identify great companies. QUESTIONS TO CONSIDER: 1. Can you name one business that you think has a "wide moat"? (one that is unlikely to have its competitive market position eroded 10 years from now). 2. Can you name one business that you think has a "narrow moat" (one that has a good business today, but whose high returns are unlikely to last 10 years from now).

3. Can you name one business that you think has "no moat" (one that is a highly competitive, bad business today and in the future as well). QUICK MATCHING GAME: Te following companies have stood the test of time, which probably indicates they have some sort of economic moat. Can you identify what their economic moat is? (brand, high switching costs, network

efect, low cost advantage) ? Coca Cola ? Bank of America ? Google ? Wal-Mart ? Exxon Mobil Hint: Tere can be more than one per company! Conclusion All businesses are not created equal, some are bad, most are average, but some are really, really good. Selling candy is better than selling rats, and even better is to sell Coca-Cola or iPhones. Te goal of the long term investor is to identify really good companies that can earn high returns on capital for decades into the future. Te only way to defend these high returns though is with a deep economic moat. Types of Economic Moats ? Intangible Assets / Brands ? High Switching Costs ? Network Efect ? Low Cost Advantage Te surest way to make money in the stock market is to invest in good companies that make exceptional returns and can defend these returns for decades into the future. In this lesson, you learned how to identify these companies. If you master this skill, you will gain one of the most valuable investing tools a great investor will ever learn. 1. Most businesses will fail. 2. Tere are some exceptional businesses out there that have an "economic moat". Warren Bufett "Time is the friend of the wonderful company, the enemy of the mediocre.

3. Great companies have the economic moats of Brand, High Switching Costs, Network Efects or a Low Cost Advantage. 4. Don't open a rat store. ACTIVITY Good businesses have something unusual about them. Tey have a product or brand image or network efect that is so strong that you can be certain they will retain their advantage for many years to come. Tis type of business has some unique characteristic(s) that can't be replicated. For example, the year is 2005. Kelly Clarkson just won American Idol. Facebook and YouTube were just launched. Brad Pitt and Jennifer Aniston were still married. Yikes. 11 years ago! Which company do you think managed to keep their return on capital (ROE) over the next decade (2005-2014), in line or higher than the previous 10 years? i.e. retained their moat

Apple: 13.7% ROE (1995-2004) Company Background: Makes computers, phones, sells sofware and apps, and operates retail stores 2005-2014: ?

Hewlett Packard: 12.2% ROE (1995-2004) Company Background: Te largest computers company in the worlds. Also sells sofware services 2005-2014: ?

Te answer of course is Apple. Apple increased from 13.7% to 30.9% return on equity (ROE) compared with HP whose ROE decreased from 12.2% to 10%. People simply like iPhones more than PCs, and Apple has a much stronger brand image, ecosystem around its products, and quality of design than HP. Specifcally, Apple benefts from the economic moats of 1) a strong brand (they price their products at a premium) and 2) high switching costs (the

Apple ecosystem makes it costly to switch to Android or Windows once you've bought movies, music and apps on iTunes). HP really just makes another run of the mill computer for cheap. And their stock prices? Stock performance follows company performance, so Apple's stock increased 975% while HP increased by a measly 40% over the time period. ALIEN INVASION ACTIVITY: Situation: Te year is 2005, and Aliens have invaded earth! Tey are going to destroy every human in the world, except they notice something they don't understand: how is it possible that some imaginary creatures, called "Companies" can be so dominant. Tey assume it will lead them to universal domination if they can discover the secret. So they make all humans a wager: if anyone is smart enough to know the secret of how to identify what companies will continue to make the same or higher return on equity over the next decade, then you get to live. If you can't, you die! You will have a series of four tests. Only one of the two companies on each list could be defned as highly defensible, exceptional businesses that can protect its return on capital. Can you identify it? Your life depends on it. Te aliens want to speak to "your leader" so you should debate on what to pick within the club, and eventually the portfolio manager will decide which stock to choose for the group. Ready earthlings!? Question 1 Walt Disney: 12.6% (1995-2004) Company Background: Operates Teme Parks, Makes Movies, Sells Merchandise, owns ESPN Networks and Disney Channel. 2005-2014: ?

Nintendo: 15.1% (1995-2004) Company Background: Makes video game systems, video games, including Nintendo Wii, and Nintendo DS. 2005-2014: ? Questions to think about: 1. What were the main things that happened to Disney and Nintendo during the next decade (2005-2014)? 2. What could you identify as Disney's moat? What about Nintendo's? 3. What is it about that businesses that makes them sticky? Is one "stickier" than the other?

Question 2 Abercrombie & Fitch: 55.0% (1995-2004) Company Background: Te most popular clothing retailer for teenagers, with very strong brand appeal 2005-2014: ? Coca Cola: 17.9% (1995-2004) Company Background: Te leading beverage company in the world with the brands Coca Cola, Sprite, Fanta, PowerAde 2005-2014: ? Question 3 Southwest Airlines: 13.2% (1995-2004) Company Background: A well-run airline that is known for lowcost airfare. 2005-2014: ?

McDonalds: 17.1% (1995-2004) Company Background: Te leading fast food operator in the world. 2005-2014: ? Question 4 Microsof: 25.2% (1995-2004) Company Background: Maker of Computer Sofware: Windows, Microsof

Ofce and Xbox Vid. 2005-2014: ? Verizon: 20.8% (1995-2004) Company Background: Leading cell phone operator in the US. Operates cable and fber optic networks. 2005-2014: ? Round-up: Did you survive? If not, what tripped you up? If you keep practicing and become a student of businesses, pretty soon you'll become a pro at identifying economic moats within companies around you. When you've learned it, it's one of the most valuable skills you will ever learn in the business world. ANSWERS TO ACTIVITES YOUNG INVESTORS SOCIETY . STOCK INVESTING 101 38 QUICK MATCHING GAME: 1). Coca Cola – Brand, Network Efect (Distribution around the world) 2). Bank of America - High Switching costs, (It's a pain to switch banks, so most people don't). 3). Google - Network Efect (the more people that use Google search, the better it becomes) 4). Wal-Mart - Low Cost (Wal-Mart's buying power allows them to buy products at the lowest cost) and Network Efect (Superior distribution and supply chain). 5). Exxon Mobil - Low Cost (Exxon has low-cost oil felds that make money in almost any oil price)

ALIEN INVASION ACTIVITY Question 1: Walt Disney vs. Nintendo? Answer: Walt Disney Results: Walt Disney went from 12.6% ROE (1995-2004) to 13.01% (2005-2014) while Nintendo went from 15.1% ROE (1995-2004) to 9.4% (2005-2014). Te stock prices? Disney was up 298% and Nintendo was down 11.5%. Rationale: Walt Disney Corporation has a strong brand of characters and theme parks; not to mention that ESPN is the most proftable television stations in the world. Teir brands are about as strong as they come, just ask any kid under the age of 10. Nintendo, on the other hand, does have a decent brand, but video games are a hit and miss business. Nintendo actually lost money in 2011 and 2013 because of poor sales.

Question 2: Abercrombie & Fitch vs. Coca Cola? Answer: Coca Cola Results: Coca Cola went from 17.9% ROE (1995-2004) to 29.5% (2005-2014) while Abercrombie & Fitch went from 55% ROE (1995-2004) to 16.4% (2005-2014). Te stock prices? Coca Cola was up 110% and Abercrombie & Fitch was down an astonishing 56%. Rationale: Coca Cola is probably one of the strongest brands ever built. Tey also have a distribution advantage (network efect) throughout the world as they dominate the sof drinks industry with over 50% of global sales. Abercrombie & Fitch is a clothing retailer, which is a very difcult business. Just think about going into a mall, there are hundreds of competitors, and the viability of the business in the future depends on staying "cool" and being on the cutting edge of fashion. Very tough to predict given the high amount of competition. Both companies would have a "brand" but this shows that one brand is much stronger than the other.

Question 3: Southwest Airlines vs. McDonalds? Answer: McDonalds Results: McDonalds went from 17.1% ROE (1995-2004) to 29.3% (2005- 2014) while Southwest Airlines went from 13.7% ROE (1995-2004) to 7.5% (2005-2014). Te stock prices? McDonalds rose 178% and Southwest Airlines actually held in there ok, up 157%. Rationale: Although you might not care for Big Macs, McDonalds is still a legendary brand, especially overseas where it is a symbol of the American lifestyle. Teir greater scale also enables them a cost advantage relative to other fast food chains. Southwest Airlines, is the best of a really terrible business: Airlines. It's an example of the investment adage "it's better to bet on a good horse than a good jockey," meaning a bad business with great managers is likely a losing bet. Airlines are capital intensive (planes are expensive!) and are highly competitive on price. During this decade, Delta Airlines, Continental, and American Airlines all went bankrupt, so at least Southwest didn't go bankrupt.

Question 4: Microsof vs. Verizon? Answer: Microsof Results: Microsof went from 26.2% ROE (1995-2004) to 35.1% (2005-2014) while Verizon went from 21.2% ROE (1995-2004) to 15.0% (2005-2014). Te stock prices? Microsof rose 78% and Verizon rose 73%. Rationale: Microsof benefts from one of the most powerful economic moats, the network efect. People use their ofce products (Microsof Word, Excel) because everyone else does, which makes it the standard. Windows is also the standard operating system for most businesses. One could argue that Microsof was one of the poorest run companies during this decade (throwing away billions of dollars into Nokia, mobile phones, Bing), but it didn't matter. Te network efect was too powerful for even incompetent management to break. Verizon, is not a bad business, with a pretty good brand and a network efect (the more friends and family that are on Verizon the more valuable it is to you), but owning fber optic cables and towers is a very capital intensive business so high returns are tougher to sustain. Not to mention Verizon was late to get the iPhone.

7

FINDING STOCKS TO INVEST IN

Picking the right stocks is essential to any share trader or investor's success. We've put together a complete, step-by-step guide to help you choose the best stocks in your chosen market.

There is no single approach to picking the best stocks to invest in. It depends on a few factors, such as the outcome you're trying to achieve, your attitude to risk, as well as the time and capital you have available. To pick the best stocks to invest in, you can follow these steps:

Do your research and understand the business. This includes fundamental and technical analysis to determine the fair value of a stock, as well as understanding the prospects of a business to make sure it's aligned to your strategy and goals

Use a mixture of quantitative and qualitative stock analysis to build your portfolio. By doing this you can create an approach that works for you

Avoid emotion when making investment decisions. Do not simply buy stock because there is hype around it – and do not rush into any buying or selling decisions

Make sure you spread your risk by diversifying your portfolio

Many investors prefer stocks that pay dividends, because they can be reinvested to increase the size of a holding. The result is that the return on investment is not only based on the capital growth relating to the initial amount deposited, but also on any dividends that are accumulated while the position is open. Others are less concerned with dividends, and like to pick stocks with strong fundamentals, following the value investing style of Warren Buffett.

How to pick stocks using fundamental analysis

There are a few steps to follow if you want to pick stocks using fundamental analysis. Firstly, keep in mind that fundamental analysis centres around estimating a stock's intrinsic value. This means you should analyse both qualitative and quantitative aspects of the economy, industries within the economy and the individual companies that make up the industry.

Qualitative factors

Qualitative factors to consider include:

Company news

Personnel changes

Financial events

Company news

News relating to the company you're looking to invest in can cause stock prices to rise or tumble. This is because good news often causes individuals to buy stock, while bad news causes them to sell the stock. This affects supply and demand and, ultimately, the share price.

Personnel changes

Personnel changes, including management restructures, are extremely relevant to those looking for stocks, because it affects the market's perception. The business's reputation could be affected by any personnel changes, which has a direct impact on stock prices.

Financial events

It's important to take note of financial events when picking stocks, as these can cause market uncertainty and heightened volatility. Economic events include interest rate decisions, scheduled changes in management, and large-scale events such as Brexit.

Quantitative factors

Quantitative factors include:

Earnings releases

Balance sheets

Dividends

Ratios

Earnings releases

Traders and investors should keep a close eye on changes in company earnings as part of their fundamental analysis. If company earnings drop and the share price does not adjust to the new earnings level, the stock price might not reflect true value.

Balance sheets

A company's balance sheet will list all its assets and liabilities. A stronger balance sheet generally means a strong stock price, because it reflects earnings potential. As mentioned, earnings also directly affect stock prices.

Dividends

Dividends are a portion of a company's profit that it chooses to return to its shareholders. They are one of the ways a shareholder can earn money from an investment without having to sell shares. You could use dividends as a deciding factor when choosing stocks, because they indicate that the company is profitable and that there is a good possibility of future earnings.

Ratios

Qualitative factors can be measured by means of various ratios. Fundamental analysis ratios include:

Price-to-earnings (P/E) ratio, which measures a stock's value by showing you how much you would have to spend to make $1 in profit. P/E ratio assists in comparing the value of one stock in a sector with another. It can also be used as a guide to determine whether a company is currently overvalued or undervalued compared with its historical averages

Debt-equity ratio (D/E), which measures a company's debt against its assets and gives you insight into how the company is performing relative to its competitors. A low ratio could mean that the company gets most of its funding from its shareholders. It's important to note that a 'good' or 'bad' ratio depends on the industry

Return on equity (ROE), which measures a company's profitability against its equity, expressed as a percentage. It shows you if the company is generating enough income by itself relative to the amount of shareholder investment

Earnings yield, which measures earnings by dividing the earnings per share (EPS) by the share price. Earnings yield is also a value indicator – the higher the earnings yield, the more likely it is that stocks are undervalued

Relative dividend yield, which measures a company's dividend yield compared to that of the entire index. If you're looking to buy stock, you should consider the relative dividend yield because it can show if stocks are overvalued or undervalued compared to competitor stocks

Current ratio, which measures a company's ability to pay off debt. It shows if liabilities can be adequately covered by the available assets. There is a link between this ratio and the stock price. The lower the current ratio, the higher the likelihood that the stock price will continue to go down

Price-earnings to growth (PEG) ratio, which measures the P/E ratio compared to the percentage growth in annual EPS. If you are deciding on which stocks to pick, you should consider the PEG ratio because it could give you an indication of the stock's fair value

Price-to-book (P/B) ratio, which measures the current market price against a company's book value. A ratio higher than one often indicates overvalued shares

The top-down and bottom-up approach

There are two approaches you can take when conducting fundamental analysis – the top-down and the bottom-up approach. The top-down approach is a faster method, preferred by those who are less experienced or prefer the bigger picture. As part of the top down approach, you may want to analyse economic growth and gross domestic product (GDP), bond prices and yields, monetary policies (including interest rates) and inflation, before choosing a sector and company to focus on.

Bottom-up analysis doesn't focus on market conditions and industry fundamentals as much as it does on how the company is performing against its competitors. If you prefer this approach, you will consider various financial ratios (mentioned above), revenue and sales, cash flow, management and products.

How to pick stocks using technical analysis

Technical analysis is completely different to fundamental analysis – when picking stocks using technical analysis, you should focus on the stock's price data and movements. This includes trends and patterns that may indicate the future movements of the market. There are a wide range of technical indicators you can use when conducting technical analysis. Your chosen technical strategy will ultimately depend on your trading style.

Moving average (MA) is used to identify the direction of a price trend, without the interference of short-term price spikes

Exponential moving average (EMA) can help confirm significant market moves and gauge their legitimacy

Stochastic oscillator shows momentum and trend strength by comparing a specific closing price of an asset to a range of its prices over time

Moving average convergence divergence (MACD) detects changes in momentum by comparing two moving averages. It can help to identify possible buy and sell opportunities around support and resistance levels

Bollinger bands are used to predict long-term price movements and useful for recognising when an asset is trading outside of its usual levels

Relative strength index (RSI) is mostly used to help identify momentum, market conditions and warning signals for dangerous price movements

Fibonacci retracement can pinpoint the degree to which a market will move against its current trend

Ichimoku cloud identifies support and resistance levels, estimates price momentum and provides you with signals to help with decision-making

Standard deviation helps you to measure the size of price moves to assist with identifying how likely volatility is to affect the price in the future

Average directional index illustrates the strength of a price trend to help you gather whether an upward or downward trend is likely to continue

Fundamental vs technical analysis: which is better?

Fundamental and technical analysis are both important when researching potential stock to trade or invest in. One method is not 'better' than the other, as there are vast differences between the two. The type of analysis you choose often depends on your strategy. Some long-term traders (position traders or investors) prefer fundamental analysis, while traders with a short-term strategy tend to focus on technical analysis. It is important to look at both forms of analysis, to ensure you do not miss any important information.

What makes a stock valuable?

A stock's value is measured by the relationship between supply and demand. A high demand generally means a higher price, and vice versa. Further to this, a stock's value is intrinsic to the return it can offer to a trader or investor. Some investors pick companies with strong fundamentals, whereas others choose smaller, under-appreciated companies with the potential to grow quickly. There are different valuation methods you can use to determine if stocks are undervalued or overvalued.

How to identify undervalued and overvalued stocks

If you want to identify undervalued or overvalued stocks, you should start with fundamental and technical analysis. You can use the eight popular ratios that form part of fundamental analysis to find undervalued or overvalued stocks and determine their true value. However, you should use both fundamental and technical analysis to get the most complete picture of the market.

Finding undervalued or overvalued stocks is not about finding cheap or expensive stocks. Instead, you should look for quality stocks that are priced below or above their fair values. The assumption is that market prices will correct over time to reflect true value, which means you could make a profit.

You would do this by going long on an undervalued stock, or short on an overvalued one.

Stocks may be undervalued or overvalued if there are changes to market conditions due to market dynamics, news, cyclical fluctuations or misjudged results.

You can take a position on stocks in two ways – by investing or by trading derivatives. If you want to buy and own the stocks, you can open an IG share dealing account and buy stocks via our share dealing service. You will need the full value of the stock upfront, and you can only profit if the share price goes up. If you own stock, you could receive dividend payments (if the company pays them) and have voting rights.

If you don't want to own the stock, or if you want to speculate on upward or downward price movements, you can do so via CFD trading or spread betting. With CFDs and spread bets, you don't need the full value of the stock upfront, because you'll trade using leverage. And, because you don't own the stock, you can go long or short.

It only takes a few minutes to create your account and you can top up your trading funds using a credit card or debit card, or via bank transfer.

If you would rather take some time to practise your trades without risking real money, you can open a demo account, which gives you £10,000 in virtual funds.

What to bear in mind when choosing stocks

Create a trading plan

Understand the market

Use a market screener

Manage your risk

Create a trading plan

Drafting a comprehensive trading plan and risk management strategy starts with writing down your goals. These goals should be specific, measurable, attainable, relevant and time-bound.

Find out how to create a successful trading plan

Your trading plan should be customised to your goals and outline the exact rules to follow when trading. Start by deciding on your trading style. There are four different styles, each with a different time frame, holding period and level of trading activity. The trading style you choose should suit your personality, skills and experience. The four different trading styles are:

Position trading: buy and hold (investing) or long-term trading with low trading activity

Swing trading: medium-term trading with average trading activity. Read more about the best strategies for swing trading

Day trading: short-term trading with high trading activity. Learn more about picking stocks for day trading

Scalping: very short-term trading with very high trading activity

Understand the market

Stocks are listed on a stock exchange, which facilitates the buying and selling of shares between parties. The stock market is moved by supply and demand. The general state of the economy, interest rates, industry trends and market sentiment also play a role in stock market changes.

Learn more about how the stock market works

Use a market screener

You can use the IG market screener to look for stocks. The screener makes it easy to compare stocks against each other. This way, you can choose the stocks that best suit your risk profile.

Remember, you should pick stocks that you know a lot about. Consider all things – including volatility, exchange opening hours, and the cost.

Manage your risk

When picking stocks, it's important to make sure they suit your risk management strategy. All markets carry some degree of risk, because stocks are continuously affected by external factors, which means the trade will not always perform as expected.

Some of the risks you may face when picking stocks include obsolete business models, poor decisions by management and new competitors. Then there's also general market risk and exchange rate risk – especially important to consider if you're investing in overseas stocks. IG offers different hedging opportunities to help you hedge against these risks.

How much trading risk you'll take on depends on your strategy, the exposure you are taking on in relation to your wider portfolio, and the risk-reward ratio you've set for yourself. Therefore, it's important to decide how much capital you're willing to risk per trade and overall.

Choosing stocks summed up

To pick the best stocks to invest in, consider factors such as the outcome you're trying to achieve, your attitude to risk, as well as the time and capital you have available

You should use fundamental and technical analysis to pick stocks

Fundamental analysis centres around estimating a stock's intrinsic value

Technical analysis looks at trends and patterns that may indicate the future movements of the market

A stock's value is measured by the relationship between supply and demand. Technical and fundamental analysis can help you to determine if stocks are overvalued or undervalued

When choosing stocks, bear in mind that you need a trading plan and a good understanding of the stock market

Looking for good stocks is a treasure hunt. Identifying an exceptional company is rare, but fnding an exceptional company that is on sale is truly a feat. But the good news is it's not impossible! Deals are almost always out there. You just need to know where to look. It requires some searching, some diligence, and a lot of homework, but it's certainly worth it. Discussion Question: Tink of things that you spend money on every month (examples: Netfix, Chipotle, video game monthly subscription, new clothes, etc.). What makes these purchases so "sticky"? Could these companies make for good investments? Besides investing in companies whose products you use, you can also fnd fantastic stock ideas by reading reports written by other investors and by doing stock screens (more on what this is later) to search for specifc variables. We'll show you how!

SECTION 1 HOW DO I COME UP WITH INVESTMENT IDEAS? Now, we're getting to the fun part - picking stocks. But where do we start? One common investment motto is to "invest in what you know." Tis is a good place to start, but we also need to be careful. Many companies we know are actually terrible investments. For example, let's go back 15 years. In the year 2000, what were the companies that the average person knew? We shopped at Sears every weekend, we surfed the internet on Netscape, we took pictures with Kodak flm, we bought GM cars and we few on Delta Airlines. Alright, sweet! Load up a portfolio of the things we know! Te problem is that all fve of those well-known companies would go bankrupt in the next decade and we would lose all our money. Just because something is well-known, doesn't mean that it's a good business. Warren Bufett taught that we do indeed want to own simple, easy to understand businesses, but that these businesses need a competitive moat around them. Te problem with all of the businesses we mentioned before is that none of them really had a protective moat around them. Sears was out-priced by Wal-Mart, Netscape lost out to Microsof Explorer, Kodak was uprooted by a change in the technology, GM's cars went out of favor, and Delta went bankrupt along with just about every other airline. (By the way, if you want a business that is good at torching piles of cash, airlines are always a good place to start!) So how do we start fnding truly good businesses? Remember back to Lesson 3 on Economic Moats. Start by asking yourself a few questions: ? What products am I happy to pay a price premium for because the service they ofer can't be replicated by another? (Brand, Quality) ? What services do I continue paying for because switching services would be too costly or a huge inconvenience? (High Switching Costs) ? What platform do I use because it is the only one where I can meet up with a certain type of people and because the network or marketplace can't even be compared to a peer? (Network Efect) ? What products have been around for generations – you can picture your parents and grandparents enjoying them and easily picture your grandkids enjoying them as well? (Sustainability, Brand)

Legendary investor Peter Lynch, who averaged a 29% return per year over 23 years at Fidelity, tells the story of his wife coming home from the grocery store and mentioning a new product – pantyhose in an egg shaped case called "L'eggs." She raved about what good products they were. He also noted that she was picking up more pantyhose than ever, because she was visiting the grocery store twice a week compared to the department store which she only visited maybe every other month. With this knowledge in hand, he began aggressively buying shares in Hanes, the maker of the L'eggs pantyhose. Te stock became a 30-bagger for his fund, meaning it didn't just double or triple, it went up 30x! He found the idea, not from the Wall Street Journal, but from paying close attention to how people were using the products around him. Peter Lynch's legendary book One Up on Wall Street is a great resource to see how one of the most successful investors of his time came up with some of his best investment ideas. ACTIVITY: CAN'T LIVE WITHOUT IT Make a list of three companies that have products that you "can't live without" considering the questions above. Do you think this company could make a good investment?

SECTION 2 STOCK SCREENS Another useful way to search out great stocks is to run a stock screen. Basically, when you run a stock screen you are running the stock market through a giant flter to sort out the characteristics that you want. It's similar to choosing a car: you know you want a blue, four-door car with good gas mileage, at a certain price, with a minimum horsepower. You put all this info into a search engine and come out with your "Goldilocks" car. Te concept is similar for a stock screener. When you know what to look for, a stock screen is a wonderful starting point. Tese are some of the fnancial characteristics that you should screen for among your initial list of investment candidates. Ideally you want to fnd a great company that is growing and you can buy cheap. Here are a couple of factors you can look for: ? A business that has very stable earnings, with little fuctuation year to year ? A company that has positive cash generation (Cash generation is the cash profts minus the investment costs to grow the business.) ? A company that consistently makes a healthy return on capital ? A company that pays a dividend that grows consistently every year One of the most popular (and free!) stock screeners out there is Google's. Below is a screenshot. https://www.google.com/fnance/stockscreener?hl=en&ei=jjr7VYH_ KdaL0ASusarQCg

Google's Stock Screener allows you drag the range for a number of diferent criteria. It also allows you to go to "Add Criteria" and customize what you want to screen. Tere are many diferent metrics to screen for, but here are some helpful starting points: (If you see terms you don't recognize below, refer to the glossary at the end of this page or investopedia.com) Go to Google Stock Screener and start playing around with the following screens.

Note, just because a company doesn't meet all of these thresholds does not automatically mean that the company is not a good investment. A very high quality company that is growing and that is very cheap is ideal, but is very rare. If you're trying to buy a new Ferrari under $10,000 you aren't likely to fnd many results. Tradeofs will ofen need to be made, but the best investors stay disciplined and fnd the best combinations.

Tere are many free stock screening tools available online. Other useful screeners are Zacks.com (screenshot in on the right), Yahoo Finance, GuruFocus (subscription required) and Uncle Stock. As you learn more about the stock market and read stories of successful investors, pay attention to what metrics they examine. For example, some successful investors look for high growth companies (companies growing more

than 20% per year) that also have high margins (gross margin above 50%). Tese would be considered growth investors. Other successful investors look for very cheap companies (Price / Book below 1x). Tese would be considered deep-value investors. Tere are many ways to successfully invest, and screening helps give you a great starting point. THE S&P 500 & THE DOW JONES: One more list that is helpful is the Dow Jones Industrial Average. Tese are 30 of the largest and most signifcant companies in the United States. Tere will be many companies on this list that you will know, and these are companies that have been leaders for decades and even centuries, such as IBM, Procter & Gamble and Nike. Next you could look at the S&P

500. Here you will fnd a list of 502 companies (not exactly 500, some companies are listed twice!) that represent the largest, most common companies in the United States. As you scan through these lists you can think to yourself: ? Does that sector look interesting? ? Do I know and like this company's products? ? Do I have certain expertise about this company's products that would give me an edge? ? Do I expect this company to grow? Or just click on a company randomly and see where it takes you. You might fnd your treasure. See a list of the current Dow Jones components in the Activity Section of this lesson. Search online for the full list of S&P 500 companies.

SECTION 3 RESEARCH REPORTS: One of the best sources of investment ideas is other investors! Remember, there's no rule in investing that says you can't own a stock that another person owns. Cherry picking is encouraged! One way to fnd ideas is to read blogs or reports on stocks. Also, successful investment managers publish quarterly investment letters where they describe their top holdings and why they own them. Here are a couple of places to start reading: ? Seeking Alpha: Seekingalpha.com is an excellent databank of investor reports on companies. Some of the writers are professional investors, some are not, but there is a plethora of articles written on companies, both large and small. ? SumZero: Similar to Seeking Alpha, sumzero.com is an online platform where investment professionals write investment reports and promote stock ideas. ? Wall Street Journal and Te Financial Times: Tese are the two newspapers that every needs investor reads each day. Most people need to pay for online access, but you can read the articles for free if you copy the article's title into Google and access it through Google directly (a legal and very useful trick!). ? Motley Fool: Fool.com is an always-interesting mix of fnancial news, investment strategies, and large doses of humor balanced by hard hitting serious news and opinion. Tom and Dave Gardner and their talented staf have been delivering their unique and informed message since 1993 and the Fool is now a full-service fnancial media enterprise. If you'd like your investing information tinged with some pleasant sarcasm and edgy laughs, the Fool might be perfect for you. ? Jim Cramer: Te host of CNBC's Mad Money and co-founder of TeStreet.com is a journalist, lawyer, and "infotainer" (his term). He's been dispensing fnancial and investment information to anyone listening since the mid-1990s. If you need a break from reading fnancial statements or waiting for your stock screener to advise you on your next hot investment, Cramer might add some zest to your day. A former hedge fund manager, Cramer has been in the investment trenches for some time. You may not agree with all that he says, but you will be informed and entertained.

? GuruFocus: GuruFocus.com tracks the stock trades of successful investment managers to see what they are buying and selling. It also provides stock recommendations based on diferent investment criteria and has a robust stock screening tool. ? Value Investors Club: Valueinvestorsclub.com is an online investment club where top investment managers come together to share their best stock ideas. ? Beyond Proxy: Beyondproxy.com is one of the most successful investment blogs. It compiles interviews with portfolio managers and stock reports. Beyond this list, there are literally thousands of investor blogs out there. Some are good, some are not, and a few are truly excellent. Te point is that there are many free sources available to provide thoughts on companies and the market. GIVING DUE DILLIGENCE ITS DUE Once we come up with a list of a few interesting companies to potentially invest in, it's time to roll up our sleeves and kick the tires. Remember that buying a stock of a company is really like buying a piece of that company – you are becoming a company owner! You would not make such a big decision before carefully considering your investment. Would you? It is funny that people ofen spend more time researching a movie to see or carefully studying the specs of a piece of electronic equipment they are planning to purchase than when buying a piece of their own company! In the early stages of the investment process, it is particularly useful to use the company's products frst-hand. Learn as much as you can about the company in which you are going to invest. Here are a couple of steps to think about when doing your company "due diligence" (as the pros call it). Make sure the company is actually investible, or publicly traded. You can search for companies' stock tickers on Yahoo Finance, or Morningstar.com. Go to the company website, click on the "Investor Relations" tab, and fnd a recent company presentation. Tis will give you an overview of the business. Read through the more in-depth Annual Report, also on the company website. Sections to focus on are the Management Discussion & Analysis and the Segment Reporting.

Read other investors' opinions on the company on resources such as seekingalpha.com. Look through the company's fnancials on sites like Morningstar.com. Evaluate the trends of the main company metrics. Remember our Golden Rule #3, DO YOUR OWN HOMEWORK. As you follow these steps and use all the resources available to you to do your detective work, you will begin to know the company inside and out. Remember, great investors see things that others don't. Tey think outside of the box. Tey do their own work and develop a conviction in their investments. Te stock market "aggregates" or adds up all the opinions and knowledge of market participants to come up with what the "consensus" (or the general market) thinks a company is worth at any given point in time. Some people will just follow the crowd and invest along with this consensus. But as a wise investor who has done your own homework, you will have a strong sense of how the company is likely to perform in the future and you can take advantage of the "misunderstandings" that take place in the stock market every single day. Scary news headlines may motivate other (perhaps less knowledgeable or prepared) investors to panic by selling the stock. If you feel you got a great price on a stock you bought for the long-term, you are more likely to hold on to it through thick and thin. In our experience, this is almost always the right thing to do with the stocks of great companies. Here it is worth making a distinction between great companies and great stocks. In some cases, and especially in the short term, these may not always be the same thing. However, in the long run, since stocks are no more than pieces of companies, great companies are really great stocks. QUESTIONS TO CONSIDER: 1. What does it mean to be a shareholder of a company? 2. How is it possible to believe in a company or know it so well that you are confdent that you are right and the market is wrong about what it is worth? 3. Why does the market get it wrong sometimes? Afer completing this lesson, you should start to use the skills you learned in Lessons 1-4 to make a list of companies you came up with by doing some detective work. You start out with products you know and like, but gather additional evidence by seeing what other consumers are doing. You begin to run your own stock screens. You know that by buying a stock, you become a part owner of the company that issued that stock. You know that it is important to really understand the company so that you feel more comfortable trying to predict its future. You are now ready to go to the next step. You need to narrow your list to the stocks you really want to buy (the companies in which you want to be an owner). And you're learning how to hunt for treasure! KEY TAKEAWAYS: 1. Finding great stocks is like a treasure hunt, a very, very rewarding treasure hunt. 2. Invest in what you know and do your homework. 3. Stock screens can be a powerful way to identify good companies. 4. Remember, there's no rule in investing that says you can't own a stock that another person owns! Reading research reports can be a great way to learn more about investing.

LESSON 5: LEARNING TO SPEAK THE LANGUAGE OF FINANCE

Introduction Suppose a friend came to you and asked you to invest in her new business. She has started a website design business and she would like more money to buy a new computer. Before you decide if you should invest in her business or not, think about the questions you would want to ask her. What questions did you come up with? Here's a few you might have thought of: ? How much cash does the company already have? ? How much revenue has the company made since it was started? In the past year? ? How much revenue does the company expect to make in the future? ? What has the company spent its cash on in the past? ? Does the company have any debt? In order to answer these questions, a good place to start would be to look at the company's fnancial statements. Learning to read Financial Statements is like learning a new language. If you want to order a good dish in a French Restaurant, you will need to speak French to read the Menu. Similarly, with companies, if you want to fnd a good stock to invest in, you will need to speak the language of fnance and read their fnancial statements. Just like learning any new language, it is difcult at frst, but the more you practice, the more fuent you will be come!

WHY DO COMPANIES PREPARE FINANCIAL STATEMENTS?

All companies need to keep track of their fnances. Tis means the company is keeping track of all of the money coming in and money going out, as well as other transactions that don't necessarily involve the exchange of money. At the end of each month, quarter (three months), and year, a company will prepare fnancial statements, which are a summary of all the fnancial transactions for that period. For a company that is publicly traded (meaning shares of the company stock are sold on a stock market) it is required that the company prepare and fle quarterly and annual fnancial statements so the government and the public can see how the company is doing. WHO USES FINANCIAL STATEMENTS? Lots of diferent parties will be interested in the fnancial statements of a company. First, the company's management and board of directors will use the fnancial statements to track performance. Te fnancial statements show how the company has done in the past, and will help management make decisions about the future. Lenders (like banks who have made loans to the company) may also want to see the fnancial statements. Some loans may have certain requirements, such as the company's debt to equity ratio cannot be more than 0.3 in order to receive that loan. Or, the lender may just want to see how much cash the company has to estimate how likely it is the company will be able to pay back the loan and interest in a timely manner. Investors are also very interested in seeing the fnancial statements. Tey are making decisions about whether to buy or sell stock in the company, so they need to know how the company is doing to help inform their decisions. Can you think of anyone else who might use the fnancial statements of a company, other than management, banks and investors?

Te balance sheet (above) is a snapshot of the business at a single point in time. Tink of it like a photograph. It is a picture of what the business looks like on the day the picture is taken. Te balance sheet shows a snapshot of the company's assets (its resources that it expects to create value in the future), liabilities (the loans and other obligations due to others), and owners' equity (also known as shareholders' equity or stockholders' equity—the stake that the owners or investors have in the business). Apple, Inc. prepared a balance sheet for the year ended September 27, 2014. Here are some of the assets the balance sheet shows: $13.8 billion Cash (in fnance terms, cash is not just dollar bills, but all money held in checking accounts, savings accounts, etc. plus actual dollar bills on hand, if any) $17.5 billion Accounts Receivable (this means someone else bought something from Apple, but instead of paying right away, they still owe the money, and Apple is expecting to receive it in the future) $2.1 billion Inventories (these are the Macs and iPhones and iPads that Apple currently has in warehouses and stores, intended to be sold to customers) $20.6 billion Property, plant and equipment (this is the amount of land, buildings, and machinery that the company owns and uses to manufacture and sell goods) Here are some of the liabilities the balance sheet shows:

$30.2 billion Accounts Payable (this is the fip side of Accounts Receivable, so in this case, Apple has bought something from others and has promised to pay them for it in the future) $18.5 billion Accrued Expenses (this could include things like the obligation to pay interest to lenders and taxes to the government) $29.0 billion Long-term Debt (this means loans from a bank) Here are some of the equity balances the balance sheet shows: $23.3 billion Common Stock (this is the stock sold to investors on the market) $87.2 billion Retained Earnings (this is the amount of profts made in previous years that has been reinvested in the business to help it grow, rather than distributed to stockholders as dividends) QUESTIONS TO CONSIDER: 1.

Why a balance sheet is important? 2. All things equal, would you rather have more liabilities or less?

ᑭᑭᑭ

THE INCOME STATEMENT Next, let's watch this video on the Income Statement by Wall Street Survivor. https://www.youtube.com/watch?v=2RupCSFcY7w Te income statement shows a business's performance over a period of time, such as a year. Tink of it like a video. It shows what happens to the business over time. Te income statement shows how much revenue the company made over the year, how much it cost to sell its main products, how much it cost to pay its employees over the year, and how much it owed in interest and taxes for the year. On a very basic level, if the company makes more revenue than it spends in costs, it is a proftable business. If the company's costs are greater than its revenues, then it is not a proftable business. It is always good to remember not to look at just one fnancial statement and think it tells the whole story of the business. A good investor should learn to read all the fnancial statements, and look at trends occurring over time, from balance sheet to balance sheet and from income statement to income statement.

Apple, Inc. prepared an Income Statement for the year ended September 27, 2014. Te income statement shows that Apple has sales of $182.8 billion during that year. Tat is how much revenue Apple made from all its sales of computers and phones and apps and songs on iTunes and everything else it sells. Tis is an increase from $170.9 billion in 2013 and $156.5 billion in 2012. Next, the Income Statement shows expenses, starting with Cost of Sales of $112.3 billion. Tis means in order to make all the products it sold for that $182.8 billion revenue, it cost Apple $112.3 billion. Other expenses include $6.0 billion research and development costs, $12.0 billion selling, general, and administrative costs, and $14.0 billion tax expense. Finally, the Income Statement shows Net Income, which is known as the bottom line because – you guessed it! – it appears at the bottom of the Income Statement. Apple's Net Income for the year ended September 27, 2014, was $39.5 billion. QUESTIONS TO CONSIDER: 1. Why the income statement is important? 2. Which two lines on the income statement do you think are the most important? THE STATEMENT OF CASH FLOWS Te third of the primary fnancial statements is the statement of cash fows. Te statement of cash fows shows how much cash came into the business and how much cash went out of the business. It's important to note here that when we use the term cash in the fnance world, we mean not only dollar bills, like you might think of, but also checks and electronic transfers and the balance in the bank account. In fact, most businesses will do a lot of their transactions through electronic transactions, but we still call this cash. Tink of cash as just meaning all forms of money. https://www.youtube.com/watch?v=9DcRJD9rbbQ Below is a snapshot of Apple's Statement of Cash Flows. Cash generated from operating activities, is one of the most important metrics to monitor. Tink of this as earnings or net proft, but the actual cash earnings. Many times if a company has big non-cash charges or gains in a year, the more accurate proft number is found on the Cash Generated from Operating Activities. Te other key metric to look out for in the Statement of Cash Flows is the Capital Expenditure (also referred to CAPEX), or the Payments for acquisition of property, plant and equipment. Total for this category is the cash used to invest in the business.

One of the best measures of the proftability of a business, according to Warren Bufett and many great investors is the Free Cash Flow. Tis is calculated by: Net Income + Depreciation – CAPEX = Free Cash Flow. Tis is how much cash the business generated that year. Activity: Can you calculate the Free Cash Flow for Apple using the statements in this lesson? *Hint, some of the metrics are found on the Income Statement and some are found on the Statement of Cash Flows.

HOW DO I FORECAST REVENUES OF A COMPANY? In its simplest form, future revenue can be calculated by multiplying the average selling price of the company's product by the number of expected products sold. However, forecasting revenue isn't that simple and can involve considering many diferent factors. For instance, Apple would see increased revenue if it sold its iPhone for more money per unit, but only if the number of phones sold didn't decrease as a result of the price increase. Apple would love for both the price per unit and the number of units sold to increase, but these two things can move in opposite directions as people tend to buy fewer units as the price of that unit increases. Apple can also increase the number of units sold by expanding geographically. If it were to begin selling phones in a new country it hadn't previously sold in, that would add revenue. Tere can be other ofsetting factors too, however. When Apple frst introduced the iPhone, iPods were quite popular, but when people began to buy iPhones, which included integrated digital music players, they began buying fewer iPods. Tis efect made it so that while Apple gained lots of revenue from the sale of its iPhones, it began losing its normal iPod revenue. Companies can also gain additional revenue by taking market share from competitors. If, for instance, the number of smartphones sold in the world is 1.2 billion per year and Apple sells 50% of those this year and 60% next year, it will see a revenue increase, all else being equal. Tis means Apple sold 600 million phones (50% of 1.2B) this year and will sell 720 million phones (60% of 1.2B) next year. Tis is known as "taking market share," as Apple essentially took a bigger piece of the pie by going from 50% of the market to 60% of the market. Another way a company can grow revenue is by being in a market where the market itself is growing. For instance, if the market (i.e., the number of smartphones sold) grew by 10% from 1.2 billion phones to 1.32 billion phones, even if Apple retained a 50% market share, it would still sell 10% more phones. Companies can also grow revenues through opening or building new stores, acquiring other companies, etc. To forecast the revenues of a company, one must evaluate the industry, the company, and its competitors. Looking at a company's revenue growth rate for many years is a good start. However, you must be careful not to assume that an abnormal period of time is in fact normal. For instance, Apple's revenue growth rate was well over 10% per year since the early 2000s, and it even reached rates of over 50% afer the company released the iPhone and iPad, but by 2013 Apple was a very large company with no new products in a long time, resulting in a growth rate of under 10% for the year. Had the analyst assumed that the company would grow revenue at 50% a year for countless years to come, he/she would've been in for a rude awakening. In conclusion, forecasting revenue involves a lot of diferent variables, but a savvy analyst who has done his/her homework should be able to generate a good forecast in time. ACTIVITY: FORECAST REVENUES Chose a company that is on your list from Lesson 4 that you can up with from screens or from a grocery store visit, or from other sources: ? How fast has this company been growing revenues over the past 5 years? ? How fast did this company grow revenues last year? ? Has this company been growing faster or slower than its competitors? ? What do you expect they will grow at over the next 5 years? Use resources such as Morningstar.com, Zacks.com and Yahoo.Finance to research these metrics. HOW DO I FORECAST MARGINS OF A COMPANY? When analyzing stocks, you will likely review the income statement, balance sheet and statement of cash fows. Te income statement provides a fnancial summary of the operating results of the frm over a period of time such as a quarter or year. Te frst section of the income statement shows gross margins, simply the total revenue (sales) minus the cost of goods sold. Financial companies and service-oriented companies tend to have high gross margins since they ofen have lower costs of goods sold. Whereas industrial and manufacturing companies have lower gross margins as they have high cost of goods sold. Does the car manufacturing company Toyota have high or low gross margins? Tat's right they have low gross margins! Car manufacturing has one of the higher cost of goods sold out of any industry, one car is made up of thousands of parts. Adding up all those parts equals a high cost of goods sold and lower gross margins. Remember the gross margin is simply subtracting the cost of goods sold from the total revenue. Which can be helpful when looking at two companies in the same industry, take Apple versus Samsung.

ᑭᑭᑭ

Tey both make wonderful cellular phones, who would you guess has higher gross margin? A. Samsung B. Apple Apple has the higher gross margin and why is that important? Whether they charge a higher price or they have lower cost of goods sold can lead to competitive advantages over the long run. Going a step further on the income statement you will notice operating incomes or EBIT. Operating Income divided by total revenues is Operating margin. Operating margin is a measure of proftability, how much of each dollar of revenue is lef over afer both cost of goods sold and operating expenses. Te operating expenses include payroll, sales commissions, marketing, transportation, travel, rent and other general expenses. It's likely easier to comprehend if you think about buying a pair of pants. You are in the mall and want to buy a pair of pants that costs $50, that's a nice pair of pants right? Tey felt so nice you go ahead and buy them, did you know it only cost $20 to make those pants. Tat's the cost of goods sold right, $20. Did you pay too much? Let's think about it. Afer the company made the pants, they had to ship the pants to the store by semi-truck, someone had to unload the shipment of pants, the company pays rent to have a store in the mall, the store has employees who put the pants on display and sold them to you, a commercial was made to promote the pants and these operating expenses add up to $25 on top of the $20 cost of goods sold. Leaving the company with a proft of $5 or gross operating margin of 10%. GROUP ACTIVITY: MARGIN MATCHING Let's play a matching game! Match the company with the operating margin they make: Walmart and Facebook. Company A has operating margin of 24% Company B has operating margin of 5% Hint, the secret behind Walmart is they ofer the lowest prices and while they make little proft per good sold, they make up for it because they sell so much more socks, shampoo, and cereal than any of their competitors. Match the operating margin to the following three companies, Coca-Cola, Nike and Boeing. Company A has operating margin of 8% Company B has operating margin of 13% Company C has operating margin of 25%

Is your head ready to explode yet? You probably feel a lot like you did in your frst week of Spanish class. A little lost with a splitting headache. But give it a bit of time and you're well on your way to being able speak the language of fnance. Whether you become a world-famous stock investor in the future, an accountant, or maybe just a dentist trying to keep the records of the business, learning to read fnancial statements is critical. Te more fuent you are, the more successful you will be in almost any industry of business. KEY TAKEAWAYS: 1. Finance has a language (accounting) that you learn how to speak. 2. Tere are three main fnancial statements, Te Balance Sheet, Te Income Statement and the Statement of Cash Flows 3. You need to be able to forecast a company's revenue and margins correctly if you want to invest in them. ACTIVITY Situation: MIXED UP FINANCIAL STATEMENTS Let's assume you landed a summer internship working for the legendary investor, Warren Bufett himself. One team will be chosen to be his next protégés, and will eventually take over his $60 billion dollar empire, Berkshire Hathaway. One morning, Bufett, comes to you in a tizzy. He explains he was doing analysis on companies and going through their fnancial statements. He printed of their balance sheets and income statements, but lost track of the names of the companies. He says, "Can you match the list of companies I was doing work on with the correct fnancial statements? I'm positive if I can match the correct companies, I will be able to fnd the next multi-billion dollar investment idea, and I will hire you to run my company!" Try to match up the correct the fnancial statements in APPENDIX A with each of the following companies. Te team with the most correct answers is the winner. NO CHEATING BY LOOKING ONLINE! Questions to Consider: (HINTS) 1. Does the company make high margins (Gross proft / Revenue)? 2. What do growth trends of revenue and net income tell you? 3. Is the business capital intensive (do they require a lot of assets to make money)? 4. Does the company hold a lot of inventories relative to their overall sales level?

5. Does the company have a high debt balance? 6. Which company makes the most sales? COMPANIES: 1). Amazon.com (ticker AMZN)– the largest eCommerce website in the world. Fast growing company, also has kindle,

Amazon Fire and cloud storage business. Because of fast growth phase, the company is currently not proftable. 2). Coca-Cola Company (ticker KO) – Te largest beverage company in the world. Coca-Cola is a high margin and high return (ROE) business (above 20%). Revenue has declined a bit in the past two years 3). Celldex Terepeutics (ticker CLDX) – an early stage biotech company working on an experimental brain cancer vaccine. Te company is spending signifcantly on research and development, but will not reap the rewards of this investment until many years down the road. 4). Freeport McMorran (FCX) – One of the largest copper and gold miners in the world. Te business has been hit due to declines in the prices of gold and copper. Tey also own some oil and gas felds. 5). Costco (COST)– Costco is one of the largest retail chains in the US, operating a warehouse model that charges a membership fee. Inventory management and increasing sales per assets (sales turnover) is an important part of the business 6). Facebook (FB) – Facebook is the largest social network in the world. Te company has few real assets (buildings, equipment) and the bulk of their costs are employees. Te company is in a high growth phase.

8

THE INVESTMENT THESIS

Successful businesses start with a clear mission statement. Marriages begin with the exchange of vows. Similarly, successful stock investors begin with a clear investment objective, called an "Investment Tesis". Tis tells you why you own the stock and what you expect to happen. When deciding what a particular stock is worth, its intrinsic value, what we are really asking is "what is it worth to you"? A horse is worth more to a farmer than a sailor. A McDonalds happy meal is worth more to kids than, well, any other rational human being. Value is always in the eye of the beholder, and when you buy a stock, the beholder is you. For example, if you need a steady cash payment every year from a stock in the form of a dividend, and a company decides to stop paying its dividend, its Investment Tesis is no longer valid. Tis is critical to know. In Lesson 4 we learned about legendary investor Peter Lynch said how he advocated buying companies that you know. He made a fortune of of buying Hanes stock because he wife liked the pantyhose. Peter Lynch said in one of his most famous quotes "Know What You Own and Know Why You Own It". In other words, when you buy a stock, you need to know the WHY. Tis is important because the value of a particular stock can rise and fall multiple times in a month, week, day and even in an hour! Instinctively, we want to buy more when a stock price is soaring, and alternatively, we want to sell as soon as possible when the price drops. But many investors get caught up in a "herd mentality" and react to price fuctuations like stampeding cattle based on the direction they perceive the market is heading. Stock prices rise and fall for various reasons as new information (good or bad, accurate or inaccurate) enters the market. In order to know whether this new information should afect your decision to buy, sell or hold stock in a particular company, it is vital that you develop your own "investment thesis."

SECTION 1 WHAT IS AN INVESTMENT THESIS? Before investing in a company, we need to have a carefully thought out "Investment Tesis." An investment thesis is basically a simple and clear description of: 1. Why you own the company. 2. What you expect to happen. 3. What you see that the market does not give the company credit for. Many experienced investors will tell you that there is hardly anything as valuable in keeping them focused and intellectually honest as this simple exercise. Remember that the principles to successful investing are simple, but the hard part is adhering to them through the ups and downs of the market. In this sense, the investment thesis becomes our anchor, even when the waters get rough or (even more difcult) when the waters stay calm for a deceivingly long time. If the thesis is still valid, nothing else matters. If the thesis may be at risk, nothing matters more. Successful value investor Martin Whitman concluded: "Based on my own personal experience – both as an investor in recent years and an expert witness in years past – rarely do more than three or four variables really count. Everything else is noise." So how do we know which variables count and which are just noise? Let's walk through an example using a company we all know, Apple. If we were going to buy stock in Apple, we would begin by understanding the competitive landscape. We would analyze their smartphone, PC and sofware peers. We would look at the company's strengths, weaknesses, opportunities and threats (also known as a "SWOT analysis"). We would analyze the fnancial statements and historical returns to shareholders. We would try to speak with someone at the company, speak with their suppliers, speak with customers, and speak with competitors. Now suppose afer all of this, we determine that Apple is a great stock to buy. Tat it has a sustainable competitive advantage, and the stock price is substantially lower than what the business is worth. We then take out a pen and paper (or smartphone) and write down the main points of why we are buying the stock.

A sample "Buy" case Investment Tesis for Apple may look something like this: ? Apple's strong brand will enable the company to sell their products at premium prices. (BRAND) ? Apple's ecosystem of inter-connected apps, videos and music fuels a loyal and sticky user base. (ECOSYSTEM) ? Smartphones and tablets are in their early stages of adoption globally, ofering signifcant growth potential. (GROWTH) ? Apple's management promotes a culture of innovation and design for consumer electronics, creating a platform for future product launches. (CULTURE) On the other hand, maybe our research uncovers some concerns about that company so that we feel that Apple's current position may not be sustainable going forward and that the company is a "Sell". We may even short the stock, hoping to proft from its decline. A "Sell" Investment Tesis for Apple may look something like this: ? Apple competes in the highly competitive industries of PC and smartphones. ? History has proven that commoditization for consumer electronics industry is inevitable, which makes Apple's premium prices and exceptionally high margins unsustainable. ? Afer the death of Steve Jobs, Apple's product innovation has noticeably deteriorated. ? Apple is heavily reliant on their supply chain of components, which they do not control, and which will limit future innovation. Which thesis do you agree with? Perhaps more important than being right, is the mere fact that you are making a choice, writing it down, and constantly keeping yourself honest by referring back to it. Of course, that being said, you also want to be right! Let's assume that you believe the frst scenario, and you go ahead and buy shares in Apple. You sit happy knowing that every time someone in the world that goes out and buys and iPhone, they are earning you a small share of that proft. You even go out and buy yourself a new iPhone using that same argument, fantastic! But then the news starts pouring in: Samsung is launching a fancy newfangled smartphone next month. Apple's quarterly earnings were 10% below expectations and suddenly the stock drops by 20%. CEO Tim Cook is having a bad hair day. What is going on?! Every day we wake up to either panic or euphoria in the news – how do we keep it all straight? Tere is one simple trick -- constantly ask yourself the same question: "Is the investment thesis still intact?" For example: Does Samsung's new smartphone have any impact on Apple's (1) brand power, (2) ecosystem, (3) growth, or (4) culture of innovation? If not, then it's just noise. Does Apple's earnings for the quarter indicate anything about the company's (1) brand power, (2) ecosystem, (3) growth, or (4) culture of innovation? If not, then it's just noise. Does Tim Cook's hairdo present any risk to the company's (1) brand power, (2) ecosystem, (3) growth, or (4) culture of innovation? Possibly, then for heaven sakes, get the man a comb! If not, then it's just noise. When we develop the habit of constantly checking new information against our investment thesis, we learn to efectively flter out the noise. But then let's say that through conversations with second-hand resellers of Apple products, we fnd out that a one-year old used iPhone that used to sell for $400 is now selling for $300. We inquire as to why, and we are told that customers are telling us that there are other phones available that are nearly as good and they simply aren't willing to pay a higher price for an iPhone. We also fnd that carriers are saying the same things. Now, we can legitimately begin to worry. Tere may be a crack forming in Point #1 ("Apple's strong brand power will enable the company to sell their products at premium prices"). If we fnd we can no longer defend a key point of the investment thesis, then we sell the company. Period. It is simply not worth the time and the risk. QUESTIONS TO CONSIDER: 1. Do you agree more with Investment Tesis of "Buy" of Apple, or "Sell"? 2. Compare the Apple today vs. Apple of 2010, before the death of Steve Jobs, has the Investment Tesis been strengthened or weakened since then? What is the evidence to support your view?

SECTION 2 Case Study: Portfolio Manager and founder of YIS, James Fletcher learned the power of the Investment Tesis early in his investment career. In 2007, he came across a company from South Korea that made online video games. Teir existing games had a remarkably sticky user base paying subscription fees every month. Te games had two powerful things that he looks for in companies: (1) a network efect -- the more kids that played the game the more attractive the game becomes and (2) high switching costs -- when someone invests seven years leveling up a character and amassing virtual items, they were unlikely to switch to another game and have to start over. Te company had a rare competitive moat that was both wide and deep. But they hadn't had a hit game in a while, so the market was rather gloomy on the company despite what was considered to be a top-notch development team. As any parent who has had to try and pick a video game for their kids, the video game industry is an unpredictable "hit or miss" industry. Trying to forecast whether a game will be a hit is very difcult. It's ofen a roll of the dice. However, James took a long-term approach and built an investment thesis on three pillars: 1). the existing games would continue to retain their loyal user base and pay handsome returns, 2). despite being a "hit-or-miss" industry, the development team would eventually get a hit, 3). the current stock price implied no probability to a new game success. Shortly afer buying the stock, the company launched a new fagship game. Here it was! Te game had all the makings of a blockbuster: substantial buzz in the gaming community, a legendary lead-developer, three full years of development, a huge marketing budget, and positive reviews. Te game hit the shelves, and then... it fopped! It just simply didn't sell. James watched the stock price fall for the company by nearly 50% in a month. He felt sick to his stomach! He stumbled back to the drawing board -- his investment thesis -- and asked himself: was the original investment premise intact? 1. Did the company still have a sticky, loyal user base on existing games? Yes. 2. Was the development team still likely to have a hit game in the future? Yes. 3. Was the stock undervalued? Yes, even more so.

Tis meant that all of the despair in the market was actually just noise. Feeling a bit more comforted afer reviewing the investment thesis, he continued to hold the stock. In 2008, the company launched another game. Tis time, expectations were even higher. Te launch was timed for the holiday season and the game was a mix between car racing and online fghting--which every industry expert believed was a sure formula for success. Te game hit the shelves and low and behold...another fop! Te game mostly sat on the shelves and everyone that bought the game ended up returning it because there was no one online to play it with. Investors were exasperated and the stock plummeted by another 40%. James' clients began to notice poor performance. At this point, to his knowledge, James's company and its clients remained the only international shareholders to continue to own the stock, which by default made them feel both stupid and lonely. Tey even had the audacity to add to our position. But here is the reason why: not one thing had changed from the original investment thesis, except for the fact that the stock price looked a whole lot more attractive now than it ever had! Some may call this sticking to your guns. Some may call this being just fat-out stubborn. Investors like to refer to this as "high conviction." Despite what you call it, however, James' conviction came from having a clearly defned investment thesis, giving him the ability to block out the noise. Te following year, the company launched another game that was largely ignored by the market because it was more of a niche game for an Asian audience. Everyone's expectations were rock bottom afer the previous failures. Te game was released and turned out to be one of the bestselling video games of all-time in Korea, and then later, a blockbuster hit in China. Te stock price shot through the roof. Two years later the company followed it up with another successful game launch, and the stock climbed even higher. From James' initial investment, he had now made over a 500% return. He and his clients were dancing in the aisles. Looking back, James recounts that the success was basically due to just one factor: "that I had written down those three simple bullet points down from the very beginning". He says if he had not he surely would have sold his shares when times get rough. Without the rock-solid conviction of why they owned it, they would have followed the herd and cut their losses. He was grateful he stayed true to his investment thesis. QUESTIONS TO CONSIDER: 1. Discuss the reasons why it's difcult to keep holding a good stock when it is going down?

2. Discuss the reasons why it's difcult to sell a stock that you bought whose investment thesis may not be valid anymore? CONCLUSION In order to invest with confdence and properly flter out noise that might intimidate you, confuse you and cause you to make emotional decisions that could cost you money, it is important that you create an investment thesis of your own for every stock that you buy. KEY TAKEAWAYS: 4. Know the stocks you own and know why you own them. 5. Creating and constantly re-evaluating an investment thesis is the most crucial tool to keep investors on-track and disciplined. 6. If news doesn't impact the investment thesis, then it is just noise. If new data gives us either higher conviction or higher concerns in our investment thesis, nothing matters more. ACTIVITY: Creating Your Own Investment Checklist Going hand in hand with creating an Investment Tesis for the each of the stocks that you own, is creating an overarching Investment Checklist. An Investment Checklist is the summary of your personal investment process. Te idea of an investment checklist was created by famed investor Mohnish Pabrai, whose fund has earned a 517% return compared to the S&P 500 up 43% since 2000. Te idea, according to Pabrai, is to create a series of Yes or No questions to ask yourself before investing in a stock to make sure you don't miss anything or make a mistake. A good Investment Checklist is like a constitution, a series of personal rules to make sure that you stay disciplined and focused. Te goal is create a series of over-arching questions that will maximize your chances of fnding great investments and minimize the chances of investing in a dud. Many successful investors such as Guy Spier and Charlie Munger (partner to Warren Bufet) also attribute the use of Investment Checklists as one of the hallmarks of their success.

9

INTRINSIC VALUE

Introduction As a value-investor your focus is to buy companies whose stock prices do not actually refect their true value, known as “intrinsic value”. If you can successfully select companies to buy whose stock price is trading below their intrinsic value, then you'll be successful. Being able to correctly estimate something's intrinsic value is one of the most important skills of a master investor. Looking at the graph below, when are the times that you want to buy to stock? When are the times that you want to sell the stock? Why do you think the market price is more volatile than the intrinsic value of a company?

Looking at the graph below, when are the times that you want to buy to stock? When are the times that you want to sell the stock? Why do you think the market price is more volatile than the intrinsic value of a company?

SECTION 1 Let's Buy a House To get your mind working, let's imagine that you are going to buy a house. We will think of buying the house in the context of its book value, market value, and its intrinsic value. Book Value When the seller of the house frst bought the house, they most likely placed a down payment, and fnanced the rest of the house with debt. Let's say for example that they bought the house for $200,000 and placed a down payment of $20,000. In essence, they paid $20,000, the bank gave them $180,000. In simple terms, we would say that the book value is the total amount of book equity plus the amount of liabilities. In this case, the book value would be $20,000 + $180,000 = $200,000. Market Value Remember that markets determine prices. Let's say we want to buy that very same house in 5 years. By this point, due to a shortage of houses and increased demand, similar houses are selling for $250,000. Tat same house, even though its book value is still $200,000 now has increased in value and the market has priced that house and similar houses at $250,000. Te market value would be $250,000. Tis is the price that you would have to pay to buy that house. Should you buy that house for the $250,000? Is it actually worth $250,000? Intrinsic Value Now, let's take a deeper dive into the $250,000 market value or wouldbe selling price of the house. You really want to know if that house is worth $250,000. If you determined the house is actually worth $250,000, you would be comfortable buying it. If you determined it was worth less than $250,000, you would not buy it. If you determined it was worth more than $250,000, you would buy it in a heart-beat and consider yourself a value investor. What are some things you should look at to determine if that house is really worth $250,000? You might look at the future housing market of that area. You might take a deeper look inside the house. You might look at the condition of the following: the kitchen, the roof, the yard, the appliances, the garage, the bathrooms, the rooms, etc. You also would need to take a look at how long that house will be able to support its residents. Afer you perform a thorough inspection of the housing market, you determine that house prices will increase

over the next couple of years and the house will have a much higher resale value. You discover that the appliances of the house are brand new, the roof has recently been replaced, the yard is in great condition, and everything else seems to be in order with the house. You run a few calculations based on the condition of the house and future prospects of the housing market, and ultimately you value the house at $300,000. Because of your inspections and belief on the future condition of the housing market, you have determined that the intrinsic value (true) value is greater than the market value of the house. You should buy the house and consider yourself a value investor. QUESTIONS TO CONSIDER: 1. Why is determining the "Intrinsic Value" of a house more difcult than the "Book Value"? 2. What is the "Market Value" and the "Book Value" of something harder to calculate, like going to college? What is the "Intrinsic Value" of going to college?

SECTION 2 Determining the Intrinsic Value of a Company Tere are many valuation metrics and techniques investors use to try to estimate a company's worth. We will teach you two: Te Discounted Cash Flow Method and the Relative Valuation method. The Discounted Cash Flows method You want to impress someone you know who works in fnance? Tell them that you built a discounted cash fows or "DCF" model in school today! It's like telling a hiker that you've hiked Mount Everest or telling an ice skater that you can do a triple axel. Yeah, doing a DFC is really that cool. And today you're going to create one! A Discounted Cash Flows model is one of the go-to ways for investors to measure the value of a company. A company's worth is the present value of all net future cash fows, or in simpler terms (I know that's a mouthful), the value of a company today is the sum of all the cash fow they will earn each year in the future, but what that cash fow is worth in today's dollars. A company's value cannot be measured entirely by its total sales, nor buy its net income. We cannot necessarily say that just because a company has more revenue or net income that it is more valuable than its counterpart. A company is only worth the amount of cash it has lef over afer it has covered all of its expenses. Tat is what we mean when we say net cash fow. Net cash fow is the cash the company receives from its sales minus total expenses minus money spent on equipment or assets to grow the business (called Capital Expenditures). Te formula is: Net Cash Flow = Revenue – Expenses – Capital Expenditures. Tis type of valuation is referred to as a discounted cash fow analysis. Question: You are given the opportunity to choose to invest in either company ABC or company XYZ. ABC has total annual revenue of $100.00 and is selling for $250/share; XYZ has total revenue of $80.00 and is selling for $300/share. Which one would you buy? Answer: It depends. You can't judge whether to buy a company based purely of of its revenue. You would need to know the present value of its future cash fows, and then determine which company to buy. Alright, are you ready to rock and roll?

Go to "Resources" Tab on the Young Investors Society website (www.younginvestorssociety.org) and download the "Intrinsic Value" Spreadsheet. Here you will fnd a template that will walk you through creating your very own calculation of the intrinsic value of a company. It may seem daunting at frst, but it's really not that complicated. And it's a powerful tool once you know how to use it. Steps to use the Discounted Cash Flow (DCF) Analysis Tool: 1. Chose a company that you would like to estimate the intrinsic value for (e.g. Apple, Google, Netfix, Ford etc.) 2. Use fnance.yahoo.com or zacks.com to input the information in the yellow boxes (name, share price, shares outstanding, revenue, net income, free cash fow). 3. Your two main assumptions are 1) the future growth rates (Row 15 & 16) and the cash fow margin (Row 26). Look at the trends the company has had in the past, think about if the future will be higher or lower, and make your best guess. Remember that most companies have fat or declining margins over time because of competition and technologic changes 4. In most cases, leave the discount rate at 12%. Also, in most cases, leave the terminal growth rate at 4 or 5%. 5. Play around with the assumptions. When you do, look at how the cash fow graph and the Intrinsic Value calculation changes. 6. In Row 33, you will see your Intrinsic Value calculated. If the Intrinsic Value is signifcantly above the Current Share price, then the stock is likely undervalued, and go BUY IT! If the Intrinsic Value is below the current share price, then the stock is likely overvalued. Below is a snapshot of how your DCF model will look. Be sure to save your sheet to your own drive for future use. And so when your dad's friend that works in fnance says "No way, you didn't really do a DCF in high-school!" You can prove it to him. He'll probably ofer you an internship on the spot.

SECTION 3 The Relative Valuation Method A simpler, better known metric, to estimate a company's valuation is its price-to-earnings (P/E) ratio. For companies with relatively stable earnings prospects, the P/E provides a reasonable approximation of the discounted value of its future earnings, as it tells the investor how many times one year's earnings the stock price is currently discounting. For example, if a stock is trading at a 15x P/E, this means that at the current year's earnings (E) it will take 15 years to get your money back. 30x P/E will take 30 years. Obviously, for an investment, the sooner the better. Tus, the P/E is a reasonable yardstick for a stock's valuation. Everything else being equal, the lower the P/E, the more attractively valued the stock is said to be. However, there are many caveats to this statement. Diferent industries have diferent P/E ranges, the more stable the industry (and the company's earnings streams), and the higher the P/E can be without necessarily making the investment "expensive." Very cyclical industries tend to present additional challenges. High growth companies tend to trade at high P/E, and low growth companies tend to trade at low P/Es.

As you can see, valuing stocks is like going to a grocery store. You get what you pay for. If you want to buy the best product, you're likely going to have to pay for it. Our job as investors is to buy as quality a product as we can (high ROE, strong economic moat business) at as low a P/E as we can. Tere are value investors who prefer to focus more on "balance sheet" related ratios, such as the price-to-book (P/B) value of a frm. Te P/B compares the stock price to the value of company's assets minus its liabilities. Are you ready to calculate Intrinsic Value using the "Relative Valuation" method? In practice, this is the method that most professional portfolio managers and analysts use to estimate the value of a company. Go back to your "Intrinsic Value" Spreadsheet and scroll down to the second section called "Relative

Valuation Analysis". Steps to use the Relative Valuation Analysis Tool: 1. Chose a company that you would like to estimate the intrinsic value for (e.g. Apple, Google, Netfix, Ford etc.) 2. If you flled in the section above in the DCF assumptions, the P/E of the company should already be calculated in C:56 (for example, 11.0). 3. You then want to think of three or four good comparable companies that operate in similar industries and have similar ROEs and growth expectations. If you are buying a house, this is like going to similar homes in the neighborhood and seeing what they sold for. 4. Look at the comparable average P/E (C:61). Is the average above or below your company? Go to Row 63, Column C and decide whether your company deserves to trade at a premium or discount to their peer average. For example, do they earn a premium ROE? Are they growing faster? Are they a more predictable business? If so, then they may warrant a premium. 5. C:64 is where you put in your Target Multiple. Use the chart above, and the comparable company table in your model to estimate a P/E ratio. Is it 15 (average), 10 (below average) or 20 (above average) company? What P/E ratio range did it trade at in the past? 6. In F:70, you will see the earnings per share estimated 3 years in the future. Review this number, and decide whether you think this is a good assumption.

7. In Row 72, you will see your Intrinsic Value calculated. If the Intrinsic Value is signifcantly above the Current Share price, then the stock is likely undervalued, and go BUY IT! If the Intrinsic Value is below the current share price, then the stock is likely overvalued.

Tere, now you've done it! Compare your DCF Intrinsic Value Calculation to the Relative Valuation Calculation. Did they reach the same conclusion? Student Teacher: Choose one student to explain the concept of "intrinsic value" to the group. Have the student briefy describe the three ways discussed above, and then choose a company that has a low P/E ratio. Why is the P/E ratio a commonly used way to value a company? QUESTIONS TO CONSIDER: 1. Referencing your Intrinsic Value calculation, why is it risky to buy a stock that trades at a high P/E ratio? 2. Why is it risky to buy a company that trades at a low P/E ratio?

CONCLUSION Intrinsic value is the true value of a company. Tis may or may not be refected in its stock price. A great investor is one that can fnd a stock that is trading at a signifcant discount to its intrinsic value. Many valuation techniques exist due to diferent preferences among investors. Two Primary Valuation Options ? Discounted Cash Flow Model ? Relative Valuation Model When measuring intrinsic value, we have to take into account a lot of random variables; therefore, the intrinsic value is ofen an estimate. Valuation is not 100 percent precise, but if you are good at it and can continuously fnd companies that are trading at a discount to their future value, you will be in great shape. Intrinsic value is a necessary lens through which we need to see our investments. KEY TAKEAWAYS: 1. Intrinsic value is what something is worth, Price is what you have to pay. Tey're not the same thing! 2. Buying stocks below their intrinsic value gives you a margin of safety and sets you up to make money in the market. 3. Te two most common methods for calculating value of stocks are the Discounted Cash Flow Model and the Relative Valuation Model.

1). Accounts Payable – a short term liability, representing money the company owes for purchases from a supplier 2). Accounts Receivable – a short term asset, representing money the company is expecting to receive from sales made to customers 3). Accrued Expenses – a liability, such as an obligation to pay interest to bank lenders or to pay taxes to the government 4). Asset – a resource that the company owns or controls 5). Book Value- Te sum of all liabilities and equity on the balance sheet 6). Balance Sheet – one of the three primary fnancial statements, which shows a snapshot of the assets, liabilities, and equity of the business at a certain point in time 7). Brokerage Firm – A fnancial institution that facilitates the buying and selling of fnancial securities (generally stocks or bonds) between buyer and seller. 8). Brand – A distinguishing symbol, mark, logo, name, word, sentence or a combination of these items that companies use to distinguish their product from others in the market. Brand equity is the positive sentiment created by a product among its target audience over time. 9). Brand – A distinguishing symbol, mark, logo, name, word, sentence or a combination of these items that companies use to distinguish their product from others in the market. Brand equity is the positive sentiment created by a product among its target audience over time. 10). Brand – A distinguishing symbol, mark, logo, name, word, sentence or a combination of these items that companies use to distinguish their product from others in the market. Brand equity is the positive sentiment created by a product among its target audience over time. 11). Cash – the money a company has on hand, whether in physical currency or in bank accounts 12). Cash Flow – Cash fow or fows is the cash generated by a company. It is diferent from earnings because does not include non-cash items. For example, a company may make a large sale to a customer, which will count as earnings, but the customer has 30 days to pay for the purchase, so it is not yet cash received by the company.

13). Creditors – Investors or institutions (such as banks, among others) to which a company owes money. 14). Capital – Another word for money. 15). Common Stock – the stock sold to investors on the market 16). Cost of Goods Sold – the costs required to produce the good or service sold to a customer 17). Dividend – Te portion of a company's profts that it pays out each year to shareholders in the form of cash. 18). Discount Price- A price that is lower than the true value 19). Discounted Cash Flow (DCF) Analysis- Forecasting future cash fows that the business will generate and then discounting them back to the present value at an appropriate discount rate. 20). Discount rate- Rate of return that investors need to receive in order to be compensated for risk 21). Diversifcation – A risk management technique that mixes a wide variety of investments within the portfolio. Te rationale behind this technique contends that a portfolio of diferent investments will, on average, yield higher returns and pose lower risk than any individual investment found within the portfolio. 22). Equity Value- Intrinsic value of equity that is found by subtracting total debt from frm value 23). Enterprise or Firm Value – Te total value of the company, including the portion of it that "belongs" to its creditors. It is calculated by adding the company's net debt to its market cap. 24). Equity – the total of all stock owned and earnings retained that belong to the owners 25). Economic Moat – Te competitive advantage that one company has over other companies in the same industry. Tis term was coined by renowned investor Warren Bufett. 26). Economic Moat – Te competitive advantage that one company has over other companies in the same industry. Tis term was coined by renowned investor Warren Bufett.

27). Economic Moat – Te competitive advantage that one company has over other companies in the same industry. Tis term was coined by renowned investor Warren Bufett. 28). Equity Portfolio or Stock Portfolio – A basket or collection of stocks. A diversifed stock portfolio includes companies from diferent industries and of diferent sizes. 29). Firm/ Enterprise Value- Intrinsic value of a company taking into account both debt and equity 30). Gross Margin – the total revenue (or sales) minus the cost of goods sold 31). Gross Margin – Te proft the company makes afer the cost of its goods are paid for. (Gross Proft / Total Revenues) 32). Intrinsic Value- the true value of a company without regards to its market value or book value 33). Income Statement – one of the three primary fnancial statements, which shows the activity of a company over a period of time, showing both revenues and expenses 34). Intrinsic Value – Te true worth of a company. Tere are many ways to estimate the intrinsic value of a company, among them are discounted cash fow analysis and relative valuation analysis. 35). Intrinsic Value – What a stock is truly worth, not necessarily what the current stock price is. 36). Inventories – products that will eventually be sold to a customer 37). Interest Coverage – Te total value of the company, including the portion of it that "belongs" to its creditors. It is calculated by adding the company's net debt to its market cap. 38). Investment Tesis – Te basic guiding principles an investor establishes to justify: 1. Why he owns the company 2. What he expects to happen 3. What he sees that the market does not give the company credit for 39). Liability – any obligation that the company owes to another entity

40). Long-term Debt – a liability such as a loan from a bank 41). Liquidity – Te degree to which an asset or security (stock) can be bought or sold in the market without afecting the asset's price or stock price. Assets that can be easily bought or sold are known as liquid assets. 42). Low Cost Advantage – A sustainable advantage driven by access to a unique process, location, scale, labor costs or access to a unique asset, which allows a company to ofer goods or services at a lower cost than competitors. 43). Low Cost Advantage – A sustainable advantage driven by access to a unique process, location, scale, labor costs or access to a unique asset, which allows a company to ofer goods or services at a lower cost than competitors. 44). Low Cost Advantage – A sustainable advantage driven by access to a unique process, location, scale, labor costs or access to a unique asset, which allows a company to ofer goods or services at a lower cost than competitors. 45). Margin of Safety – Only purchase stocks when the market price is signifcantly below the intrinsic value. For example, a company owns land, equipment, cash and other assets that are worth $20 per share, yet the stock price is trading at $15 per share in the market. Buying this company at $15 provides a 25% discount or margin of safety. 46). Mutual Fund – Professionally managed stock portfolio. Instead of investing in individual stocks yourself, you can invest money in a mutual fund, where professionals pick stocks for you. 47). Market Value- the sum of the market cap (shares outstanding times total shares) and the debt 48). Market Share – the percentage of a certain industry or market (e.g. the athletic shoe market) that a certain company's sales are 49). Margins – Te percentage of proft the company makes for every dollar of revenues. For example, a 50% proft margin means the company earns $0.5 of proft for every $1 of revenue earned. 50). Market Capitalization (also known as market cap) – Total market value of the company's equity. It is calculated by multiplying the stock price of the company times the number of shares outstanding.

51). Network Efect – A phenomenon whereby a good or service becomes more valuable when more people use it. 52). Network Efect – A phenomenon whereby a good or service becomes more valuable when more people use it. 53). Network Efect – A phenomenon whereby a good or service becomes more valuable when more people use it. 54). Net Debt – Te company's total debt adjusted by its cash on hand (total debt minus cash). 55). Operating Expenses – the costs associated with operating the business, such as payroll, sales commissions, marketing, transportation, travel, and rent expenses 56). Operating Income – the income afer subtracting both cost of goods sold and operating expenses from total revenuesOperating Margin – calculated by dividing operating income by total revenues 57). Operating Margin (EBIT Margin) – Te proft the company makes afer paying for its cost of goods sold and the cost of salaries, utilities, and depreciation. (Operating Proft / Total Revenues) 58). Proft Margins – Te ratio of profts made per dollar of revenue. Te higher the proft margin the better. 59). Portfolio Manager – Te manager of a portfolio of stocks. Tey do extensive research to make investment decisions for a fund or group of funds under their control. Based on their research, the Portfolio Manager will buy and sell stocks. 60). P/E Ratio – One measure of how expensive a stock is. In general, a high P/E suggests that investors are expecting higher earnings growth to be high in the future. A low P/E can indicate either that a company may currently be undervalued or that the company's profts are expected to decline. Te price-earnings ratio can be calculated as: Market Value per Share (Stock Price) / Earnings per Share or Market Capitalization / Profts 61). Property, Plant, & Equipment – the long-term physical assets owned by a company, including land, buildings, furnishings, and machinery

62). Price to Book – A ratio used to compare a stock's market value to its book value. It is calculated by dividing the current closing price of the stock by the latest quarter's book value per share. 63). Profts – Proft is the money a business makes afer accounting for all the expenses. Regardless of whether the business is a couple of kids running a lemonade stand or a publicly traded multinational company, consistently earning proft is every company's goal. Net Profts = Total Revenue – Total Expenses 64). Profts – Proft is the money a business makes afer accounting for all the expenses. Regardless of whether the business is a couple of kids running a lemonade stand or a publicly traded multinational company, consistently earning proft is every company's goal. Net Profts = Total Revenue – Total Expenses

65). Retained Earnings – income generated by the business that has been reinvested in the business, rather than distributed to owners in a dividend 66). Revenue – Te amount of money that a company actually receives during a specifc period. It is referred to as the "top line" because it is the total amount of sales before you start to factor in the costs of the business. 67). Revenue (or Sales) – the total amount generated by sales to customers 68). Return on Invested Capital – A calculation used to assess a company's efciency at allocating capital under its control to proftable investments. 69). Return on Capital – Return on Capital is a useful metric for comparing proftability across companies based on the amount of capital they use. 70). Return on Equity (ROE) – Perhaps the most useful fnancial metric or all, it is used to compare a company's profts based on the total capital. Return on Equity = Net Income / Shareholder's Equity 71). Revenue – Te amount of money that a company actually receives during a specifc period. It is referred to as the "top line" because it is the total amount of sales before you start to factor in the costs of the business.

72). Return on Equity (ROE) – Perhaps the most useful fnancial metric of all, it is used to compare a company's profts based on the total capital. Return on Equity = Net Income / Shareholder's Equity 73). Statement of Cash Flows – one of the three primary fnancial statements, which shows all the sources and uses of cash over a period of time 74). Stock – Stock is a unit of ownership in a company. When you buy a stock you become a shareholder, which means you own part of the company. 75). Switching Costs – Te inconveniences that dissuade a customer from switching to a competitor's products. Te negative costs that a consumer incurs as a result of changing suppliers, brands or products. Although most prevalent switching costs are monetary in nature, there are also psychological, efort- and time-based switching costs. 76). Stock Market – Te market in which shares of publicly-held companies are issued and traded, either through exchanges or over-the-counter markets. Also known as the equity market, it provides companies with access to capital (money) in exchange for giving investors a slice of ownership in a company. 77). Switching Costs – Te inconveniences that dissuade a customer from switching to a competitor. Te negative costs that a consumer incurs as a result of changing suppliers, brands or products. Although most prevalent switching costs are monetary in nature, there are also psychological, efort and time-based switching costs. 78). Shareholder – Any person, company, or other institution that owns at least one share of a company's stock. Shareholders are a company's owners. 79). Stock Ticker or Symbol – An identifer (usually from 1 to 4 letters for US companies) for a stock. Tis symbol is the name under which a company's stock trades in the stock market. 80). Shareholders – Owners of company stock. 81). SWOT Analysis – A comprehensive analysis of a company's Strengths, Weaknesses, Opportunities and Treats. 82). Shorting a stock – Borrowing against the shares of stock, you proft when the stock price goes down.

83). Switching Costs – Te inconveniences that dissuade a customer from switching to a competitor. Te negative costs that a consumer incurs as a result of changing suppliers, brands or products. Although most prevalent switching costs are monetary in nature, there are also psychological, efort and time-based switching costs. 84). Ticker – Te abbreviation that a company is listed on the stock exchange. For example, Google has the ticker GOOG and Apple has the ticker AAPL. 85). Valuations – A way to gauge how expensive a stock is. Commonly used methods are the price of the share relative to earnings per share (P/E Ratio) and the price per share relative to the book value per share (P/ Book ratio). Te higher the valuations, the more growth you need to justify the investment.

ÞÞÞ

ÞÞÞ

10

How to Read Charts Like a Pro and Improve Your Selection and Timing

In the world of medicine, X-rays, MRIs, and brain scans are "pictures" that doctors study to help them diagnose what's going on in the human body. EKGs and ultrasound waves are recorded on paper or shown on TV-like monitors to illustrate what's happening to the human heart. Similarly, maps are plotted and set to scale to help people understand exactly where they are and how to get to where they want to go. And seismic data are traced on charts to help geologists study which structures or patterns seem most likely to contain oil. In almost every field, there are tools available to help people evaluate current conditions correctly and receive accurate information. The same is true in investing. Economic indicators are plotted on graphs to assist in their interpretation. A stock's price and volume history are recorded on charts to help investors determine whether the stock is strong, healthy, and under accumulation or whether it's weak and behaving abnormally. Would you allow a doctor to open you up and perform heart surgery if he had not utilized the critical necessary tools? Of course not. That would be just plain irresponsible. However, many investors do exactly that when they buy and sell stocks without first consulting stock charts. Just as doctors would be irresponsible not to use X-rays, CAT scans, and EKGs on their patients, investors are just plain foolish if they don't learn to interpret the price and volume patterns found on stock charts. If nothing else, charts can tell you when a stock is not acting right and should be sold. Individual investors can lose a lot of money if they don't know how to recognize when a stock tops and starts into a significant correction or if they have been depending on someone else who also doesn't know this. Chart Reading Basics Charts record the factual price performance of thousands of stocks. Price changes are the result of daily supply and demand in the largest auction marketplace in the world. Investors who train themselves to decode price movements on charts properly have an enormous advantage over those who either refuse to learn, just don't know any better, or are a bit lazy. Would you fly in a plane without instruments or take a long cross-country trip in your car without a road map? Charts are your investment road map. In fact, the distinguished economists Milton and Rose Friedman devoted the first 28 pages of their excellent book Free to Choose to the power of market facts and the unique ability of prices to provide important and accurate information to decision makers. Chart patterns, or "bases," are simply areas of price correction and consolidation after an earlier price advance. Most of them (80% to 90%) are created and formed as a result of corrections in the general market. The skill you need to learn in order to analyze these bases is how to diagnose whether the price and volume movements are normal or abnormal. Do they signal strength or weakness? Major advances occur off strong, recognizable price patterns (discussed later in this chapter). Failures can always be traced to bases that are faulty or too obvious to the typical investor. Fortunes are made every year by those who take the time to learn to interpret charts properly. Professionals who don't make use of charts are confessing their ignorance of highly valuable measurement and timing mechanisms. To further emphasize this point: I have seen many high-level investment professionals ultimately lose their jobs as a result of weak performance. When this happens, their poor records are often a direct result of not knowing very much about market action and chart reading. Universities that teach finance or investment courses and dismiss charts as irrelevant or unimportant are demonstrating their complete lack of knowledge and understanding of how the market really works and how the best professionals operate. As an individual investor, you too need to study and benefit from stock charts. It's not enough to buy a stock simply because it has good fundamental characteristics, like strong earnings and sales. In fact, no Investor's Business Daily® reader should ever buy a stock based solely on IBD's proprietary SmartSelect® Ratings. A stock's chart must always be checked to determine whether the stock is in a proper position to buy, or whether it is the stock of a sound, leading company but is too far extended in price above a solid basing area and thus should temporarily be avoided. As the number of investors in the market has increased over recent years, simple price and volume charts have become more readily available. (Investor's Business Daily subscribers have free access to 10,000 daily and weekly charts on the Web at investors.com.) Chart books and online chart services can help you follow hundreds and even thousands of stocks in a highly organized, time-saving way. Some are more advanced than others, offering both fundamental and technical data in addition to price and volume movement. Subscribe to one of the better chart services, and you'll have at your fingertips valuable information that is not easily available elsewhere. History Repeats Itself: Learn to Use Historical Precedents As mentioned in the introduction, and as shown on the annotated charts of history's best winners in Chapter 1, our system for selecting winning stocks is based on how the market actually operates, not on my or anyone else's personal opinions or academic theories. We analyzed the greatest winning stocks of the past and discovered they all had seven common characteristics, which can be summarized in the two easy-to-remember words CAN SLIM. We also discovered there were a number of successful price patterns and consolidation structures that repeated themselves over and over again. In the stock market, history repeats itself. This is because human nature doesn't change. Neither does the law of supply and demand. Price patterns of the great stocks of the past can clearly serve as models for your future selections. There are several price patterns you'll want to look for when you're analyzing a stock for purchase. I'll also go over some signals to watch out for that indicate that a price pattern may be faulty and unsound. The Most Common Chart Pattern: "Cup with Handle" One of the most important price patterns looks like a cup with a handle when the outline of the cup is viewed from the side. Cup patterns can last from 7 weeks to as long as 65 weeks, but most of them last for three to six months. The usual correction from the absolute peak (the top of the cup) to the low point (the bottom of the cup) of this price pattern varies from around the 12% to 15% range to upwards of 33%. A strong price pattern of any type should always have a clear and definite price uptrend prior to the beginning of its base pattern. You should look for at least a 30% increase in price in the prior uptrend, together with improving relative strength and a very substantial increase in trading volume at some points in the prior uptrend. In most, but not all, cases, the bottom part of the cup should be rounded and give the appearance of a "U" rather than a very narrow "V." This characteristic allows the stock time to proceed through a needed natural correction, with two or three final little weak spells around the lows of the cup. The "U" area is important because it scares out or wears out the remaining weak holders and takes other speculators' attention away from the stock. A more solid foundation of strong owners who are much less apt to sell during the next advance is thereby established. The accompanying chart from Daily Graphs Online® shows the daily price and volume movements for Apple Computer in February 2004. It's normal for growth stocks to create cup patterns during intermediate declines in the general market and to correct 1½ to 2½ times the market averages. Your best choices are generally stocks with base patterns that deteriorate the least during an intermediate market decline. Whether you're in a bull market or a bear market, stock downturns that exceed 2½ times the market averages are usually too wide and loose and must be regarded with suspicion. Dozens of former high-tech leaders, such as JDS Uniphase, formed wide, loose, and deep cup patterns in the second and third quarters of 2000. These were almost all faulty, failure-prone patterns signaling that the stocks should have been avoided when they attempted to break out to new highs. A very small number of volatile leaders can plunge by as much as 40% or 50% in a bull market. Chart patterns that correct by more than this amount during bull markets have a higher rate of failure if they try to make new price highs and resume their advance. The reason? A downswing of over 50% from a peak to a low means that the stock must increase more than 100% from its low to get back to its old high. Historical research has shown that stocks that make new price highs after such huge moves tend to fail 5% to 15% beyond their breakout prices. Stocks that come straight off the bottom into new highs off cups can be more risky because they had no pullbacks. Sea Containers was a glowing exception. It descended about 50% during an intermediate decline in the 1975 bull market. It then formed a perfectly shaped cup-with-handle price structure and proceeded to increase 554% in the next 101 weeks. This stock, with its 54% earnings growth rate and its latest quarterly results up 192%, was one of several classic cup-with-handle stocks that I presented to Fidelity Research & Management in Boston during a monthly meeting in early June 1975. Upon seeing such big numbers, one of the portfolio managers was instantly interested. As you can see by this example, some patterns that have corrected 50% to 60% or more coming out of an intermediate bull market decline or a major bear market can succeed. (See the charts for Sea Containers and The Limited.) In these cases, the percent of decline is a function of the severity of the general market decline and the tremendous extent of the stock's prior price run-up. Basic Characteristics of a Cup's Handle Area The formation of the handle area generally takes more than one or two weeks and has a downward price drift or "shakeout" (where the price drops below a prior low point in the handle made a few weeks earlier), usually near the end of its down-drifting price movement. Volume may dry up noticeably near the lows in the handle's price pullback phase. During a bull market, volume in the majority of cases should not pick up during a correction in the handle, although there have been some exceptions. Although cups without handles have a somewhat higher failure rate, many stocks can advance successfully without forming a handle. Also, some of the more volatile technology names in 1999 formed handles of only one or two weeks before they began their major price advances. When handles do occur, they almost always form in the upper half of the overall base structure, as measured from the absolute peak of the entire base to the absolute low of the cup. The handle should also be above the stock's 10-week moving average price line. Handles that form in the lower half of an overall base or completely below the stock's 10-week line are weak and failureprone. Demand up to that point has not been strong enough to enable the stock to recover more than half its prior decline. Additionally, handles that consistently wedge up (drift upward along their price lows or just go straight sideways along their lows rather than drifting down) have a much higher probability of failing when they break out to new highs. This upward-wedging behavior along low points in the handle doesn't let the stock undergo the needed shakeout or sharp price pullback after having advanced from the low of the base into the upper half of the pattern. This highrisk trait tends to occur in third- or fourth-stage bases, in laggard stock bases, or in very active market leaders that become too widely followed and therefore too obvious. You should beware of wedging handles. A price drop in a proper handle should be contained within 8% to 12% of its peak during bull markets unless the stock forms a very large cup, as in the rather unusual case of Sea Containers in 1975. Downturns in handles that exceed this percentage during bull markets look wide and erratic and in most cases are improper and risky. However, if you're in the last shake-out area of a bear market bottom, the unusual general market weakness will cause some handle areas to quickly decline around 20% to 30%, but the price pattern can still be sound if the general market then follows through on the upside, creating a new major uptrend.

Constructive Patterns Have Tight Price Areas There should also be at least some tight areas in the price patterns of stocks under accumulation. On a weekly chart, tightness is defined as small price variations from high to low for the week, with several consecutive weeks' prices closing unchanged or remarkably near the previous week's close. If the base pattern has a wide spread between the week's high and low points every week, it's been constantly in the market's eye and frequently will not succeed when it breaks out. However, amateur chartists typically will not notice the difference, and the stock can run up 5% to 15%, drawing in less-discriminating traders, before it breaks badly and fails. Find Pivot Points and Watch "Volume Percent Change" When a stock forms a proper cup-with-handle chart pattern and then charges through an upside buy point, which Jesse Livermore referred to as the "pivot point" or "line of least resistance," the day's volume should increase at least 40% to 50% above normal. During major breakouts, it's not uncommon for new market leaders to show volume spikes 200%, 500%, or 1,000% greater than the average daily volume. In almost all cases, it's professional institutional buying that causes the big, above-average volume increases in the better-priced, betterquality growth-oriented stocks at pivot breakouts. A full 95 percent of the general public is usually afraid to buy at such points because it's scary and it seems risky and rather absurd to buy stocks at their highest prices. Your objective isn't to buy at the cheapest price or near the low, but to begin buying at exactly the right time, when your chances for success are greatest. This means that you have to learn to wait for a stock to move up and trade at your buy point before you make an initial commitment. If you work and cannot watch the market constantly, small quote devices or quotes available on cell phones and Web sites will help you stay on top of potential breakout points. The winning individual investor waits to buy at these precise pivot points. This is where the real move generally starts and all the exciting action begins. If you try to buy before this point, you may be premature. In many cases the stock will never get to its breakout point, but rather will stall or actually decrease in price. You want a stock to prove its strength to you before you invest in it. Also, if you buy at more than 5% to 10% past the precise buy point, you are buying late and will more than likely get caught in the next price correction. Your automatic 8% loss-cutting rule.

"When You Must Sell and Cut Every Loss ... Without Exception") will then force you to sell because the stock was extended in price and didn't have enough room to go through a perfectly normal sharp but minor correction.

So don't get into the bad habit of chasing stocks up too high. Pivot buy points in correct chart base patterns are not typically based on a stock's old high price. Most of them occur at 5% to 10% below the prior peak. The peak price in the handle area is what determines most buy points, and this is almost always somewhat below the base's actual high. This is very important to remember. If you wait for an actual new high price, you will often buy too late. Sometimes you can get a slight head start by drawing a downtrend line from the overall pattern's absolute peak downward across the peak where the stock begins building the handle. Then begin your purchase when the trend line is broken on the upside a few weeks later. However, you have to be right in your chart and stock analysis to get away with this. Look for Volume Dry-Ups Near the Lows of a Price Pattern Nearly all proper bases will show a dramatic drying up of volume for one or two weeks along the very low of the base pattern and in the low area or few last weeks of the handle. This means that all of the selling has been exhausted and there is very little stock coming into the marketplace. Healthy stocks that are under accumulation almost always show this symptom. The combination of tightness in prices (daily or weekly price closes being very near each other) and dried-up volume at key points is generally quite constructive. Big Volume Clues Are Valuable Another clue that is valuable to the trained chart specialist is the occurrence of big daily and weekly volume spikes. Microsoft is an example of an outstanding stock that flashed heavy accumulation just before a huge run-up. Weeks of advancing prices on heavy volume, followed in other weeks by extreme volume dry-ups, are also a very constructive sign.

A Few Normal-Size Cups with Handles Texas Instruments, Apple, General Cable, and Precision Castparts were all similar-size patterns in length and depth. Can you recognize the similarity between Apple and Precision Castparts? As you learn to do this with greater skill, you will in the future be able to spot many cup with handles just like these past winners. The Value of Market Corrections Since 80% to 90% percent of price patterns are created during periods of market corrections, you should never get discouraged and give up on the stock market's potential during intermediate-term sell-offs or short or prolonged bear markets. America always comes back because of its inventors and entrepreneurs and the total freedom and unlimited opportunity that do not exist in communist or dictator-controlled countries. Bear markets can last as little as three, six, or nine months or as long as two or, in very rare cases, three years. If you follow the sell rules in this book carefully, you will sell and nail down most of your profits, cut short any losses, raise significant cash, and move off margin (borrowed money) in the early stages of each new bear market (see the success stories at the end of the book). In fact, Investor's Business Daily conducted four surveys in late 2008 that indicated that about 60% of IBD subscribers used our rules to sell and raise cash in December 2007 or June 2008 and thereby preserved most of their capital prior to the more serious decline in late 2008 that resulted from the subprime loan debacle. Even if you sell out completely and move to cash, you never want to throw in the towel on stock investing because bear markets create new bases in new stocks, some of which could be the next cycle's 1,000% winners. You don't foolishly give up while the greatest opportunities of a lifetime are setting up and may sooner or later be just around the corner. A bear market is the time to do a postanalysis of your prior decisions. Plot on daily or weekly charts exactly where you bought and sold all the stocks you traded in the past year. Study your decisions and write out some new rules that will let you avoid the mistakes you made in the past cycle. Then study several of the biggest winners that you missed or mishandled. Develop some rules to make sure that you buy the real leaders and handle them right in the next bull market cycle. They will be there, and this is the time to be watching for them as they begin to form bases. The question is whether you will be there with a carefully thought-through game plan to totally capitalize on them.

Definition of a "Flat-Base" Price Structure A flat base is another rewarding price structure. It is usually a second-stage base that occurs after a stock has advanced 20% or more off a cup with handle, saucer with handle, or double bottom. The flat base moves straight sideways in a fairly tight price range for at least five or six weeks, and it does not correct more than 10% to 15%. Standard Oil of Ohio in May 1979, Smith-Kline in March 1978, and Dollar General in 1982 are good examples of flat bases. Pep Boys in March 1981 formed a longer flat base. If you miss a stock's initial breakout from a cup with handle, you should keep your eye on it. In time it may form a flat base and give you a second opportunity to get on board. Here are a few more recent examples: Surgical Care Affiliates, CB Richard Ellis, and Deckers Outdoor. Here's a New Base We've Dubbed a Square Box After moving up from a cup with handle or double bottom, this formation typically lasts from four to seven weeks; doesn't correct too much, usually only 10% to 15%; and has a square, boxy look. I've noted this over recent years, but finally we've studied, measured, and classified it. Here are some examples: Lorillard, Korvette, Texas Instruments, Home Depot, Dell, and

Taro. High, Tight Flags Are Rare A "high, tight flag" price pattern is rare, occurring in no more than a few stocks during a bull market. It begins with the stock moving generally 100% to 120% in a very short period of time (four to eight weeks). It then corrects sideways no more than 10% to 25%, usually in three, four, or five weeks. This is the strongest of patterns, but it's also very risky and difficult to interpret correctly. Many stocks can skyrocket 200% or more off this formation. (See the charts for Bethlehem Steel, May 1915; American Chain & Cable, October 1935; E. L. Bruce, June 1958; Zenith, October 1958; Universal Controls, November 1958; Certain-teed, January 1961; Syntex, July 1963; Rollins, July 1964; Simmonds Precision, November 1965; Accustaff, January 1995; Emulex, October 1999; JDS Uniphase, October 1999; Qualcomm, December 1999; Taser International, November 2003; and Google, September 2004. Each earlier pattern serves as a precedent for each later pattern, so study them carefully.

The E. L. Bruce pattern in the second quarter of 1958, at around $50, provided a perfect chart pattern precedent for the Certain-teed advance that occurred in 1961. Certain-teed, in turn, became the chart model that I used to buy my first super winner, Syntex, in July 1963. What Is a Base on Top of a Base? During the latter stages of a bear market, a seemingly negative condition flags what may be aggressive new leadership in the new bull phase. I call this unusual case a "base on top of a base." What happens is that a powerful stock breaks out of its base and advances, but is unable to increase a normal 20% to 30% because the general market begins another leg down. The stock therefore pulls back in price and builds a second back-and-forth price consolidation area just on top of its previous base while the general market averages keep making new lows. When the bearish phase in the overall market ends, as it always does at some point, this stock is apt to be one of the first to emerge at a new high en route to a huge gain. It's like a spring that is being held down by the pressure of a heavy object. Once the object (in this case, a bear market) is removed, the spring is free to do what it wanted to do all along. This is another example of why it's foolhardy to get upset and emotional with the market or lose your confidence. The next big race could be just a few months away. Two of our institutional services firm's best ideas in 1978—M/A-Com and Boeing—showed base-on-top-of-a-base patterns. One advanced 180%, the other 950%. Ascend Communications and Oracle were other examples of a base on top of a base. After breaking out at the bear market bottom of December 1994, Ascend bolted almost 1,500% in 17 months. Oracle repeated the same base-onbase pattern in October 1999 and zoomed nearly 300%. Coming out of the Depression in 1934, Coca-Cola did the same thing. Ascending Bases Ascending bases, like flat bases, occur midway along a move up after a stock has broken out of a cup-with-handle or double-bottom base. They have three pullbacks of from 10% to 20%, with each low point during the sell-off in price being higher than the preceding one, which is why I call them ascending bases. Each of the pullbacks usually occurs because the general market is declining at that time. Boeing formed a 13-week ascending base in the second quarter of 1954 and then doubled in price. Redman Industries, a builder of mobile homes, had an 11- week ascending base in the first quarter of 1968 and proceeded to increase 500% in just 37 weeks. America Online created the same type of base in the first quarter of 1999 and resumed what turned out to be a 500% run-up from the breakout of a 14-week cup with handle in October 1998. So you see, history does repeat itself. The more historical patterns you know and come to recognize, the more money you should be able to make in future markets. (See the chart examples in Chapter 1, and also Simmonds Precision, Monogram Industries, Redman Industries, America Online, and Titanium Metals. Wide-and-Loose Price Structures Are Failure Prone Wide-and-loose-looking charts usually fail but can tighten up later. New England Nuclear and Houston Oil & Minerals are two cases of stocks that tightened up following wide, loose, and erratic price movements. I cite them because I missed both of them at the time. It's always wise to review big winners that you missed to find out why you didn't recognize them when they were exactly right and ready to soar. New England Nuclear formed a wide, loose, and faulty price pattern that looked like a double bottom from points A, B, C, D, and E. It declined about 40% from the beginning at point A to point D. That was excessive, and it took too much time—almost six months—to hit bottom. Note the additional clue provided by the declining trend of its relative strength line (RS) throughout the faulty pattern. Buying at point E was wrong. The handle was also too short and did not drift down to create a shakeout. It wedged up along its low points. New England Nuclear then formed a second base from points E to F to G. But if you tried to buy at point G, you were wrong again. It was premature because the price pattern was still wide and loose. The move from point E to point F was a prolonged decline, with relative strength deteriorating badly. The rise straight up from the bottom at point F to the bogus breakout point G was too fast and erratic, taking only three months. Three months of improving relative strength versus the prior 17 months of decline weren't enough to turn the previous poor trend into a positive one. The stock then declined from point G to point H to form what appeared to be a handle area for the possible cup formation from points E to F to G. If you bought at point I on the breakout attempt, the stock failed again. Reason: the handle was too loose; it degenerated 20%. However, after failing that time, the stock at last tightened up its price structure from points I to J to K, and 15 weeks later, at point K, it broke out of a tight, sound base and nearly tripled in price afterwards. Note the stock's strong uptrend and materially improved relative strength line for 11 months from point K back to point F. So, there really is a right time and a wrong time to buy a stock, but understanding the difference requires some study. There's no such thing as being an overnight success in the stock market, and success has nothing to do with listening to tips from other people or being lucky. You have to study and prepare yourself so that you can become successful on your own with your investing. So make yourself more knowledgeable. It isn't easy at first, but it can be very rewarding. Anyone can learn to do it. You can do it. Believe in your ability to learn. Unlearn past assumptions that didn't work. Here are some faulty wide-and-loose patterns that faked people into buying during the prolonged bear market that began in March 2000: Veritas Software on October 20, 2000; Anaren Microwave on December 28, 2000; and Comverse Technology on January 24, 2001. The aforementioned Houston Oil & Minerals is an even more dramatic example of the handle correction from point F to point G being a wide-and-loose pattern that later tightened up into a constructive price formation (see the accompanying chart). A to B to C was extremely wide, loose, and erratic (the percent decline was too great). B to C was straight up from the bottom without any pullback in price. Points C and D were false attempts to break out of a faulty price pattern, and so was point H, which tried to break out of a wide-and-loose cup with handle. Afterward, a tight nine-week base formed from points H to I to J. (Note the extreme volume dry-up along the December 1975 lows.) An alert stockbroker in Hartford, Connecticut, called this structure to my attention. However, I'd been so conditioned by the two prior years of poor price patterns and less-than-desirable earnings that my mind was slow to change when the stock suddenly altered its behavior in only nine weeks. I was probably also intimidated by the tremendous price increase that had occurred in Houston Oil in the earlier 1973 bull market. This proves that opinions and feelings are frequently wrong, but markets rarely are. It also points out a very important principle: it takes time for all of us to change opinions that we have built up over a substantial period. In this instance, even the current quarterly earnings turning up 357% after three down quarters didn't change my incorrect bearish view of the stock to a bullish one. The right buy point was in January 1976. In August 1994, PeopleSoft repeated the New England Nuclear and Houston Oil patterns. It failed in its breakout attempt from a wide, loose, wedgingupward pattern in September 1993. It then failed a second time in its breakout attempt in March 1994, when its handle area formed in the lower half of its cup-with-handle pattern. Finally, when the chart pattern and the general market were right, PeopleSoft skyrocketed starting in August 1994. In the first week of January 1999, San Diego–based Qualcomm followed PeopleSoft's three-phased precedent. In October 1997, Qualcomm charged into new-high ground straight up from a loose, faulty base with too much of its base in its lower half. It then built a second faulty base, broke out of a handle in the lower part, and failed. The third base was the charm: a properly formed cup with handle that worked in the first week in January 1999. Qualcomm went straight through the roof from a split-adjusted $7.50 to $200 in only one year. Maybe you should spend more time studying historical precedents. What do you think? If you had invested $7,500 in Qualcomm, a year later it would have been worth $200,000. Detecting Faulty Price Patterns and Base Structures Unfortunately, no original or thorough research on price pattern analysis has been done in the last 78 years. In 1930, Richard Schabacker, a financial editor of Forbes, wrote a book, Stock Market Theory and Practice. In it he discussed many patterns, including triangles, coils, and pennants. Our detailed model building and investigations of price structure over the years have shown these patterns to be unreliable and risky. They probably worked in the latter part of the "Roaring '20s," when most stocks ran up in a wild, climactic frenzy. Something similar happened in 1999 and the first quarter of 2000, when many loose, faulty patterns at first seemed to work, but then failed. These periods were just like the Dutch tulip bulb craze of the seventeenth century, during which rampant speculation caused varieties of tulip bulbs to skyrocket to astronomical prices and then crash. Our studies show that, with the exception of high, tight flags, which are extremely rare and hard to interpret, flat bases of five or six weeks, and the square box of four to seven weeks, the most reliable base patterns must have a minimum of seven to eight weeks of price consolidation. Most coils, triangles, and pennants are simply weak foundations without sufficient time or price correction to become proper bases. One-, two-, and three-week bases are risky. In almost all cases, they should be avoided. In 1948, John McGee and Robert D. Edwards wrote Technical Analysis of Stock Trends, a book that discusses many of the same faulty patterns presented in Schabacker's earlier work. In 1962, William Jiler wrote an easy-to-read book, How Charts Can Help You in the Stock Market, that explains many of the correct principles behind technical analysis. However, it too seems to have continued the display and discussion of certain failure-prone patterns of the pre-Depression era.

Triple bottoms and head-and-shoulders bottoms are patterns that are widely mentioned in several books on technical analysis. We have found these to be weaker patterns as well. A head-and-shoulders bottom may succeed in a few instances, but it has no strong prior uptrend, which is essential for most powerful market leaders. When it comes to signifying a top in a stock, however, head-and-shoulders top patterns are among the most reliable. Be careful: if you have only a little knowledge of charts, you can misinterpret what is a correct head-and-shoulders top. Many pros don't interpret the pattern properly. The right (second) shoulder must be slightly below the left shoulder (see the chart for Alexander & Alexander).

A triple bottom is a looser, weaker, and less-attractive base pattern than a double bottom. The reason is that the stock corrects and falls back sharply to its absolute low three times rather than twice, as with a double bottom, or once, as in the strong cup with handle. As mentioned earlier, a cup with a wedging handle is also usually a faulty, failure-prone pattern, as you can see in the Global Crossing Ltd. chart example. A competent chart reader would have avoided or sold Global Crossing, which later went bankrupt. How to Use Relative Price Strength Correctly Many fundamental securities analysts think that technical analysis means buying those stocks with the strongest relative price strength. Others think that technical research refers only to the buying of "high-momentum" stocks. Both views are incorrect. It's not enough to just buy stocks that show the highest relative price strength on some list of best performers. You should buy stocks that are performing .

What Is Overhead Supply? A critically important concept to learn in analyzing price movements is the principle of overhead supply. Overhead supply is when there are significant areas of price resistance in a stock as it moves up after experiencing a downtrend. These areas of resistance represent prior purchases of a stock and serve to limit and frustrate its upward movement because the investors who made these purchases are motivated to sell when the price returns to their entry point. (See the chart for At Home.) For example, if a stock advances from $25 to $40, then declines back to $30, most of the people who bought it in the upper $30s and at $40 will have a loss in the stock unless they were quick to sell and cut their loss (which most people don't do). If the stock later climbs back to the high $30s or $40 area, the investors who had losses can now get out and break even. These are the holders who promised themselves: "If I can just get out even, I will sell." Human nature doesn't change. So it's normal for a number of these people to sell when they see a chance to get their money back after having been down a large amount. Good chartists know how to recognize the price zones that represent heavy areas of overhead supply. They will never make the fatal mistake of buying a stock that has a large amount of recent overhead supply. This is a serious mistake that many analysts who are concerned solely with fundamentals sometimes make. A stock that's able to fight its way through its overhead supply, however, may be safer to buy, even though the price is a little higher. It has proved to have sufficient demand to absorb the supply and move past its level of resistance. Supply areas more than two years old create less resistance. Of course, a stock that has just broken out into new high ground for the first time has no overhead supply to contend with, which adds to its appeal. Excellent Opportunities in Unfamiliar, Newer Stocks Alert investors should have a way of keeping track of all the new stock issues that have emerged over the last 10 years. This is important because some of these newer and younger companies will be among the most stunning performers of the next year or two. Most of these issues trade on the Nasdaq market. Some new issues move up a small amount and then retreat to new price lows during a bear market, making a poor initial impression. But when the next bull market begins, a few of these forgotten newcomers will sneak back up unnoticed, form base patterns, and suddenly take off and double or triple in price if they have earnings and sales that are good and improving. Most investors miss these outstanding price moves because they occur in new names that are largely unknown to most people. A charting service can help you spot these unfamiliar, newer companies, but make sure that your service follows a large number of stocks (not just one or two thousand). Successful, young growth stocks tend to enjoy their fastest earnings growth between their fifth and tenth years in business, so keep an eye on them during their early growth periods. To summarize, improve your stock selection and overall portfolio performance by learning to read and use charts. They provide a gold mine of information. It will take some time and study on your part to become good at this, but interpreting charts is easier than you think. A Loud Warning to the Wise about Bear Markets!!! Let me offer one last bit of judicious guidance. If you are new to the stock market or the historically tested and proven strategies outlined in this book, or, more importantly, if you are reading this book for the first time near the beginning or middle of a bear market, do not expect the presumed buy patterns to work. Most of them will definitely be defective. You absolutely do not buy break-outs during a bear market. Most of them will fail. The price patterns will be too deep, wide, and loose in appearance compared to earlier patterns. They will be third- and fourth-stage bases; have wedging or loose, sloppy handles; have handles in the lower half of the base; or show narrow "V" formations moving straight up from the bottom of a base into new highs, without any handle forming. Some patterns may show laggard stocks with declining relative strength lines and price patterns with too much adverse volume activity or every week's price spread wide. It isn't that bases, breakouts, or the method isn't working anymore; it's that the timing and the stocks are simply all wrong. The price and volume patterns are phony, faulty, and unsound. The general market is turning negative. It is selling time. Be patient, keep studying, and be 100% prepared. Later, at the least expected time, when all the news is terrible, winter will ultimately pass and a great new bull market will suddenly spring to life. The practical techniques and proven disciplines discussed here should work for you for many, many future economic cycles. So get prepared and do your homework. Create your own buy and sell rules that you will constantly use.

11

Accelerating Quarterly Earnings and Sales per Share

Dell Computer, Cisco Systems, America Online–why, among the thousands of stocks that trade each day, did these three perform so well during the 1990s, posting gains of 1,780%, 1,467%, and 557%, respectively? Or for that matter, what about Google, which started trading at $85 a share in August 2004 and didn't stop climbing until it peaked at over $700 in 2007? Or Apple, which had emerged from a perfect cup-with-handle pattern six months earlier at a split-adjusted $12 a share and reached $202 in 45 months? What key traits, among the hundreds that can move stocks up and down, did these companies all have in common? These are not idle questions. The answers unlock the secret to true success in the stock market. Our study of all the stock market superstars from the last century and a quarter found that they did indeed share common characteristics. None of these characteristics, however, stood out as boldly as the profits each big winner reported in the latest quarter or two before its major price advance. For example: Dell's earnings per share surged 74% and 108% in the two quarters prior to its price increase from November 1996. Cisco posted earnings gains of 150% and 155% in the two quarters ending October 1990, prior to its giant run-up over the next three years. America Online's earnings were up 900% and 283% before its six-month burst from October 1998. Google showed earnings gains of 112% and 123% in the two quarters before it made its spectacular debut as a public company. Apple's earnings were up 350% in the quarter before it took off, and its next quarter was up another 300%. But this isn't just a recent phenomenon. Explosive earnings have accompanied big stock moves throughout the stock market's great history in America. Studebaker's earnings were up 296% before it sped from $45 to $190 in eight months in 1914, and Cuban American Sugar's earnings soared 1,175% in 1916, the same year its stock climbed from $35 to $230. In the summer of 1919, Stutz Motor Car was showing an earnings gain of 70% before the prestigious manufacturer of high-performance sports cars—you remember the Bearcat, don't you?—raced from $75 to $385 in just 40 weeks. Earnings at U.S. Cast Iron Pipe rose from $1.51 a share at the end of 1922 to $21.92 at the end of 1923, an increase of 1,352%. In late 1923, the stock traded at $30; by early 1925, it went for $250. And in March of 1926, du Pont de Nemours showed earnings up 259% before its stock took off from $41 that July and got to $230 before the 1929 break. In fact, if you look down a list of the market's biggest winners year-in and year-out, you'll instantly see the relationship between booming profits and booming stocks. And you'll see why our studies have concluded that The stocks you select should show a major percentage increase in current quarterly earnings per share (the most recently reported quarter) when compared to the prior year's same quarter. Seek Stocks Showing Huge Current Earnings Increases In our models of the 600 best-performing stocks from 1952 to 2001, three out of four showed earnings increases averaging more than 70% in the latest publicly reported quarter before they began their major advances. Those that did not show solid current quarterly earnings increases did so in the very next quarter, with an average earnings increase of 90%! Priceline.com was showing earnings up "only" 34% in the June quarter of 2006, when its stock began a move from $30 to $140. But its earnings accelerated, rising 53%, 107%, and 126%, in the quarters that followed. From 1910 to 1950, most of the very best performers showed earnings gains ranging from 40% to 400% before their big price moves. So, if the best stocks had profit increases of this magnitude before they advanced rapidly in price, why should you settle for anything less? You may find that only 2% of all stocks listed on Nasdaq or the New York Stock Exchange will show earnings gains of this size. But remember: you're looking for stocks that are exceptional, not lackluster. Don't worry; they're out there. As with any search, however, there can be traps and pitfalls along the way, and you need to know how to avoid them. The earnings per share (EPS) number you want to focus on is calculated by dividing a company's total after-tax profits by the number of common shares outstanding. This percentage change in EPS is the single most important element in stock selection today. The greater the percentage increase, the better. And yet during the Internet boom of the wild late 1990s, some people bought stocks based on nothing more than big stories of profits and riches to come, as most Internet and dot-com companies had shown only deficits to date. Given that companies such as AOL and Yahoo! were actually showing earnings, risking your hard-earned money in other, unproven stocks was simply not necessary. AOL and Yahoo! were the real leaders at that time. When the inevitable market correction (downturn) hit, lower-grade, more speculative companies with no earnings rapidly suffered the largest declines. You don't need that added risk. I am continually amazed at how some professional money managers, let alone individual investors, buy common stocks when the current reported quarter's earnings are flat (no change) or down. There is absolutely no good reason for a stock to go anywhere in a big, sustainable way if its current earnings are poor. Even profit gains of 5% to 10% are insufficient to fuel a major price movement in a stock. Besides, a company showing an increase of as little as 8% or 10% is more likely to suddenly report lower or slower earnings the next quarter. Unlike some institutional investors such as mutual funds, banks, and insurance companies, which have billions under management and which may be restricted by the size of their funds, individual investors have the luxury of investing in only the very best stocks in each bull cycle. While some companies with no earnings (like Amazon.com and Priceline.com) had big moves in their stocks in 1998–1999, most investors in that time period would have been better off buying stocks like America Online and Charles Schwab, both of which had strong earnings. Following the CAN SLIM strategy's emphasis on earnings ensures that an investor will always be led to the strongest stocks in any market cycle, regardless of any temporary, highly speculative "bubbles" or euphoria. Of course, you don't buy on earnings growth alone. Several other factors, which we'll cover in the chapters that follow, are almost as important. It's just that EPS is the most important. Watch Out for Misleading Earnings Reports Have you ever read a corporation's quarterly earnings report that went like this: We had a terrible first three months. Prospects for our company are turning down because of inefficiencies at the home office. Our competition just came out with a better product, which will adversely affect our sales. Furthermore, we are losing our shirt on the new Midwestern operation, which was a real blunder on management's part. No way! Here's what you see instead: Greatshakes Corporation reports record sales of $7.2 million versus $6 million (+20%) for the quarter ended March 31. If you're a Greatshakes stockholder, this sounds like wonderful news. You certainly aren't going to be disappointed. After all, you believe that this is a fine company (if you didn't, you wouldn't have invested in it in the first place), and the report confirms your thinking. But is this "record-breaking" sales announcement a good report? Let's suppose the company also had record earnings of $2.10 per share, up 5% from the $2.00 per share reported for the same quarter a year ago. Is it even better now? The question you have to ask is, why were sales up 20% but earnings ahead only 5%? What does this say about the company's profit margins? Most investors are impressed with what they read, and companies love to put their best foot forward in their press releases and TV appearances. However, even though this company's sales grew 20% to an all-time high, it didn't mean much for the company's profits. The key question for the winning investor must always be: How much are the current quarter's earnings per share up (in percentage terms) from the same quarter the year before? Let's say your company discloses that sales climbed 10% and net income advanced 12%. Sound good? Not necessarily. You shouldn't be concerned with the company's total net income. You don't own the whole organization; you own shares in it. Over the last 12 months, the company might have issued additional shares or "diluted" the common stock in other ways. So while net income may be up 12%, earnings per share—your main focus as an investor—may have edged up only 5% or 6%. You must be able to see through slanted presentations. Don't let the use of words like sales and net income divert your attention from the truly vital facts like current quarterly earnings. To further clarify this point: You should always compare a company's earnings per share to the same quarter a year earlier, not to the prior quarter, to avoid any distortion resulting from seasonality. In other words, you don't compare the December quarter's earnings per share to the prior September quarter's earnings per share. Rather, compare the December quarter to the December quarter of the previous year for a more accurate evaluation. Omit a Company's One-Time Extraordinary Gains The winning investor should avoid the trap of being influenced by nonrecurring profits. For example, if a computer maker reports earnings for the last quarter that include nonrecurring profits from activities such as the sale of real estate, this portion of earnings should be subtracted from the report. Such earnings represent a one-time event, not the true, ongoing profitability of corporate operations. Ignore the earnings that result from such events. Is it possible that the earnings of New York's Citigroup bank may have been propped up at times during the 1990s by nonrecurring sales of commercial real estate prior to the bank's later leveraged involvement in the subprime disaster? Set a Minimum Level for Current Earnings Increases Whether you're a new or an experienced investor, I would advise against buying any stock that doesn't show earnings per share up at least 18% or 20% in the most recent quarter versus the same quarter the year before. In our study of the greatest winning companies, we found that they all had this in common prior to their big price moves. Many successful investors use 25% or 30% as their minimum earnings parameter. To be even safer, insist that both of the last two quarters show significant earnings gains. During bull markets (major market uptrends), I prefer to concentrate on stocks that show powerful earnings gains of 40% to 500% or more. You have thousands of stocks to choose from. Why not buy the very best merchandise available? To further sharpen your stock selection process, look ahead to the next quarter or two and check the earnings that were reported for those same quarters the previous year. See if the company will be coming up against unusually large or small earnings achieved a year ago. When the unusual year-earlier results are not caused by seasonal factors, this step may help you anticipate a strong or poor earnings report in the coming months. Also, be sure to check consensus earnings estimates (projections that combine the earnings estimates of a large group of analysts) for the next several quarters —and for the next year or two—to make sure the company is projected to be on a positive track. Some earnings estimate services even show an estimated annual earnings growth rate for the next five years for many companies. Many individuals and even some institutional investors buy stocks whose earnings were down in the most recently reported quarter because they like the company and think that its stock price is "cheap." Usually they accept the story that earnings will rebound strongly in the near future. In some cases this may be true, but in many cases it isn't. Again, the point is that you have the choice of investing in thousands of companies, many of which are actually showing strong operating results. You don't have to accept promises of earnings that may never occur. Requiring that current quarterly earnings be up a hefty amount is just another smart way for the intelligent investor to reduce the risk of mistakes in stock selection. But you must also understand that in the late stage of a bull market, some or even many leaders that have had long runs may top out even though their earnings are up 100%. This usually fools investors and analysts alike. It pays to know your market history. Avoid Big Older Companies with Maintainer Management In fact, many older American corporations have mediocre management that continually produces second-rate earnings results. I call these people the "entrenched maintainers" or "caretaker management." You want to avoid these companies until someone has the courage to change the top executives. Not coincidentally, they are generally the companies that strain to pump up their current earnings a still-dull 8% or 10%. True growth companies with outstanding new products or improved management do not have to inflate their current results. Look for Accelerating Quarterly Earnings Growth Our analysis of the most successful stocks also showed that, in almost every case, earnings growth accelerated sometime in the 10 quarters before a towering price move began. In other words, it's not just increased earnings and the size of the increase that cause a big move. It's also that the increase represents an improvement from the company's prior rate of earnings growth. If a company's earnings have been up 15% a year and suddenly begin spurting 40% to 50% or more—what Wall Street usually calls "earnings surprises"—this usually creates the conditions for important stock price improvement. Other valuable ways to track a stock's earnings include determining how many times in recent months analysts have raised their estimates for the company plus the percentage by which several previous quarterly earnings reports have actually beaten the estimates. Look for Sales Growth as Well as Earnings Growth Strong and improving quarterly earnings should always be supported by sales growth of at least 25% for the latest quarter, or at least an acceleration in the rate of sales percentage improvement over the last three quarters. Certain newer issues (initial public offerings) may show sales growth averaging 100% or more in each of the last 8, 10, or 12 quarters. Check all these stocks out. Take particular note if the growth of both sales and earnings has accelerated for the last three quarters. You don't want to get impatient and sell your stock if it shows this type of acceleration. Stick to your position. Some professional investors bought Waste Management at $50 in early 1998 because earnings had jumped three quarters in a row from 24% to 75% and 268%. But sales were up only 5%. Several months later, the stock collapsed to $15 a share. This demonstrates that companies can inflate earnings for a few quarters by reducing costs or spending less on advertising, research and development, and other constructive activities. To be sustainable, however, earnings growth must be supported by higher sales. Such was not the case with Waste Management. It also helps improve your batting average if the latest quarter's after-tax profit margins for your stock selections are either at or near a new high and among the very best in the company's own industry. Yes, you have to do a little homework if you want to really improve your results. No pain, no gain. Two Quarters of Major Earnings Deceleration Can Be Trouble for Your Stock Just as it's important to recognize when quarterly earnings growth is accelerating, it's also important to know when earnings begin to decelerate, or slow down significantly. If a company that has been growing at a quarterly rate of 50% suddenly reports earnings gains of only 15%, that might spell trouble, and you may want to avoid that company. Even the best organizations can have a slow quarter every once in a while. So before turning negative on a company's earnings, I prefer to see two consecutive quarters of material slowdown. This usually means a decline of two-thirds or greater from the previous rate—a slowdown from 100% earnings growth to 30%, for example, or from 50% to 15%. Consult Log-Scale Weekly Graphs Understanding the principle of earnings acceleration or deceleration is essential. Securities analysts who recommend stocks because of the absolute level of earnings expected for the following year could be looking at the wrong set of numbers. The fact that a stock earned $5 per share and expects to report $6 the next year (a "favorable" 20% increase) could be misleading unless you know the previous trend in the percentage rate of earnings change. What if earnings were previously up 60%? This partially explains why so few investors make significant money following the buy and sell recommendations of securities analysts. Logarithmic-scale graphs are of great value in analyzing stocks because they clearly show the acceleration or deceleration in the percentage rate of quarterly earnings increases. One inch anywhere on the price or earnings scale represents the same percentage change. This is not true of arithmetically scaled charts. On an arithmetically scaled chart, a 100% price increase from $10 to $20 a share shows the same space change as a 50% increase from $20 to $30 a share. In contrast, a log-scale graph would show the 100% increase as being twice as large as the 50% increase. As a do-it-yourself investor, you can take the latest quarterly earnings per share along with the prior three quarters' EPS, and plot them on a logarithmicscale graph to get a clear picture of earnings acceleration or deceleration. For the best companies, plotting the most recent 12-month earnings each quarter should put the earnings per share point close to or already at new highs. Check Other Stocks in the Group For additional validation, check the earnings of other companies in your stock's industry group. If you can't find at least one other impressive stock displaying strong earnings in the group, chances are you may have selected the wrong investment. Where to Find Current Quarterly Earnings Reports Quarterly corporate earnings statements used to be published in the business sections of most local newspapers and financial publications every day. But many publications are downsizing their business sections these days, dropping data right and left. As a result, they no longer adequately cover the most important thing that investors need to know. This is not true of Investor's Business Daily. IBD not only continues to provide detailed earnings coverage, but goes a step further and separates all new earnings reports into companies with "up" earnings and those reporting "down" results, so you can easily see who produced excellent gains and who didn't. Chart services such as Daily Graphs® and Daily Graphs Online also show earnings reported during the week as well as the most recent earnings figures for every stock they chart. Once you locate the percentage change in earnings per share when compared to the same year-ago quarter, also compare the percentage change in EPS on a quarter-by-quarter basis. Looking at the March quarter and then at the June, September, and December quarters will tell you if a company's earnings growth is accelerating or decelerating. You now have the first critical rule for improving your stock selection: Current quarterly earnings per share should be up a major percentage– 25% to 50% at a minimum—over the same quarter the previous year. The best companies might show earnings up 100% to 500% or more! A mediocre 10% or 12% isn't enough. When you're picking winning stocks, it's the bottom line that counts.

12

Look for Big Growth

Any company can report a good earnings quarter every once in a while. And as we've seen, strong current quarterly earnings are critical to picking most of the market's biggest winners. But they're not enough. To make sure the latest results aren't just a flash in the pan, and the company you're looking at is of high quality, you must insist on more proof. The way to do that is by reviewing the company's annual earnings growth rate. Look for annual earnings per share that have increased in each of the last three years. You normally don't want the second year's earnings to be down, even if the results in the following year rebound to the highest level yet. It's the combination of strong earnings in the last several quarters plus a record of solid growth in recent years that creates a superb stock, or at least one with a higher probability of success during an uptrending general market.
Select Stocks with 25% to 50% and Higher Annual Earnings Growth Rates
The annual rate of earnings growth for the companies you pick should be 25%, 50%, or even 100% or more. Between 1980 and 2000, the median annual growth rate of all outstanding stocks in our study at their early emerging stage was 36%. Three out of four big winners showed at least some positive annual growth over the three years, and in some cases the five years, preceding the stocks' big run-ups. A typical earnings per share progression for the five years preceding the stock's move might be something like $0.70, $1.15, $1.85, $2.65, and $4.00. In a few cases, you might accept one down year in five as long as the following year's earnings move back to new high ground. It's possible a company could earn $4.00 a share one year, $5.00 the next, $6.00 the next, and then $3.00 a share. If the next annual earnings statement was, say, $4.00 per share versus the prior year's $3.00, this would not be a good report despite the 33% increase over the prior year. The only

reason it might seem positive is that the previous year's earnings ($3.00 a share) were so depressed that any improvement would look good. The point is, profits are recovering slowly and are still well below the company's peak annual earnings of $6.00 a share. The consensus among analysts on what earnings will be for the next year should also be up—the more, the better. But remember: estimates are personal opinions, and opinions may be wrong (too high or too low). Actual reported earnings are facts. Look for a Big Return on Equity You should also be aware of two other measurements of profitability and growth: return on equity and cash flow per share. Return on equity, or ROE, is calculated by dividing net income by shareholders' equity. This shows how efficiently a company uses its money, thereby helping to separate well-managed firms from those that are poorly managed. Our studies show that nearly all the greatest growth stocks of the past 50 years had ROEs of at least 17%. (The really superior growth situations will sport 25% to 50% ROEs.) To determine cash flow, add back the amount of depreciation the company shows to reflect the amount of cash that is being generated internally. Some growth stocks can also show annual cash flow per share that is at least 20% greater than actual earnings per share. Check the Stability of a Company's Three-Year Earnings Record Through our research, we've determined another factor that has proved important in selecting growth stocks: the stability and consistency of annual earnings growth over the past three years. Our stability measurement, which is expressed on a scale of 1 to 99, is calculated differently from most statistics. The lower the figure, the more stable the past earnings record. The figures are calculated by plotting quarterly earnings for the past three or five years and fitting a trend line around the plotted points to determine the degree of deviation from the basic growth trend. Growth stocks with steady earnings tend to have a stability figure below 20 or 25. Companies with stability ratings over 30 are more cyclical and a little less dependable in terms of their growth. All other things being equal, you may want to look for stocks showing a greater degree of sustainability, consistency, and stability in past earnings growth. Some companies that are growing 25% per year could have a stability rating of 1, 2, or 3. When the quarterly earnings for several years are plotted on a log-scale chart, the earnings line should be nearly straight, consistently moving up. In most cases there will be some acceleration in the rate of increase in recent quarters. Earnings stability numbers are customarily shown right after a company's annual growth rate, but most analysts and investment services don't bother to make the calculation. We show them in many of our institutional products as well as in Daily Graphs and Daily Graphs Online, which are designed for individual investors. If you restrict your stock selections to ventures with proven growth records, you will avoid the hundreds of investments with erratic histories or cyclical recoveries in profits. A few such stocks could "top out" as they approach the peaks of their prior earnings cycle. What Is a Normal Stock Market Cycle? History demonstrates most bull (up) markets last two to four years and are followed by a recession or a bear (down) market. Then another bull market starts. In the beginning phase of a new bull market, growth stocks are usually the first to lead and make new price highs. These are companies whose profits have grown quarter to quarter, but whose stocks have been held back by the poor general market conditions. The combination of a general market decline and a stock's continued profit growth will have compressed the price/earnings (P/E) ratio to a point where it is attractive to institutional investors, for whom P/Es are important. Cyclical stocks in basic industries such as steel, chemicals, paper, rubber, autos, and machinery usually lag in the new bull market's early phase. Young growth stocks will typically dominate for at least two bull market cycles. Then the emphasis may change to cyclicals, turnarounds, or other newly improved sectors for a short period. While three out of four big market winners in the past were growth stocks, one in four was a cyclical or turnaround situation. In 1982, Chrysler and Ford were two such spirited turnaround plays. Cyclical and turnaround opportunities led in the market waves of 1953–1955, 1963–1965, and 1974–1975. Cyclicals including paper, aluminum, autos, chemicals, and plastics returned to the fore in 1987, and home-building stocks, which are also cyclical, have led in other periods. Examples of turnaround situations include IBM in 1994 and Apple in 2003. Yet even when cyclical stocks are in favor, some pretty dramatic young growth issues are also available. Cyclical stocks in the United States are often those in older, less-efficient industries. Some of these companies weren't competitive until the demand for steel, copper, chemicals, and oil surged as a result of the rapid buildup of basic industries in China. That's why cyclicals were resurrected aggressively after the 2000 bear market ended in 2003. They are still cyclical stocks, however, and they may not represent America's true future. In addition, large, old-line companies in America frequently have the added disadvantage of size: they are simply too large to be able to innovate and continually renew themselves so that they can compete with nimble foreign rivals and with America's young new entrepreneurs. Rallies in cyclical stocks may tend to be more short-lived and prone to falter at the first hint of a recession or an earnings slowdown. Should you decide to buy a turnaround stock, look for annual earnings growth of at least 5% to 10% and two straight quarters of sharp earnings recovery that lift results for the latest 12 months into or very near new high ground. Check the 12-month earnings line on a stock chart; the sharper the angle of the earnings upswing, the better. If the profit upswing is so dramatic that it reaches a new high, one quarter of earnings turnaround will sometimes suffice. Cleveland Cliffs, a supplier of iron ore pellets to the steel industry (and now known as Cliffs Natural Resources), came from a deficit position to dramatically accelerate quarterly earnings in 2004 by 64% and then by 241%. With that impetus, the stock rapidly advanced 170% in the next eight months. How to Weed Out the Losers in a Group Insisting on three years of earnings growth will help you quickly weed out 80% of the stocks in any industry group. Growth rates for most stocks in most groups are lackluster or nonexistent—unlike, for example, Xerox, which was growing at a 32% annual rate before its shares soared 700% from March 1963 to June 1966 Wal-Mart Stores, which consistently created an annual growth rate of 43% before rocketing 11,200% from 1977 to 1990 Cisco Systems, whose earnings were exploding at a 257% rate in October 1990, and Microsoft, which was growing at a 99% clip in October 1986, before their enormous advances Priceline.com, which from 2004 to 2006 more than doubled its earnings from 96 cents a share to $2.03, before it tripled in price in the next five quarters Google, which had already expanded its earnings from 55 cents a share in 2002 to $2.51 a share in 2004 before its stock climbed from $200 to $700 by 2007 Keep in mind that an annual growth record doesn't necessarily make a company a solid growth stock. In fact, some so-called growth stocks report substantially slower growth than they did in earlier market periods. Many growth leaders in one cycle do not repeat in the next cycle. The stock of a company that has an outstanding three-year growth record of 30% but whose earnings growth has slowed to 10% or 15% in the last several quarters acts like a fully mature growth stock. Older and larger organizations are usually characterized by slower growth, and many of them should be avoided. America is continually led and driven by new innovative entrepreneurial companies. They, and not our government, create our new industries. Insist on Both Annual and Current Quarterly Earnings Being Excellent A standout stock needs both a sound growth record in recent years and a strong current earnings record in the last several quarters. It's the powerful combination of these two critical factors, rather than one or the other, that creates a super stock, or at least one that has a higher chance for true success. The fastest way to find a company with strong and accelerating current earnings and solid three-year growth is by checking the proprietary Earnings per Share (EPS) Rating provided for every stock listed in Investor's Business Daily's research stock tables. The EPS Rating measures a company's two most recent quarters of earnings growth against the same quarters the year before and examines its growth rate over the last three years. The results are then compared with those of all other publicly traded companies and rated on a scale from 1 to 99, with 99 being best. An EPS Rating of 99 means a company has outperformed 99% of all other companies in terms of both annual and recent quarterly earnings performance. If the stock is newly issued and the company doesn't have a three-year earnings record, look for big earnings increases and even bigger sales growth over the last five or six quarters. One or two quarters of profitability are often not enough and indicate a less-proven stock that might fall apart somewhere down the line. Are Price/ Earnings Ratios Really Important? If you're like most investors, you've probably learned the most important thing you need to know about a stock is its P/E ratio. Well, prepare yourself for a bubble-bursting surprise. For years, analysts have used P/E ratios as their basic measurement tool in deciding whether a stock is undervalued (has a low P/E) and should be bought, or is overvalued (has a high P/E) and should be sold. But our ongoing analysis of the most successful stocks from 1880 to the present shows that, contrary to most investors' beliefs, P/E ratios were not a relevant factor in price movement and have very little to do with whether a stock should be bought or sold. Much more crucial, we found, was the percentage increase in earnings per share. To say that a security is "undervalued" because it's selling at a low P/E or because it's in the low end of its historical P/E range can be nonsense. Primary consideration should be given to whether the rate of change in earnings is substantially increasing or decreasing. From 1953 through 1985, the average P/E ratio for the best-performing stocks at their early emerging stage was 20. (The average P/E of the Dow Jones Industrials over the same period was 15.) As they advanced, the biggest winners expanded their P/Es by 125%, to about 45. From 1990 to 1995, the real leaders began with an average P/E of 36 and expanded into the 80s. But these were just the averages. Beginning P/Es for most big winners ranged from 25 to 50, and the P/E expansions varied from 60 to 115. In the market euphoria of the late 1990s, these valuations increased to even greater levels. Value buyers missed almost all of these tremendous investments. Why You Missed Some Fabulous Stocks! These findings strongly suggest that if you weren't willing to buy growth stocks at 25 to 50 times earnings, or even much more, you automatically eliminated most of the best investments available! You missed Microsoft, Cisco Systems, Home Depot, America Online, and many, many others during their periods of greatest market performance. Our studies suggest P/E ratios are an end effect of accelerating earnings that, in turn, attract big institutional buyers, resulting in strong price performance. P/Es are not a cause of excellent performance. High P/Es, for example, were found to occur because of bull markets. Low P/Es, with the exception of those on cyclical stocks, generally occurred because of bear markets. In a roaring bull market, don't overlook a stock just because its P/E seems too high. It could be the next great winner. And never buy a stock just because the P/E ratio makes it look like a bargain. There are usually good reasons why the P/E is low, and there's no golden rule that prevents a stock that sells at 8 or 10 times earnings from going even lower and selling at 4 or 5 times earnings. Many years ago, when I first began to study the market, I bought Northrop at 4 times earnings and watched in disbelief as the stock declined to a P/E ratio of 2. How Price/Earnings Ratios Are Misused Many Wall Street analysts put a stock on their "buy" list because it's selling at the low end of its historical P/E range. They'll also recommend a stock when the price starts to drop, thereby lowering the P/E and making it seem like an even bigger bargain. In 1998, Gillette and Coca-Cola looked like great buys because they had sold off several points and their P/Es looked more attractive. In actuality, the earnings at both companies were showing a material deceleration that justified a lower valuation. A great deal of P/E analysis is based on personal opinions and theories that have been handed down through the years by analysts, academicians, and others, whose track records when it comes to making money in the market are both questionable and undocumented. In 2008, some Wall Street analysts recommended buying Bank of America all the way down. There are no safe, sure things in the market. That's why you need avoid or sell rules as well as buy rules. Reliance on P/E ratios often ignores more basic trends. The general market, for example, may have topped, in which case all stocks are headed lower. To say a company is undervalued because at one time it was selling at 22 times earnings and it can now be bought for 15 is ridiculous and somewhat naive. One way I do sometimes use P/E ratios is to estimate the potential price objective for a growth stock over the next 6 to 18 months based on its estimated future earnings. I may take the earnings estimate for the next two years and multiply it by the stock's P/E ratio at the initial chart base buy point, then multiply the result by 100% or slightly more. This is the degree of P/E expansion possible on average if a growth stock has a major price move. This tells me what a growth stock could potentially sell for during bull market conditions. However, there are some bull markets and certain growth stocks that may have little or no P/E expansion. For example, if Charles Schwab's stock breaks out of its first base at $43.75 per share (as it did in late 1998) and its P/E ratio at the beginning buy point is 40, multiply 40 by 130% to see that the P/E ratio could possibly expand to 92 if the stock has a huge price move. Next, multiply the potential P/E ratio of 92 by the consensus earnings estimate two years out of $1.45 per share. This tells you what a possible price objective for your growth stock might be. The Wrong Way to Analyze Companies in an Industry Another faulty use of P/E ratios, by amateurs and professionals alike, is to evaluate the stocks in an industry and conclude the one selling at the cheapest P/E is always undervalued and therefore the most attractive purchase. The reality is, the lowest P/E usually belongs to the company with the most ghastly earnings record. The simple truth is that at any given time, stocks usually sell near their current value. The stock that sells at 20 times earnings is at that level for one set of reasons, and the stock that trades at 15 times earnings is at that level for another set of reasons. A stock selling at, say, 7 times earnings does so because its overall record is more deficient than that of a stock with a higher P/E ratio. Also, keep in mind that cyclical stocks normally have lower P/Es, and that, even in good periods, they do not show the P/E expansion that occurs in growth stocks. You can't buy a Mercedes for the price of a Chevrolet, and you can't buy oceanfront property for the same price you'd pay for land a couple of miles inland. Everything sells for about what it's worth at the time based on the law of supply and demand. The increased value of great paintings was brought about almost singlehandedly many years ago by a fine-arts dealer named Joseph Duveen. He would travel to Europe and buy one-of-a-kind paintings by Rembrandt and others, paying more than the market price. He would then bring them back to the United States and sell them to Henry Ford and other industrialists of that era for substantially more than he had paid. In other words, Lord Duveen bought the one-of-a-kind masterpieces high and sold them much higher. The point is, anyone can buy a mediocre piece of art for a low price, but the very best costs more. The very best stocks, like the very best art, usually command a higher price. If a company's price and P/E ratio change in the near future, it's because conditions, events, psychology, and earnings have continued to improve or started to deteriorate. Eventually, a stock's P/E will reach a peak, but this normally occurs when the general market averages are topping out and starting a significant decline. It could also be a signal the company's rate of earnings growth is about to weaken. It's true high-P/E stocks will be more volatile, particularly if they're in the high-tech area. The price of a high-P/E stock can also temporarily get ahead of itself, but the same can be said for lower-P/E stocks. Examples of High P/Es That Were Great Bargains In situations where small but captivating growth companies have revolutionary new products, what seems like a high P/E ratio can actually be low. For instance, Xerox, which introduced the first dry copier in 1959, sold for 100 times earnings in 1960—before it advanced 3,300% in price (from a split-adjusted $5 to $170). Syntex, the first company to submit a patent for a birth control pill, sold for 45 times earnings in July 1963—before it advanced 400%. Genentech, a pioneer in the use of genetic information to develop new wonder drugs and the first biotech company to go public, was initially priced at 200 times earnings in November 1985. In five months, the new stock bolted 300%. America Online, whose software gave millions access to the revolutionary new world of the Internet, sold for over 100 times earnings in November 1994 before climbing 14,900% to its peak in December 1999. Google's P/E was in the 50s and 60s from $115 a share in September 2004 until it hit $475 a share in early January 2006. The fact is, investors with a bias against what they consider to be high P/Es will miss out on some of the greatest opportunities of this or any other time. During bull markets, in particular, such a bias could literally cost you a fortune. Don't Sell High-P/E Stocks Short In June 1962, when the stock market was at rock bottom, a big Beverly Hills investor barged into the office of a broker friend of mine and shouted that, at 50 times earnings, Xerox was drastically overpriced. He proceeded to sell 2,000 shares short at $88 (borrowing stock from his broker to sell in hopes the stock would decline and he could later buy it back cheaper, making money on the difference in price). Sure enough, the stock took off at once and ultimately reached a price of $1,300 (before adjusting for splits) with a P/E ratio that topped 80. So much for opinions about P/Es being too high! Investors' personal opinions are usually wrong; the market is almost always right. So stop fighting and arguing with the market. Concentrate on stocks with proven records of significant earnings growth in each of the last three years plus strong recent quarterly improvements.

Don't accept anything less.

13

New Highs off Properly Formed Bases

It takes something new to produce a startling advance in the price of a stock. It can be an important new product or service that sells rapidly and causes earnings to accelerate faster than previous rates of increase. Or it can be a change of management that brings new vigor, new ideas, or at least a new broom to sweep everything clean. New industry conditions—such as supply shortages, price increases, or the introduction of revolutionary technologies—can also have a positive effect on most stocks in an industry group. In our study of the greatest stock market winners, which now spans the period from 1880 through 2008, we discovered that more than 95% of successful stocks with stunning growth in American industry fell into at least one of these categories. In the late 1800s, there was the new railroad industry connecting every part of our country, electricity, the telephone, and George Eastman's camera. Edison created the phonograph, the motion picture camera, and the lightbulb. Next came the auto, the airplane, and then the radio. The refrigerator replaced the icebox. Television, the computer, jet planes, the personal computer, fax machines, the Internet, cell phones ... America's relentless inventors and entrepreneurs never quit. They built and created America's amazing growth record with their new products and new companies. These, in turn, created millions and millions of new jobs and a higher standard of living for the vast majority of Americans. In spite of bumps in the road, most Americans are far better off than they or their parents were 30 or 50 years ago. New Products That Created Super Successes The way a company can achieve enormous success, thereby enjoying large gains in its stock price, is by introducing dramatic new products into the marketplace. I'm not talking about a new formula for dish soap. I'm talking about products that revolutionize the way we live. Here are just a few of the thousands of entrepreneurial companies that drove America and, during their time in the sun, created millions of jobs and a higher standard of living in the United States than in other areas of the world: 1. Northern Pacific was chartered as the first transcontinental railroad. Around 1900, its stock rocketed more than 4,000% in just 197 weeks. 2. General Motors began as the Buick Motor Company. In 1913–1914, GM stock increased 1,368%. 3. RCA, by 1926, had captured the market for commercial radio. Then, from June 1927, when the stock traded at $50, it advanced on a presplit basis to $575 before the market collapsed in 1929. 4. After World War II, Rexall's new Tupperware division helped push the company's stock to $50 a share in 1958, from $16. 5. Thiokol came out with new rocket fuels for missiles in 1957–1959, propelling its shares from $48 to the equivalent of $355. 6. Syntex marketed the oral contraceptive pill in 1963. In six months, the stock soared from $100 to $550. 7. McDonald's, with low-priced fast-food franchising, snowballed from 1967 to 1971 to create an 1,100% profit for stockholders. 8. Levitz Furniture's stock soared 660% in 1970–1971 on the popularity of the company's giant warehouse discount-furniture centers. 9. Houston Oil & Gas, with a major new oil field, ran up 968% in 61 weeks in 1972–1973 and picked up another 367% in 1976. 10. Computervision's stock advanced 1,235% in 1978–1980 with the introduction of its new CAD-CAM factory-automation equipment. 11. Wang Labs' Class B shares grew 1,350% in 1978–1980 on the development of its new word-processing office machines. 12. Price Company's stock shot up more than 15 times in 1982–1986 with the opening of a southern California chain of innovative wholesale warehouse membership stores. 13. Amgen developed two successful new biotech drugs, Epogen and Neupogen, and the stock raced ahead from $60 in 1990 to the equivalent of $460 in early 1992. 14. Cisco Systems, yet another California company, created routers and networking equipment that enabled companies to link up geographically dispersed local area computer networks. The stock rose nearly 2,000% from November 1990 to March 1994. In 10 years—1990 to 2000—it soared an unbelievable 75,000%. 15. International Game Technology surged 1,600% in 1991–1993 with new microprocessor-based gaming products. 16. Microsoft stock was carried up almost 1,800% from March 1993 to the end of 1999 as its innovative Windows software products dominated the personal computer market. 17. PeopleSoft, the number one maker of personnel software, achieved a 20-fold increase in the 3½ years starting in August 1994. 18. Dell Computer, the leader and innovator in build-to-order, direct PC sales, advanced 1,780% from November 1996 to January 1999. 19. EMC, with superior computer memory devices, capitalized on the everincreasing need for network storage and raced up 478% in the 15 months starting in January 1998. 20. AOL and Yahoo!, the two top Internet leaders providing consumers with the new "portals" needed to access the wealth of services and information on the Internet, both produced 500% gains from the fall of 1998 to their peaks in 1999. 21. Oracle's database and e-business applications software drove its stock from $20 to $90 in only 29 weeks, starting in 1999. 22. Charles Schwab, the number one online discount broker, racked up a 414% gain in just six months starting in late 1998, a period that saw a shift to online trading, 23. Hansen Natural's "Monster" energy fruit drinks were a hit with the workout crowd, and its stock bolted 1,219% in only 86 weeks beginning in late 2004. 24. Google gave the world instant information via the Internet, and its stock advanced 536% from its initial offering in 2004. 25. Apple and the new iPod music player created a sensation that carried the company's stock up 1,580% from a classic cup-with-handle base price pattern that was easy to spot on February 27, 2004—if you used charts. And if you missed that last golden opportunity, you had four more classic base pattern chances to buy Apple: on August 27, 2004; July 15, 2005; September 1, 2006; and April 27, 2007—if you checked a chart book each week. In the years ahead, hundreds and thousands of new creative leaders just like these will continue to surface and be available for you to purchase. People from all over the world come to America to capitalize on its freedom and opportunity. That's one secret of our success that many countries do not have. So don't ever get discouraged and give up on the lifetime opportunity that the stock market will provide. If you study, save, prepare, and educate yourself, you too will be able to recognize many of the future big winners as they appear. You can do it, if you have the necessary drive and determination. It doesn't make any difference who you are or where you came from or your current position in life. It's all up to you. Do you want to get ahead? The Stock Market's "Great Paradox" There is another fascinating phenomenon we found in the early stage of all winning stocks. We call it the "Great Paradox." Before I tell you what it is, I want you to look at the accompanying graphs of three typical stocks. Which one looks like the best buy to you, A, B, or C? Which would you avoid? We'll give you the answer at the end of this chapter. The staggering majority of individual investors, whether new or experienced, take delightful comfort in buying stocks that are down substantially from their peaks, thinking that they're getting a bargain. Among the hundreds of thousands of individual investors attending my investment lectures in the 1970s, 1980s, 1990s, and 2000s, many said that they do not buy stocks that are making new highs in price. This bias is not limited to individual investors, however. I have provided extensive historical precedent research for more than 600 major institutional investors, and I have found that a number of them are also "bottom buyers." They, too, feel it's safer to buy stocks that look like bargains because they're either down a lot in price or actually selling near their lows. Our study of the greatest stock market winners proved that the old adage "buy low, sell high" was completely wrong. In fact, our study proved the exact opposite. The hard-to-believe Great Paradox in the stock market is What seems too high in price and risky to the majority usually goes higher eventually, and what seems low and cheap usually goes lower. Are you finding this "high-altitude paradox" a little difficult to act upon? Let me cite another study we conducted. In this one, we analyzed two groups of stocks—those that made new highs and those that made new lows—over many bull market periods. The results were conclusive: stocks on the new-high list tended to go higher in price, while those on the newlow list tended to go lower. Based on our research, a stock on Investor's Business Daily's "new price low" list tends to be a pretty poor prospect and should be avoided. In fact, decisive investors should sell such stocks long before they ever get near the new-low list. A stock making the new-high list—especially one making the list for the first time while trading on big volume during a bull market—might be a prospect with big potential.

14

Supply and Demand: Big Volume Demand at Key Points

The price of almost everything in your daily life is determined by the law of supply and demand. What you pay for your lettuce, tomatoes, eggs, and beef depends on how much of each is available and how many people want these items. Even in former Communist countries, where the difference between haves and have-nots was theoretically nonexistent, supply and demand held sway. There, state-owned goods were always in short supply and were often available only to the privileged class or on the black market to those who could pay the exorbitant prices. This basic principle of supply and demand also applies to the stock market, where it is more important than the opinions of all the analysts on Wall Street, no matter what schools they attended, what degrees they earned, or how high their IQs. Big or Small Supply of Stock It's hard to budge the price of a stock that has 5 billion shares outstanding because the supply is so large. Producing a rousing rally in these shares would require a huge volume of buying, or demand. On the other hand, it takes only a reasonable amount of buying to push up the price of a stock with 50 million shares outstanding, a relatively smaller supply. So if you're choosing between two stocks to buy, one with 5 billion shares outstanding and the other with 50 million, the smaller one will usually be the better performer, if other factors are equal. However, since smaller-capitalization stocks are less liquid, they can come down as fast as they go up, sometimes even faster. In other words, with greater opportunity comes significant additional risk. But there are definite ways of minimizing your risk

The total number of shares outstanding in a company's capital structure represents the potential amount of stock available. But market professionals also look at the "floating supply"—the number of shares that are available for possible purchase after subtracting stock that is closely held. Companies in which top management owns a large percentage of the stock (at least 1% to 3% in a large company, and more in small companies) generally are better prospects because the managers have a vested interest in the stock. There's another fundamental reason, besides supply and demand, why companies with a large number of shares outstanding frequently produce slower results: the companies themselves may be much older and growing at a slower rate. They are simply too big and sluggish. In the 1990s, however, bigger-capitalization stocks outperformed small-cap issues for several years. This was in part related to the size problem experienced by the mutual fund community. It suddenly found itself awash in new cash as more and more people bought funds. As a result, larger funds were forced to buy more bigger-cap stocks. This need to put their new money to work made it appear that they favored bigger-cap issues. But this was contrary to the normal supply/demand effect, which favors smaller-cap stocks with fewer shares available to meet increases in institutional investor demand. Big-cap stocks do have some advantages: greater liquidity, generally less downside volatility, better quality, and in some cases less risk. And the immense buying power that large funds have these days can make top-notch big stocks advance nearly as fast as shares of smaller companies. Pick Entrepreneurial Management Rather than Caretakers Big companies may seem to have a great deal of power and influence, but size often begets a lack of imagination and productive efficiency. Large companies are often run by older and more conservative "caretaker managements" that are less willing to innovate, take risks, and move quickly and wisely to keep up with rapidly changing times. In most cases, top managers of large companies don't own a lot of their company's stock. This is a serious deficiency that should be corrected. To the savvy investor, it suggests that the company's management and employees don't have a personal interest in seeing the company succeed. In some cases, large companies also have multiple layers of management that separate senior executives from what's going on at the customer level. And for companies competing in a capitalist economy, the ultimate boss is the customer. Communication of information continues to change at an ever-faster rate. A company that has a hot new product today will find its sales slipping within two or three years if it doesn't continue to bring relevant, superior new products to market. Most new products, services, and inventions come from young, hungry, and innovative small- and medium-sized companies with entrepreneurial management. Not coincidentally, these smaller public and nonpublic companies grow faster and create somewhere between 80% and 90% of the new jobs in the United States. Many of them are in the service or technology and information industries. This is possibly where the great future growth of America lies. Microsoft, Cisco Systems, and Oracle are just a few examples of dynamic smallcap innovators of the 1980s and 1990s that continually grew and eventually became big-cap stocks. If a mammoth older company creates an important new product, it may not help the stock materially because the product will probably account for only a small percentage of the company's total sales and earnings. The product is simply a small drop in a bucket that's now just too big. Excessive Stock Splits May Hurt From time to time, companies make the mistake of splitting their stocks excessively. This is sometimes done on advice from Wall Street investment bankers. In my opinion, it's usually better for a company to split its shares 2-for1 or 3-for-2 than to split them 3-for-1 or 5-for-1. (When a stock splits 2-for-1, you get two shares for each share you previously held, but the new shares sell for half the price.) Oversized splits create a substantially larger supply and may put a company in the more lethargic, big-cap status sooner. Incidentally, a stock will usually end up moving higher after its first split in a new bull market. But before it moves up, it will go through a correction for a period of weeks. It may be unwise for a company whose stock has gone up in price for a year or two to declare an extravagant split near the end of a bull market or in the early stage of a bear market. Yet this is exactly what many corporations do. Generally speaking, these companies feel that lowering the share price of their stock will attract more buyers. This may be the case with some smaller buyers, but it also may produce the opposite result—more sellers—especially if it's the second split within a year or two. Knowledgeable pros and a few shrewd individual traders will probably use the excitement generated by the oversized split as an opportunity to sell and take their profits. In addition, large holders who are thinking of selling might figure it will be easier to unload their 100,000 shares before a 3-for-1 split than to sell 300,000 shares afterward. And smart short sellers pick on stocks that are heavily owned by institutions and are starting to falter after huge price run-ups. A stock will often reach a price top around the second or third time it splits. Our study of the biggest winners found that only 18% of them had splits in the year preceding their great price advances. Qualcomm topped in December 1999, just after its 4-for-1 stock split. Look for Companies Buying Their Own Stock in the Open Market In most but not all cases, it's usually a good sign when a company, especially a small- to medium-sized growth company that meets the CAN SLIM criteria, buys its own stock in the open market consistently over a period of time. (A 10% buyback would be considered big.) This reduces the number of shares and usually implies that the company expects improved sales and earnings in the future. As a result of the buyback, the company's net income will be divided by a smaller number of shares, thereby increasing earnings per share. And as already noted, the percentage increase in earnings per share is one of the principal driving forces behind outstanding stocks. From the mid-1970s to the early 1980s, Tandy, Teledyne, and Metromedia successfully repurchased their own stock, and all three achieved higher EPS growth and spectacular stock gains. Charles Tandy once told me that when the market went into a correction, and his stock was down, he would go to the bank and borrow money to buy back his stock, then repay the loans after the market recovered. Of course, this was also when his company was reporting steady growth in earnings. Tandy's (split-adjusted) stock increased from $2.75 to $60 in 1983, Metromedia's soared from $30 in 1971 to $560 in 1977, and Teledyne zoomed from $8 in 1971 to $190 in 1984. Teledyne used eight separate buybacks to shrink its capitalization from 88 million shares to 15 million and increase its earnings from $0.61 a share to nearly $20. In 1989 and 1990, International Game Technology announced that it was buying back 20% of its stock. By September 1993, IGT had advanced more than 20 times. Another big winner, home builder NVR Inc., had large buy-backs in 2001. All these were growth companies. I'm not sure that company buybacks when earnings are not growing are all that sound. A Low Corporate Debt-to-Equity Ratio Is Generally Better After you've found a stock with a reasonable number of shares, check the percentage of the company's total capitalization represented by long-term debt or bonds. Usually, the lower the debt ratio, the safer and better the company. The earnings per share of companies with high debt-to-equity ratios could be clobbered in difficult periods when interest rates are high or during more severe recessions. These highly leveraged companies are generally of lower quality and carry substantially higher risk. The use of extreme leverage of up to 40-to-1 or 50-to-1 was common among banks, brokers, mortgage lenders, and quasi-government agencies like Fannie Mae and Freddie Mac starting in 1995 and continuing until 2007. These institutions were strongly encouraged by the federal government's actions to invest large amounts of money in subprime loans to lower-income buyers, which ultimately led to the financial and credit crisis in 2008. Rule 1 for all competent investors and homeowners is never ever borrow more than you can pay back. Excessive debt hurts all people, companies, and governments. A corporation that's been reducing its debt as a percentage of equity over the last two or three years is worth considering. If nothing else, interest costs will be sharply reduced, helping to generate higher earnings per share. Another thing to watch for is the presence of convertible bonds in the capital structure; earnings could be diluted if and when the bonds are converted into shares of common stock. Evaluating Supply and Demand The best way to measure a stock's supply and demand is by watching its daily trading volume. This is exceptionally important, and it's why Investor's Business Daily's stock tables show both a stock's volume of trading for the day and the percentage that volume is above or below the stock's average daily volume over the last three months. These measurements, plus a proprietary rating of the degree of recent accumulation or distribution in the stock, are invaluable pieces of information that are available in no other daily publication, including the Wall Street Journal. When a stock pulls back in price, you typically want to see volume dry up at some point, indicating that there is no further significant selling pressure. When the stock rallies in price, in most situations you want to see volume rise, which usually represents buying by institutions, not the public. When a stock breaks out of a price consolidation area (see Chapter 2 on chart reading and identifying the price patterns of winning stocks), trading volume should be at least 40% or 50% above normal. In many cases, it will increase 100% or much more for the day, indicating solid buying of the stock and the possibility for further increases in price. Using daily and weekly charts helps you analyze and interpret a stock's price and volume action. Monthly charts are also of value. You should analyze a stock's base pattern week by week, beginning with the first week that the stock closes down in a newly formed base and continuing each week until you get to the current week, where you believe it may break out of the base. You want to judge how much price progress up or down the stock made during each week and whether it was on increased or decreased volume from the prior week. You also want to note where the stock closed within the price spread of each week's high and low. You both do a week-by-week check and evaluate the pattern's overall shape to see if it is a sound pattern that's been under accumulation or if it has too many defects. Remember: Stock of any size capitalization can be bought using the CAN SLIM system. But small-cap stocks will be substantially more volatile, both on the upside and on the downside. From time to time, the market will shift its emphasis from small to large caps and vice versa. Companies that are buying back their stock in the open market and that show considerable stock ownership by management are preferred.

15

Leader or Laggard: Which Is Your Stock?

People tend to buy stocks that make them feel either good or comfortable. But in a bull market populated by dynamic leaders that just keep surprising on the upside, these sentimental favorites often turn out to be the dullest laggards. Suppose you want to own a stock in the computer industry. If you buy the best performer in the group, and your timing is right, you have a crack at real price appreciation. But if you buy a stock that hasn't moved much, or that has even fallen to a price that makes it seem like a bargain and therefore safer, chances are that you've picked a stock with little potential. There's a reason, after all, that it's at the bottom of the pile. Don't just dabble in stocks, buying what you like for whatever reason. Dig in, do some detective work, and find out what makes some stocks go up much more than others. You can do it, if you work at it. Buy Among the Best Two or Three Stocks in a Group The top one, two, or three stocks in a strong industry group can have unbelievable growth, while others in the pack may hardly stir. The great computer stocks in the bull market of 1979 and 1980—Wang Labs, Prime Computer, Datapoint, Rolm, and Tandy—had five-, six-, and sevenfold advances before they topped and retreated. But the sentimental favorite, grand old IBM, just sat there, and giants Burroughs, NCR, and Sperry Rand were just as lifeless. In the bull market of 1981–1983, however, IBM sprang to life and produced excellent results. In the retail sector, Home Depot advanced 10 times from 1988 to 1992, while the laggards in the home-improvement niche, Waban and Hechinger, dramatically underperformed. You should buy the really great companies—those that lead their industries and are number one in their particular fields. All of my best big winners—

Syntex in 1963, Pic 'N' Save from 1976 to 1983, Price Co. from 1982 to 1985, Franklin Resources from 1985 to 1986, Genentech from 1986 to 1987, Amgen from 1990 to 1991, America Online from 1998 to 1999, Charles Schwab from 1998 to 1999, Sun Microsystems from 1998 to 1999, Qualcomm in 1999, eBay from 2002 to 2004, Google from 2004 to 2007, and Apple from 2004 to 2007— were the number one companies in their industry space at the time I purchased them. By number one, I don't mean the largest company or the one with the most recognized brand name. I mean the one with the best quarterly and annual earnings growth, the highest return on equity, the widest profit margins, the strongest sales growth, and the most dynamic stock-price action. This type of company will also have a unique and superior product or service and be gaining market share from its older, less-innovative competitors. Avoid Sympathy Stock Moves Our studies show that very little in the stock market is really new; history just keeps repeating itself. When I first bought stock in Syntex, the developer of the birth-control pill, in July 1963 off a high, tight flag pattern (and it then rapidly shot up 400%), most people wouldn't touch it. The stock had just made a new price high at $100 on the American Stock Exchange, and its price plus its P/E ratio, 45, made it seem too high and scary. No brokerage firms had research reports on it then, and the only mutual fund that owned it—a Value Line fund—had sold it the prior quarter when it began moving up. Instead, several Wall Street investment firms later recommended G. D. Searle as a "sympathy play." Searle had a product similar to Syntex's, and its stock looked much cheaper because it hadn't gone up as much. But its stock failed to produce the same results. Syntex was the leader; Searle the laggard. A sympathy play is a stock in the same industry group that is bought in the hope that the luster of the real leader will rub off on it. But the profits of such companies usually pale in comparison. The stocks will eventually try to move up "in sympathy" with the leader, but they never do as well. In 1970, Levitz Furniture, the leader in the then-new warehouse business, became an electrifying market winner. Wickes Corp. copied Levitz, and many people bought its shares because they were "cheaper," but Wickes never performed and ultimately got into financial trouble. Levitz, meanwhile, appreciated 900% before it finally topped. As steel industry pioneer Andrew Carnegie said in his autobiography: "The first man gets the oyster; the second, the shell." Each new business cycle in America is driven by new innovators, inventors, and entrepreneurs. If our government really wants to create jobs and not welfare packages, the most powerful way would be to provide strong tax incentives for the first two or three years to people who want to start new, small entrepreneurial businesses. Our data show that in the last 25 years, small businesses in America were responsible for creating 80% to 90% of all new jobs. This is a significantly higher percentage than that shown in government data, where new jobs are not accounted for in a realistic, comprehensive manner. For example, the Small Business Administration defines a small business as one with fewer than 500 people. Yes, when Sam Walton started Wal-Mart and Bill Gates started Microsoft, each company had maybe 30 or 40 people. A year later they had maybe 75, the next year 120, then 200, then 320, then 501. From that point on, they were no longer considered to be small companies. But over the next 10 or 15 years, one of them created more than a million jobs and the other 500,000 jobs. Those jobs were all created by a dynamic entrepreneur who started a brand-new company, and they should be recognized and counted as such. We have a huge database on all public companies. In the past 25 years, big business created no net new jobs. When a big business buys another company, thereby instantly padding its payrolls, it doesn't create new jobs. In fact, it usually consolidates and lays off people in duplicative positions. Many such companies also downsize over time. Our inefficient, bureaucratic government needs to start counting all jobs created by new or small businesses during their first 15 or 20 years in business. How to Separate the Leaders from the Laggards: Using Relative Price Strength If you own a portfolio of stocks, you must learn to sell the worst performers first and keep the best a little longer. In other words, always sell your mistakes while the loss is still small, and watch your better selections to see if they progress into your big winners. Human nature being what it is, most people do it backwards: they hold their losers and sell their winners, a formula that always leads to bigger losses. How do you tell which stock is better and which is worse? The fastest and easiest way is by checking its Relative Price Strength (RS) Rating in Investor's Business Daily. The proprietary RS Rating measures the price performance of a given stock against the rest of the market for the past 52 weeks. Every stock in the market is assigned a rating from 1 to 99, with 99 being best. An RS Rating of 99 means that the stock has outperformed 99% of all other companies in terms of price performance. A RS of 50 means that half of all other stocks have done better and half have done worse. If your stock's RS Rating is below 70, it is lagging the better-performing stocks in the overall market. That doesn't mean that it can't go up in price. It just means that if by some chance it does go up, it'll probably go up less. From the early 1950s through 2008, the average RS Rating of the bestperforming stocks before their major run-ups was 87. In other words, the best stocks were already doing better than nearly 9 out of 10 others when they were starting out on their most explosive advance yet. So the rule for those who are determined to be big winners in the stock market is: look for the genuine leaders and avoid laggards and sympathy plays. Don't buy stocks with Relative Strength Ratings in the 40s, 50s, or 60s. The Relative Price Strength Rating is shown each day for all stocks listed in Investor's Business Daily's stock tables. You can't find this information in any other daily business or local newspaper. Updated RS Ratings are also shown on the Daily Graphs Online charting service. A stock's relative strength can also be plotted on a chart. If the RS line has been sinking for seven months or more, or if the line has an abnormally sharp decline for four months or more, the stock's price behavior is highly questionable, and it should probably be sold. Pick 80s and 90s That Are in Sound and Proper Chart Base Patterns If you want to upgrade your stock selection so that you're zeroing in on the leaders, restrict your purchases to companies showing RS Ratings of 80 or higher. There's no point in buying a stock that's straggling behind. Yet that's exactly what many investors do—including some who work at America's largest investment firms. I don't like to buy stocks with Relative Price Strength Ratings less than 80. In fact, the really big moneymakers generally have RS Ratings of 90 or higher just before they break out of their first or second base structure. The RS Rating of a potential winning stock should be in the same league as a pitcher's fastball. The average big-league fastball is clocked at 86 miles per hour, and the best pitchers throw "heat" in the 90s. When you buy a stock, make absolutely sure that it's coming out of a sound base or price consolidation area. Also make sure that you buy it at its exact buy, or pivot, point. As mentioned before, avoid buying stocks that are extended more than 5% or 10% above the precise initial buy point. This will keep you from chasing stocks that race up in price too rapidly and makes it less likely that you will be shaken out during sharp market sell-offs. The unwillingness of investors to set and follow minimum standards for stock selection reminds me of doctors years ago who were ignorant of the need to sterilize their instruments before each operation. They kept killing off patients until surgeons finally and begrudgingly accepted studies by researchers Louis Pasteur and Joseph Lister. Ignorance rarely pays off in any walk of life, and it's no different in the stock market. Finding New Leaders during Market Corrections Corrections, or price declines, in the general market can help you recognize new leaders—if you know what to look for. The more desirable growth stocks normally correct 1½ to 2½ times the general market averages. In other words, if the overall market comes down 10%, the better growth stocks will correct 15% to 25%. However, in a correction during a bull, or upward-trending, market, the growth stocks that decline the least (percentagewise) are usually your best selections. Those that drop the most are normally the weakest. Say the general market average suffers an intermediate-term correction of 10%, and three of your successful growth stocks come off 15%, 25%, and 35%. The two that are off only 15% or 25% are likely to be your best investments after they recover. A stock that slides 35% to 40% in a general market decline of 10% could be flashing a warning signal. In most cases, you should heed it. Once a general market decline is definitely over, the first stocks that bounce back to new price highs are almost always your authentic leaders. These chart breakouts continue week by week for about 13 weeks. The best ones usually come out in the first three or four weeks. This is the ideal period to buy stocks ... you absolutely don't want to miss it. Be sure to read the chapter on general market direction carefully to learn how you determine it. Pros Make Many Mistakes Too Many professional investment managers make the serious mistake of buying stocks that have just suffered unusually large price drops. Our studies indicate that this is a surefire way to get yourself in trouble. In June 1972, an otherwise capable institutional investor in Maryland bought Levitz Furniture after its first abnormal price break—a one-week drop from $60 to around $40. The stock rallied for a few weeks, then rolled over and broke to $18. In October 1978, several institutional investors bought Memorex, a leading supplier of computer peripheral equipment, when it had its first unusual price break and looked to be a real value. It later plunged. In September 1981, certain money managers in New York bought Dome Petroleum on a break from $16 to $12. To them, it seemed cheap, and a favorable story about the stock was going around Wall Street. Months later, Dome sold for $1. Institutional buyers snapped up Lucent Technologies, a Wall Street darling after it was spun off from AT&T in the mid-1990s, after it broke from $78 to $50. Later that year, it collapsed to $5. Also in 2000, many people bought Cisco Systems when it dropped to 50 from its early-year high of 82. The maker of computer networking equipment had been a huge winner in the 1990s, when it soared 75,000%, so it looked cheap at $50. It went to $8 and never got back to $50. In 2008, eight years after those buyers saw value at $50, Cisco was selling for only $17. To do well in the stock market, you've got to stop doing what got you into trouble in the past and create new and far better rules and methods to guide you in the future. Suppose Joe Investor missed buying Crocs, the footwear company, at a splitadjusted $15 as it came out of the perfect cup-with-handle pattern in September 2006. Suppose he also missed the next cup pattern in April 2007 at 28. Then the stock roars up to $75 by October, with earnings up 100% every quarter. A month later, however, the stock drops to 47, and Joe sees his chance to get into this big winner that he missed all the way up and that's now at a cheaper price. But the stock just keeps falling, and by January 2009 it's trading at $1. Buying stocks on the way down is dangerous. You can get wiped out. So stop this risky bad habit. How about buying a blue chip, a top-flight bank that's a leader in its industry —Bank of America? In December 2006, it was $55 a share, but you could have gotten it cheaper a year later at $40. Another year later, however, it had plunged to $6. But you're still a long-term investor, getting your 4-cent dividend. This is why I say don't buy a supposed good stock on the way down and why we recommend cutting all losses at 7% or 8%. Any stock can do anything. You must have rules to protect your hard-earned money. We all make mistakes. You must learn to correct yours without vacillating. None of the pros or individual investors who owned or bought Cisco, Crocs, or BofA when they were falling recognized the difference between normal price declines and highly abnormal big-volume corrections that can signal potential disaster. But the real problem was they relied on stories they'd heard and a method of fundamental analysis that equates lower P/E ratios with "value." They didn't heed the market action that could have told them what was really going on. Those who listen and learn the difference between normal and abnormal action are said to have a "good feel for the market." Those who ignore what the market says usually pay a heavy price. Anyone who buys stocks on the way down in price because they look cheap will learn the hard way this is how you can lose a lot of money. Look for Abnormal Strength on a Weak Market Day In the spring of 1967, I remember walking through a broker's office in New York on a day when the Dow Jones Industrial Average was down more than 12 points. That was a lot in those days, when the Dow was around 800 compared with 8,000 in 2008. When I looked up at the electronic ticker tape moving across the wall and showing prices, I saw that Control Data—a pioneer in supercomputers—was trading at $62, up 3½ points on heavy volume. I bought the stock at once. I knew Control Data well, and this was highly abnormal strength in the face of a weak overall market. The stock later ran up to $150. In April 1981, just as the 1981 bear market was getting underway, MCI Communications, a telecommunications stock trading in the over-the-counter market, broke out of a price base at $15. It advanced to the equivalent of $90 in 21 months. This was another great example of highly abnormal strength during a weak market. Lorillard, the tobacco company, did the same thing in the 1957 bear market, Software Toolworks soared in the down market of early 1990, wireless telecom firm Qualcomm made big progress even during the difficult midyear market of 1999, and Taro Pharmaceutical late in 2000 bucked the bear market that had begun that spring. Also in 2000, home builder NVR took off at $50 and rode steadily lower interest rates up to $360 by March 2003. The new bull market in 2003 uncovered many leaders, including Apple, Google, Research in Motion, Potash, and several Chinese stocks. So don't forget: It seldom pays to invest in laggard stocks, even if they look tantalizingly cheap. Look for, and confine your purchases to, market leaders. Get out of your laggard losers if you're down 8% below the price you paid so that you won't risk getting badly hurt.

16

Institutional Sponsorship

It takes big demand to push up prices, and by far the biggest source of demand for stocks is institutional investors, such as mutual funds, pension funds, hedge funds, insurance companies, large investment counselors, bank trust departments, and state, charitable, and educational institutions. These large investors account for the lion's share of each day's market activity. What Is Institutional Sponsorship? Institutional sponsorship refers to the shares of any stock owned by such institutions. For measurement purposes, I have never considered brokerage research reports or analyst recommendations as institutional sponsorship, although a few may exert short-term influence on some securities for a few days. Investment advisory services and market newsletters also aren't considered to be institutional or professional sponsorship by this definition because they lack the concentrated or sustained buying or selling power of institutional investors. A winning stock doesn't need a huge number of institutional owners, but it should have several at a minimum. Twenty might be a reasonable minimum number in a few rare cases involving small or newer companies, although most stocks have many, many more. If a stock has no professional sponsorship, chances are that its performance will be more run-of-the-mill, as this means that at least some of the more than 10,000 institutional investors have looked at the stock and passed over it. Even if they're wrong, it still takes large buying volume to stimulate an important price increase. Look for Both Quality and Increasing Numbers of Buyers Diligent investors dig down yet another level. They want to know not only how many institutional sponsors a stock has, whether that number has steadily increased in recent quarters, and, more importantly, whether the most recent quarter showed a materially larger increase in the number of owners.

They also want to know who those sponsors are, as shown by services reporting this information. They look for stocks that are held by at least one or two of the more savvy portfolio managers who have the best performance records. This is referred to as analyzing the quality of sponsorship. In analyzing the recorded quality of a stock's institutional sponsorship, the latest 12 months plus the last three years of the investment performance of mutual fund sponsors are usually most relevant. A quick and easy way to get this information is by checking a mutual fund's 36-Month Performance Rating in Investor's Business Daily. An A+ rating indicates that a fund is in the top 5% in terms of performance. Funds with ratings of B+ or higher are considered the better performers. Keep in mind that the rating of a good growth stock mutual fund may be a little lower during a bear market, when most growth stocks will definitely correct. Results may change significantly, however, if key portfolio managers leave one money-management firm and go to another. The leaders in the ratings of top institutional mutual funds generally rotate and change slowly as the years go by. Several financial services publish fund holdings and the investment performance records of various institutions. For example, you can learn the top 25 holdings of each fund plus other data at Morningstar.com. In the past, mutual funds tended to be more aggressive in the market. More recently, new "entrepreneurial-type" investment-counseling firms have cropped up to manage public and institutional money. Buy Companies That Show Increasing Sponsorship As mentioned earlier, it's less crucial to know how many institutions own a stock than to know which of the limited number of better-performing institutions own a stock or have bought it recently. It's also key to know whether the total number of sponsors is increasing or decreasing. The main thing to look for is the recent quarterly trend. It's always best to buy stocks showing strong earnings and sales and an increasing number of institutional owners over several recent quarters. Note New Stock Positions Bought in the Last Quarter A significant new position taken by an institutional investor in the most recently reported period is generally more relevant than existing positions that have been held for some time. When a fund establishes a new position, chances are that it will continue to add to that position and be less likely to sell it in the near future. Reports on such activities are available about six weeks after the end of a fund's three- or six-month period. They are helpful to those who can identify the wiser picks and who understand correct timing and proper analysis of daily and weekly charts. Many investors feel that disclosures of a fund's new commitments are published too long after the fact to be of any real value. But these individual opinions typically aren't correct. Institutional trades also tend to show up on some ticker tapes as transactions of from 1,000 to 100,000 shares or more. Institutional buying and selling can account for up to 70% of the activity in the stocks of most leading companies. This is the sustained force behind most major price moves. About half of the institutional buying that shows up on the New York Stock Exchange ticker tape may be in humdrum stocks. Much of it may also be wrong. But out of the other half, you may have several truly phenomenal selections. Your task, then, is to separate intelligent, highly informed institutional buying from poor, faulty buying. This is hard at first, but it will get easier as you learn to apply and follow the proven rules, guidelines, and principles presented in this book. To get a better sense for what works in the market, it's important to study the investment strategies of a well-managed mutual fund. When reviewing the tables in Investor's Business Daily, look for growth funds with A, A-, or B+ ratings during bull markets and then call to obtain a prospectus. From the prospectus, you'll learn the investment philosophy and techniques used by the individual funds as well as the type and caliber of stocks they've purchased. For example: Fidelity's Contrafund, managed by Will Danoff, has been the bestperforming large, multibillion-dollar fund for a number of years. He scours the country and international equities to get in early on every new concept or story in a stock. Jim Stower's American Century Heritage and Gift Trust funds use computers to find aggressive stocks with accelerating percentage increases in recent sales and earnings. Ken Heebner's CGM Focus and CGM Mutual have both had superior results for many years. His Focus fund concentrates in only 20 stocks. This makes it more volatile, but Ken likes to make big sector bets that in most cases have worked very well for him. Jeff Vinick was a top-flight manager at Fidelity who left and started what is regarded as one of the country's best-performing hedge funds. Janus 20, headquartered in Denver, runs a concentrated portfolio of fewer than 30 growth stocks. Some funds buy on new highs; others buy around lows and may sell on new highs. Is Your Stock "Overowned" by Institutions? It's possible for a stock to have too much institutional sponsorship. Overowned is a term we coined in 1969 to describe stocks in which institutional ownership has become excessive. The danger is that excessive sponsorship might translate into large potential selling if something goes wrong at the company or if a bear market begins. Janus Funds alone owned more than 250 million shares of Nokia and 100 million shares of America Online, which contributed to an adverse supply/demand imbalance in 2000 and 2001. WorldCom (in 1999) and JDS Uniphase and Cisco Systems (in 2000 and 2001) were other examples of overowned stocks. Thus, the "Favorite 50" and other widely owned institutional stocks can be poor, risky prospects. By the time a company's strong performance is so obvious that almost all institutions own the stock, it's probably too late to climb aboard. The heart is already out of the watermelon. Look how many institutions thought Citigroup should be a core holding in the late 1990s and 2000s. At one point during the 2008 bank subprime loan and credit crisis, the stock of this leading New York City bank got down to $3.00 and later $1.00. Only two years earlier it was $57. This is why, since its first edition, How to Make Money in Stocks has always had two detailed chapters on the subject of when to sell your stock. Most investors have no rules or plan for when to sell. That is a serious mistake. The same goes for American International Group. In 2008, AIG had more than 3,600 institutional owners when it tanked to 50 cents from the over $100 it had sold for in 2000. The government-sponsored Fannie Mae collapsed to less than a dollar during the same financial fiasco. America Online in the summer of 2001 and Cisco Systems in the summer of 2000 were also overowned by more than a thousand institutions. This potential heavy supply can adversely affect a stock during bear market periods. Many funds will pile into certain leaders on the way up and pile out on the way down. An Unassailable Institutional Growth Stock Tops Some stocks may seem invincible, but the old saying is true: what goes up must eventually come down. No company is forever immune to management problems, economic slowdowns, and changes in market direction. Savvy investors know that in the stock market, there are few "sacred cows." And there are certainly no guarantees. In June 1974, few people could believe it when William O'Neil + Co. put Xerox on its institutional avoid or sell list at $115. Until then, Xerox had been one of the most amazingly successful and widely held institutional stocks, but our data indicated that it had topped and was headed down. It was also overowned. Institutional investors went on to make Xerox their most widely purchased stock for that year. But when the stock tumbled in price, it showed the true condition of the company at that time. That episode called attention to our institutional services firm and got us our first major insurance company account in New York City. The firm had been buying Xerox in the $80s on the way down until we persuaded it that it should be selling instead. We also received a lot of resistance in 1998 when we put Gillette, another sacred cow, on our avoid list near $60 before it tanked. Enron was removed from our new ideas list on November 29, 2000, at $72.91, and we stopped following it. (Six months later it was $45, and six months after that it was below $5 and headed for bankruptcy.) Here is a list of some of the technology stocks that were removed from our New Stock Market Ideas (NSMI) institutional service potential new ideas list in 2000, when most analysts were incorrectly calling them buys. The lesson: don't be swayed by a stock's broad-based popularity or an analyst advising investors to buy stocks on the way down in price. Institutional Sponsorship Means Market Liquidity Another benefit to you as an individual investor is that institutional sponsorship provides buying support when you want to sell your investment. If there's no sponsorship, and you try to sell your stock in a poor market, you may have problems finding someone to buy it. Daily marketability is one of the big advantages of owning high-quality stocks in the United States. (Real estate is far less liquid, and sales commissions and fees are much higher.) Good institutional sponsorship provides continuous liquidity for you. In a poor real estate market, there is no guarantee that you can find a willing buyer when you want to sell. It could take you six months to a year, and you could sell for a much lower price than you expected.

> *"buy only those stocks that have at least a few institutional sponsors with better-than-average recent performance records and that have added institutional owners in recent quarters. If I find that a stock has a large number of sponsors, but that none of the sponsors is on my list of the 10 or so excellent-performing funds, in the majority of cases I will pass over the stock. Institutional sponsorship is one more important tool to use as you analyze a stock for purchase."*

17

Market Direction

three out of four of your stocks will plummet along with the market averages, and you will certainly lose money big time, as many people did in 2000 and again in 2008. Therefore, in your analytical tool kit, you absolutely must have a proven, reliable method to accurately determine whether you're in a bull (uptrending) market or a bear (downtrending) market. Very few investors or stockbrokers have such an essential tool. Many investors depend on someone else to help them with their investments. Do these other advisors or helpers have a sound set of rules to determine when the general market is starting to get into trouble? That's not enough, however. If you're in a bull market, you need to know whether it's in the early stage or a later stage. And more importantly, you need to know what the market is doing right now. Is it weak and acting badly, or is it merely going through a normal intermediate decline (typically 8% to 12%)? Is it doing just what it should be, considering the basic current conditions in the country, or is it acting abnormally strong or weak? To answer these and other vital questions, you'll want to learn to analyze the overall market correctly, and to do that, you must start at the most logical point. The market direction method that we discovered and developed many years ago is such a key element in successful investing that you'll want to reread this chapter several times until you understand and can apply it on a day-to-day basis for the rest of your investment life. If you learn to do this well, you should never in the future find your investment portfolio down 30% to 50% or more in a bad bear market. The best way for you to determine the direction of the market is to look carefully at, follow, interpret, and understand the daily charts of the three or four major general market averages and what their price and volume changes are doing on a day-to-day basis. This might sound intimidating at first, but with patience and practice, you'll soon be analyzing the market like a true pro. This is the most important lesson you can learn if you want to stop losing and start winning. Are you ready to get smarter? Are your future peace of mind and financial independence worth some extra effort and determination on your part? Don't ever let anyone tell you that you can't time the market. This is a giant myth passed on mainly by Wall Street, the media, and those who have never been able to do it, so they think it's impossible. We've heard from thousands of readers of this chapter and Investor's Business Daily's The Big Picture column who have learned how to do it. They took the time to read the rules and do their homework so that they were prepared and knew exactly what facts to look for. As a result, they had the foresight and understanding to sell stocks and raise cash in March 2000 and from November 2007 to January 2008 and June 2008, protecting much of the gains they made during 1998 and 1999 and in the strong five-year bull market in stocks that lasted from March 2003 to June 2008. The erroneous belief that you can't time the market—that it's simply impossible, that no one can do it—evolved more than 40 years ago after a few mutual fund managers tried it unsuccessfully. They had to both sell at exactly the right time and then get back into the market at exactly the right time. But because of their asset size problems, and because they had no system, it took a number of weeks for them to believe the turn and finally reenter the market. They relied on their personal judgments and feelings to determine when the market finally hit bottom and turned up for real. At the bottom, the news is all negative. So these managers, being human, hesitated to act. Their funds therefore lost some relative performance during the fast turnarounds that frequently happen at market bottoms. For this reason, and despite the fact that twice in the 1950s, Jack Dreyfus successfully raised cash in his Dreyfus Fund at the start of a bear market, top management at most mutual funds imposed rigid rules on money managers that required them to remain fully invested (95% to 100% of assets). This possibly fits well with the sound concept that mutual funds are truly long-term investments. Also, because funds are typically widely diversified (owning a hundred or more stocks spread among many industries), in time they will always recover when the market recovers. So owning them for 15 or 20 years has always been extremely rewarding in the past and should continue to be in the future. However, you, as an individual investor owning 5, 10, or 20 stocks, don't have a large size handicap. Some of your stocks can drop substantially and maybe never come back or take years to do so. Learning when it's wise to raise cash is very important for you ... so study and learn how to successfully use this technique to your advantage. What Is the General Market? The general market is a term referring to the most commonly used market indexes. These broad indexes tell you the approximate strength or weakness in each day's overall trading activity and can be one of your earliest indications of emerging trends. They include The Standard & Poor's (S&P) 500. Consisting of 500 companies, this index is a broader, more modern representation of market action than the Dow. The Nasdaq Composite. This has been a somewhat more volatile and relevant index in recent years. The Nasdaq is home to many of the market's younger, more innovative, and faster-growing companies that trade via the Nasdaq network of market makers. It's a little more weighted toward the technology sector. The Dow Jones Industrial Average (DJIA). This index consists of 30 widely traded big-cap stocks. It used to focus primarily on large, cyclical, industrial issues, but it has broadened a little in recent years to include companies such as Coca-Cola and Home Depot. It's a simple but rather out-of-date average to study because it's dominated by large, established, old-line companies that grow more slowly than today's more entrepreneurial concerns. It can also be easily manipulated over short time periods because it's limited to only 30 stocks. The NYSE Composite. This is a market-value-weighted index of all stocks listed on the New York Stock Exchange. All these key indexes are shown in Investor's Business Daily in large, easy-toanalyze charts that also feature a moving average and an Accumulation/ Distribution Rating (ACC/DIS RTG®) for each index. The Accumulation/ Distribution Rating tells you if the index has been getting buying support recently or is undergoing significant selling. I always try to check these indexes every day because a key change can occur over just a few weeks, and you don't want to be asleep at the switch and not see it. IBD's "The Big Picture" column also evaluates these indexes daily to materially help you in deciphering the market's current condition and direction. Why Is Skilled, Careful Market Observation So Important? A Harvard professor once asked his students to do a special report on fish. His scholars went to the library, read books about fish, and then wrote their expositions. But after turning in their papers, the students were shocked when the professor tore them up and threw them in the wastebasket. When they asked him what was wrong with the reports, the professor said, "If you want to learn anything about fish, sit in front of a fishbowl and look at fish." He made his students sit and watch fish for hours. Then they rewrote their assignment solely on their observations of the objects themselves. Being a student of the market is like being a student in this professor's class: if you want to learn about the market, you must observe and study the major indexes carefully. In doing so, you'll come to recognize when the daily market averages are changing at key turning points—such as major market tops and bottoms—and learn to capitalize on this with real knowledge and confidence. There's an important lesson here. To be highly accurate in any pursuit, you must observe and analyze the objects themselves carefully. If you want to know about tigers, you need to watch tigers—not the weather, not the vegetation, and not the other animals on the mountain. Years ago, when Lou Brock set his mind to breaking baseball's stolen base record, he had all the big-league pitchers photographed with high-speed film from the seats behind first base. Then he studied the film to learn what part of each pitcher's body moved first when he threw to first base. The pitcher was the object that Brock was trying to beat, so it was the pitchers themselves that he studied in great detail. In the 2003 Super Bowl, the Tampa Bay Buccaneers were able to intercept five Oakland Raider passes by first studying and then concentrating on the eye movements and body language of Oakland's quarterback. They "read" where he was going to throw. Christopher Columbus didn't accept the conventional wisdom about the earth being flat because he himself had observed ships at sea disappearing over the horizon in a way that told him otherwise. The government uses wiretaps, spy planes, unmanned drones, and satellite photos to observe and analyze objects that could threaten our security. That's how we discovered Soviet missiles in Cuba. It's the same with the stock market. To know which way it's going, you must observe and analyze the major general market indexes daily. Don't ever, ever ask anyone: "What do you think the market's going to do?" Learn to accurately read what the market is actually doing each day as it is doing it. Recognizing when the market has hit a top or has bottomed out is frequently 50% of the whole complicated investment ball game. It's also the key investing skill virtually all investors, whether amateur or professional, seem to lack. In fact, Wall Street analysts completely missed calling the market top in 2000, particularly the tops in every one of the high-technology leaders. They didn't do much better in 2008. We conducted four surveys of IBD subscribers in 2008 and also received hundreds of letters from subscribers that led us to believe that 60% of IBD readers sold stock and raised cash in either December 2007 or June 2008 with the help of "The Big Picture" column and by applying and acting on our rule about five or six distribution days over any four- or five-week period. They preserved their capital and avoided the brunt of the dramatic and costly market collapse in the fall of 2008 that resulted from excessive problems in the market for subprime mortgage real estate loans (which had been sponsored and strongly encouraged by the government). You may have seen some of our subscribers' comments in IBD at the top of a page space titled "You Can Do It Too." You'll learn exactly how to apply IBD's general market distribution rules later in this chapter. The Stages of a Stock Market Cycle The winning investor should understand how a normal business cycle unfolds and over what period of time. The investor should pay particular attention to recent cycles. There's no guarantee that just because cycles lasted three or four years in the past, they'll last that long in the future. Bull and bear markets don't end easily. It usually takes two or three tricky pullbacks up or down to fake out or shake out the few remaining speculators. After everyone who can be run in or run out has thrown in the towel, there isn't anyone left to take action in the same market direction. Then the market will finally turn and begin a whole new trend. Most of this is crowd psychology constantly at work. Bear markets usually end while business is still in a downtrend. The reason is that stocks are anticipating, or "discounting," all economic, political, and worldwide events many months in advance. The stock market is a leading economic indicator, not a coincident or lagging indicator, in our govern-ment's series of key economic indicators. The market is exceptionally perceptive, taking all events and basic conditions into account. It will react to what is taking place and what it can mean for the nation. The market is not controlled by Wall Street. Its action is determined by millions of investors all across the country and thousands of large institutions and is a consensus conclusion on whether it likes or doesn't like what it foresees—such as what our government is doing or about to do and what the consequences could be. Similarly, bull markets usually top out and turn down before a recession sets in. For this reason, looking at economic indicators is a poor way to determine when to buy or sell stocks and is not recommended. Yet, some investment firms do this very thing. The predictions of many economists also leave a lot to be desired. A few of our nation's presidents have had to learn this lesson the hard way. In early 1983, for example, just as the economy was in its first few months of recovery, the head of President Reagan's Council of Economic Advisers was concerned that the capital goods sector was not very strong. This was the first hint that this advisor might not be as sound as he should be. Had he understood historical trends, he would have seen that capital goods demand has never been strong in the early stage of a recovery. This was especially true in the first quarter of 1983, when U.S. plants were operating at a low percentage of capacity. You should check earlier cycles to learn the sequence of industry-group moves at various stages of the market cycle. If you do, you'll see that railroad equipment, machinery, and other capital goods industries are late movers in a business or stock market cycle. This knowledge can help you get a fix on where you are now. When these groups start running up, you know you're near the end. In early 2000, computer companies supplying Internet capital goods and infrastructure were the last-stage movers, along with telecommunications equipment suppliers. Dedicated students of the market who want to learn more about cycles and the longer-term history of U.S. economic growth may want to write to Securities Research Company, 27 Wareham Street, #401, Boston, MA 02118, and purchase one of the company's long-term wall charts. Also, in 2008, Daily Graphs, Inc., created a 1900 to 2008 stock market wall chart that shows major market and economic events. Some charts of market averages also include major news events over the last 12 months. These can be very valuable, especially if you keep and review back copies. You then have a history of both the market averages and the events that have influenced their direction. It helps to know, for example, how the market has reacted to new faces in the White House, rumors of war, controls on wages and prices, changes in discount rates, or just loss of confidence and "panics" in general. The accompanying chart of the S&P 500 Index shows several past cycles with the bear markets shaded. You Should Study the General Market Indexes Each Day In bear markets, stocks usually open strong and close weak. In bull markets, they tend to open weak and close strong. The general market averages need to be checked every day, since reverses in trends can begin on any given few days. Relying on these primary indexes is a more direct, practical, and effective method for analyzing the market's behavior and determining its direction. Don't rely on other, subsidiary indicators because they haven't been proven to be effective at timing. Listening to the many market newsletter writers, technical analysts, or strategists who pore over 30 to 50 different technical or economic indicators and then tell you what they think the market should be doing is generally a very costly waste of time. Investment newsletters can create doubt and confusion in an investor's mind. Interestingly enough, history shows that the market tends to go up just when the news is all bad and these experts are most skeptical and uncertain. When the general market tops, you must sell to raise at least some cash and to get off margin (the use of borrowed money) to protect your account. As an individual investor, you can easily raise cash and get out in one or two days, and you can likewise reenter later when the market is finally right. If you don't sell and raise cash when the general market tops, your diversified list of former market leaders can decline sharply. Several of them may never recover to their former levels. Your best bet is to learn to interpret daily price and volume charts of the key general market averages. If you do, you can't get too far off-track, and you won't need much else. It doesn't pay to argue with the market. Experience teaches that second-guessing the market can be a very expensive mistake. The Prolonged Two-Year Bear Market of 1973–1974 The combination of the Watergate scandal and hearings and the 1974 oil embargo by OPEC made 1973–1974 the worst stock market catastrophe up to that time since the 1929–1933 depression. The Dow corrected 50%, but the average stock plummeted more than 70%. This was a big lesson for stockholders and was almost as severe as the 90% correction the average stock showed from 1929 to 1933. However, in 1933, industrial production was only 56% of the 1929 level, and more than 13 million Americans were unemployed. The peak unemployment rate in the 1930s was 25%. It remained in double digits throughout the entire decade and was 20% in 1939. The markets were so demoralized in the prolonged 1973–1974 bear market that most members on the floor of the New York Stock Exchange were afraid the exchange might not survive as a viable institution. This is why it's absolutely critical that you study the market averages and learn how to protect yourself against catastrophic losses, for the sake of your health as well as your portfolio. You can learn to do this. Anyone can do it, if they get serious and apply themselves. Is your money important to you? A 33% Drop Requires a 50% Rise to Break Even The importance of knowing the direction of the general market cannot be overemphasized. If you have a 33% loss in a portfolio of stocks, you need a 50% gain just to get to your breakeven point. If, for example, you've allowed a $10,000 portfolio to drop to $6,666 (a 33% decline), it has to rise $3,333 (or 50%) just to get you back where you started. In the 2007–2008 bear market, the S&P 500 fell more than 50%, meaning that a 100% rebound will be needed for the index to fully recover. And how easy is it for you to make 100%? Maybe it's time for you to learn what you're doing, adopt new rules and methods, and stop doing things that create 50% losses. You positively must always act to preserve as much as possible of the profit that you've built up during the bull market rather than ride your investments back down through difficult bear market periods. To do this, you have to learn historically proven selling rules. (See Chapters 10 and 11 for more on selling rules.) The Myths about "Long-Term Investing" and Being Fully Invested Many investors like to think of, or at least describe, themselves as "long-term investors." Their strategy is to stay fully invested through thick and thin. Most institutions do the same thing. But such an inflexible approach can have tragic results, particularly for individual investors. Individuals and institutions alike may get away with standing pat through relatively mild (25% or less) bear markets, but many bear markets are not mild. Some, such as 1973–1974, 2000– 2002, and 2007–2008, are downright devastating. The challenge always comes at the beginning, when you start to sense an impending bear market. In most cases, you cannot project how bad economic conditions might become or how long those bad conditions could linger. The war in Vietnam, inflation, and a tight money supply helped turn the 1969–1970 correction into a two-year decline of 36.9%. Before that, bear markets averaged only nine months and took the averages down 26%. Most stocks fall during a bear market, but not all of them recover. If you hold on during even a modest bear correction, you can get stuck with damaged merchandise that may never see its former highs. You definitely must learn to sell and raise at least some cash when the overall environment changes and your stocks are not working. Buy-and-hold investors fell in love with Coca-Cola during the 1980s and 1990s. The soft-drink giant chugged higher year after year, rising and falling with the market. But it stopped working in 1998, as did Gillette, another favorite of long-term holders. When the market slipped into its mild bear correction that summer, Coke followed along. Two years later—after some of the market's most exciting gains in decades—Coke was still stuck in a downtrend. In some instances, stocks of this kind may come back. But this much is certain: Coke investors missed huge advances in 1998 and 1999 in names such as America Online and Qualcomm. The buy-and-hold strategy was also disastrous to anyone who held technology stocks from 2000 through 2002. Many highfliers lost 75% to 90% of their value, and some may never return to their prior highs. Take a look now at Time Warner, Corning, Yahoo!, Intel, JDS Uniphase, and EMC, former market leaders in 1998–2000. Protecting Yourself from Market Downturns Napoleon once wrote that never hesitating in battle gave him an advantage over his opponents, and for many years he was undefeated. In the battlefield that is the stock market, there are the quick and there are the dead! After you see the first several definite indications of a market top, don't wait around. Sell quickly before real weakness develops. When market indexes peak and begin major downside reversals, you should act immediately by putting 25% or more of your portfolio in cash, selling your stocks at market prices. The use of limit orders (buying or selling at a specific price, rather than buying or selling at market prices using market orders) is not recommended. Focus on your ability to get into or out of a stock when you need to. Quibbling over an eighth- or quarterpoint (or their decimal equivalents) could make you miss an opportunity to buy or sell a stock. Lightning-fast action is even more critical if your stock account is on margin. If your portfolio is fully margined, with half of the money in your stocks borrowed from your broker, a 20% decline in the price of your stocks will cause you to lose 40% of your money. A 50% decline in your stocks could wipe you out! Never try to ride through a bear market on margin. In the final analysis, there are really only two things you can do when a new bear market begins: sell and retreat or go short. When you retreat, you should stay out until the bear market is over. This usually means five or six months or more. In the prolonged, problem-ridden 1969–1970 and 1973–1974 periods, however, it meant up to two years. The bear market that began in March 2000 during the last year of the Clinton administration lasted longer and was far more severe than normal. Nine out of ten investors lost a lot of money, particularly in high-tech stocks. It was the end of a period of many excesses during the late 1990s, a decade when America got careless and let down its guard. It was the "anything goes" period, with stocks running wild. Selling short can be profitable, but be forewarned: it's a very difficult and highly specialized skill that should be attempted only during bear markets. Few people make money at it.

> *"If you use stop-loss orders or mentally record a selling price and act upon it, a market that is starting to top out will mechanically force you, robotlike, out of many of your stocks. A stop-loss order instructs the specialist in the stock on the exchange floor that once the stock has dropped to your specified price, the order becomes a market order, and the stock will be sold out on the next transaction. It's usually better not to enter stop-loss orders. In doing so, you and other similarly minded investors are showing your hand to market makers, and at times they might drop the stock to shake out stop-loss orders. Instead, watch your stocks closely and know ahead of time the exact price at which you will*

> *immediately sell to cut a loss. However, some people travel a lot and aren't able to watch their stocks closely, and others have a hard time making sell decisions and getting out when they are losing. In such cases, stop-loss orders help compensate for distance and indecisiveness. If you use a stop-loss order, remember to cancel it if you change your mind and sell a stock before the order is executed. Otherwise, you could later accidentally sell a stock that you no longer own. Such errors can be costly.*"

How You Can Learn to Identify Stock Market Tops To detect a market top, keep a close eye on the daily S&P 500, NYSE Composite, Dow 30, and Nasdaq Composite as they work their way higher. On one of the days in the uptrend, volume for the market as a whole will increase from the day before, but the index itself will show stalling action (a significantly smaller price increase for the day compared with the prior day's price increase). I call this "heavy volume without further price progress up." The average doesn't have to close down for the day, but in most instances it will, making the distribution (selling) as professional investors liquidate stock must easier to see. The spread from the average's daily high to its daily low may in some cases be a little wider than on previous days. Normal liquidation near the market peak will usually occur on three to five specific days over a period of four or five weeks. In other words, the market comes under distribution while it's advancing! This is one reason so few people know how to recognize distribution. After four or five days of definite distribution over any span of four or five weeks, the general market will almost always turn down. Four days of distribution, if correctly spotted over a two- or three-week period, are sometimes enough to turn a previously advancing market into a decline. Sometimes distribution can be spread over six weeks if the market attempts at some point to rally back to new highs. If you are asleep or unaware and you miss the topping signals given off by the S&P 500, the NYSE Composite, the Nasdaq, or the Dow (which is easy to do, since they sometimes occur on only a few days), you could be wrong about the market direction and therefore wrong on almost everything you do. One of the biggest problems is the time it takes to reverse investors' positive personal opinions and views. If you always sell and cut your losses 7% or 8% below your buy points, you may automatically be forced to sell at least one or two stocks as a correction in the general market starts to develop. This should get you into a questioning, defensive frame of mind sooner. Following this one simple but powerful rule of ours saved a lot of people big money in 2000's devastating decline in technology leaders and in the 2008 subprime loan bear market. It takes only one of the indexes to give you a valid repeated signal of too much distribution. You don't normally need to see several of the major indexes showing four or five distribution days. Also, if one of the indexes is down for the day on volume larger than the prior day's volume, it should decline more than 0.2% for this to be counted as a distribution day. After the Initial Decline off the Top, Track Each Rally Attempt on the Way Down After the required number of days of increased volume distribution around the top and the first decline resulting from this, there will be either a poor rally in the market averages, followed by a rally failure, or a positive and powerful followthrough day up on price and volume. You should learn in detail exactly what signals to look for and remain unbiased about the market. Let the day-by-day averages tell you what the market has been doing and is doing. (See "How You Can Spot Stock Market Bottoms" later in this chapter for a further discussion of market rallies.) Three Signs the First Rally Attempt May Fail After the market does top out, it typically will rally feebly and then fail. After the first day's rebound, for instance, the second day will open strongly but suddenly turn down near the end of the session. The abrupt failure of the market to follow through on its first recovery attempt should probably be met with further selling on your part. You'll know that the initial bounce back is feeble if (1) the index advances in price on the third, fourth, or fifth rally day, but on volume that is lower than that of the day before, (2) the average makes little net upward price progress compared with its progress the day before, or (3) the market average recovers less than half of the initial drop from its former absolute intraday high. When you see these weak rallies and failures, further selling is advisable. How CAN SLIM and IBD Red-Flagged the March 2000 Nasdaq Top In October 1999, the market took off on a furious advance. Fears of a Y2K meltdown on January 1, 2000, had faded. Companies were announcing strong profits for the third quarter just ended. Both leading tech stocks and speculative Internet and biotechnology issues racked up huge gains in just five months. But cracks started to appear in early March 2000. On March 7, the Nasdaq closed lower on higher volume, the first time it had done so in more than six weeks. That's unusual action during a roaring bull market, but one day of distribution isn't significant on its own. Still, it was the first yellow flag and was worth watching carefully. Three days later, the Nasdaq bolted up more than 85 points to a new high in the morning. But it reversed in the afternoon and finished the day up only 2 points on heavy volume that was 13% above average. This was the second warning sign.

Follow the Leaders for Clues to a Market Top

The second most important indicator of a primary change in market direction, after the daily averages, is the way leading stocks act. After the market has advanced for a couple of years, you can be fairly sure that it's headed for trouble if most of the individual stock leaders start acting abnormally. One example of abnormal activity can be seen when leading stocks break out of third- or fourth-stage chart base formations on the way up. Most of these base structures will be faulty, with price fluctuations appearing much wider and looser. A faulty base (wide, loose, and erratic) can best be recognized and analyzed by studying charts of a stock's daily or weekly price and volume history. Another sign of abnormal activity is the "climax" top. Here, a leading stock will run up more rapidly for two or three weeks in a row, after having advanced for many months.

A few leaders will have their first abnormal price break off the top on heavy volume but then be unable to rally more than a small amount from the lows of their correction. Still others will show a serious loss of upward momentum in their most recent quarterly earnings reports. Shifts in market direction can also be detected by reviewing the last four or five stock purchases in your own portfolio. If you haven't made a dime on any of them, you could be picking up signs of a new downtrend. Investors who use charts and understand market action know that very few leading stocks will be attractive around market tops. There simply aren't any stocks coming out of sound, properly formed chart bases. The best merchandise has been bought, played, and well picked over. Most bases will be wide and loose—a big sign of real danger that you must learn to understand and obey. All that's left to show strength at this stage are laggard stocks. The sight of sluggish or low-priced, lower-quality laggards strengthening is a signal to the wise market operator the up market may be near its end. Even turkeys can try to fly in a windstorm. During the early phase of a bear market, certain leading stocks will seem to be bucking the trend by holding up in price, creating the impression of strength, but what you're seeing is just a postponement of the inevitable. When they raid the house, they usually get everyone, and eventually all the leaders will succumb to the selling. This is exactly what happened in the 2000 bear market. Cisco and other high-tech leaders all eventually collapsed in spite of the many analysts who incorrectly said that they should be bought. That's also what happened at the top of the Nasdaq in June and July of 2008. The steels, fertilizers, and oils that had led the 2003–2007 bull market all rolled over and finally broke down after they appeared to be bucking the overall market top that actually began with at least five distribution days in October of 2007. U.S. Steel tanked even though its next two quarterly earnings reports were up over 100%. Potash topped when its current quarter was up 181% and its next quarter was up 220%. This fooled most analysts, who were focused on the big earnings that had been reported or were expected. They had not studied all past historical tops and didn't realize that many past leaders had topped when earnings were up 100%. Why did these stocks finally cave in? They were in a bear market that had begun eight months earlier, in late 2007. Market tops, whether intermediate (usually 8% to 12% declines) or primary bull market peaks, sometimes occur five, six, or seven months after the last major buy point in leading stocks and in the averages. Thus, top reversals are usually late signals—the last straw before a cave-in. In most cases, distribution, or selling, has been going on for days or even weeks in individual market leaders. Use of individual stock selling rules,

Other Bear Market Warnings If the original market leaders begin to falter, and lower-priced, lower-quality, more-speculative stocks begin to move up, watch out! When the old dogs begin to bark, the market is on its last feeble leg. Laggards can't lead the market higher. Among the telltale signs are the poor-quality stocks that start to dominate the most-active list on market "up" days. This is simply a matter of weak leadership trying to command the market. If the best ones can't lead, the worst certainly aren't going to do so for very long. Many top reversals (when the market closes at the bottom of its trading range after making a new high that day) have occurred between the third and the ninth day of a rally after the averages moved into new high ground off small chart bases (meaning that the time span from the start to the end of the pattern was really too short). It's important to note that the conditions under which the tops occurred were all about the same. At other times, a topping market will recover for a couple of months and get back nearly to its old high or even above it before breaking down in earnest. This occurred in December 1976, January 1981, and January 1984. There's an important psychological reason for this: the majority of people in the market can't be exactly right at exactly the right time. In 1994, the Nasdaq didn't top until weeks after the Dow did. A similar thing happened in early 2000. The majority of people in the stock market, including both professional and individual investors, will be fooled first. It's all about human psychology and emotions. If you were smart enough to sell or sell short in January 1981, the powerful rebound in February and March probably forced you to cover your short sales at a loss or buy some stocks back during the strong rally. It was an example of how treacherous the market really can be at turning points. Don't Jump Back In Too Early I didn't have much problem recognizing and acting upon the early signs of the many bear markets from 1962 through 2008. But a few times I made the mistake of buying back too early. When you make a mistake in the stock market, the only sound thing to do is to correct it. Don't fight it. Pride and ego never pay off; neither does vacillation when losses start to show up. The typical bear market (and some aren't typical) usually has three separate phases, or legs, of decline interrupted by a couple of rallies that last just long enough to convince investors to begin buying. In 1969 and 1974, a few of these phony, drawn-out rallies lasted up to 15 weeks. Most don't last that long. Many institutional investors love to "bottom fish." They'll start buying stocks off a supposed bottom and help make the rally convincing enough to draw you in. You're better off staying on the sidelines in cash until a new bull market really starts. How You Can Spot Stock Market Bottoms Once you've recognized a bear market and have scaled back your stock holdings, the big question is how long you should remain on the sidelines. If you plunge back into the market too soon, the apparent rally may fade, and you'll lose money. But if you hesitate at the brink of the eventual roaring recovery, opportunities will pass you by. Again, the daily general market averages provide the best answer by far. Markets are always more reliable than most investors' emotions or personal opinions. At some point in every correction—whether that correction is mild or severe —the stock market will always attempt to rally. Don't jump back in right away. Wait for the market itself to confirm the new uptrend. A rally attempt begins when a major market average closes higher after a decline that happened either earlier in the day or during the previous session. For example, the Dow plummets 3% in the morning but then recovers later in the day and closes higher. Or the Dow closes down 2% and then rebounds the next day. We typically call the session in which the Dow finally closes higher the first day of the attempted rally, although there have been some exceptions. For example, the first day of the early October market bottom in 1998 was actually down on heavy volume, but it closed in the upper half of that day's price range. Sit tight and be patient. The first few days of improvement can't tell you whether the rally will succeed. Starting on the fourth day of the attempted rally, look for one of the major averages to "follow through" with a booming gain on heavier volume than the day before. This tells you the rally is far more likely to be real. The most powerful follow-throughs usually occur on the fourth to seventh days of the rally. The 1998 bottom just mentioned followed through on the fifth day of the attempted rally. The market was up 2.1%. A follow-through day should give the feeling of an explosive rally that is strong, decisive, and conclusive—not begrudging and on the fence or barely up 1½%. The market's volume for the day should in most cases be above its average daily volume, in addition to always being higher than the prior day's trading. Occasionally, but rarely, a follow-through occurs as early as the third day of the rally. In such a case, the first, second, and third days must all be very powerful, with a major average up 1½% to 2% or more each session in heavy volume. I used to consider 1% to be the percentage increase for a valid follow-through day. However, in recent years, as institutional investors have learned of our system, we've moved the requirement up a significant amount for the Nasdaq and the Dow. By doing this, we are trying to minimize the possibility that professionals will manipulate a few of the 30 stocks in the Dow Jones average to create false or faulty follow-through days. There will be cases in which confirmed rallies fail. A few large institutional investors, armed with their immense buying power, can run up the averages on a particular day and create the impression of a follow-through. Unless the smart buyers are getting back on board, however, the rally will implode—sometimes crashing on heavy volume within the next several days. However, just because the market corrects the day after a follow-through doesn't mean the follow-through was false. When a bear market bottoms, it frequently pulls back and settles above or near the lows made during the previous few weeks. It is more constructive when these pullbacks or "tests" hold at least a little above the absolute intraday lows made recently in the market averages. A follow-through signal doesn't mean you should rush out and buy with abandon. It just gives you the go-ahead to begin buying high-quality stocks with strong sales and earnings as they break out of sound price bases, and it is a vital second confirmation the attempted rally is succeeding. Remember, no new bull market has ever started without a strong price and volume follow-through confirmation. It pays to wait and listen to the market. The following graphs are examples of several bottoms in the stock market between 1974 and 2003.

The Big Money Is Made in the First Two Years

The really big money is usually made in the first one or two years of a normal new bull market cycle. It is at this point that you must always recognize, and fully capitalize upon, the golden opportunities presented. The rest of the "up" cycle usually consists of back-and-forth movement in the market averages, followed by a bear market. The year 1965 was one of the few exceptions, but that strong market in the third year of a new cycle was caused by the beginning of the Vietnam War. In the first or second year of a new bull market, there should be a few intermediate-term declines in the market averages. These usually last a couple of months, with the market indexes dropping by from 8% to an occasional 12% or 15%. After several sharp downward adjustments of this nature, and after at least two years of a bull market have passed, heavy volume without further upside progress in the daily market averages could indicate the early beginning of the next bear market. Since the market is governed by supply and demand, you can interpret a chart of the general market averages about the same way you read the chart of an individual stock. The Dow Jones Industrial Average and the S&P 500 are usually displayed in the better publications. Investor's Business Daily displays the Nasdaq Composite, the New York Stock Exchange Composite, and the S&P 500, with large-size daily price and volume charts stacked one on top of the other for ease of comparing the three. These charts should show the high, low, and close of the market averages day by day for at least six months, together with the daily NYSE and Nasdaq volume in millions of shares traded. Incidentally, when I began in the market about 50 years ago, an average day on the New York Stock Exchange was 3.5 million shares. Today, 1.5 billion shares are traded on average each day—an incredible 150-fold increase that clearly demonstrates beyond any question the amazing growth and success of our free enterprise, capitalist system. Its unparalleled freedom and opportunity have consistently attracted millions of ambitious people from all around the world who have materially increased our productivity and inventiveness. It has led to an unprecedented increase in our standard of living, so that the vast majority of Americans and all areas of our population are better off than they were before. There are always problems that need to be recognized and solved. But our system is the most successful in the world, and it offers remarkable opportunities to grow and advance to those who are willing to work, train, and educate themselves.Normal bear markets show three legs of price movement down, but there's no rule saying you can't have four or even five down legs. You have to evaluate overall conditions and events in the country objectively and let the market averages tell their own story. And you have to understand what that story is.

> *"Look for Divergence of Key Averages Several averages should be checked at market turning points to see if there are significant divergences, meaning that they are moving in different directions (one up and one down) or that one index is advancing or declining at a much greater rate than another. For example, if the Dow is up 100 and the S&P 500 is up only the equivalent of 20 on the Dow for the day (the S&P 500 being a broader index), it would indicate the rally is not as broad and strong as it appears. To compare the change in the S&P 500 to that in the Dow, divide the S&P 500 into the Dow average and then multiply by the change in the S&P 500. For example, if the Dow closed at 9,000 and the S&P 500 finished at 900, the 9,000 Dow would be 10 times the S&P 500. Therefore, if the Dow, on a particular day, is up 100 points and the S&P 500 is up 5 points, you can multiply the 5 by 10 and find that the S&P 500 was up only the equivalent of 50 points on the Dow. The Dow's new high in January 1984 was accompanied by a divergence in the indexes: the broader-based, more significant S&P 500 did not hit a new high. This is the reason most professionals plot the key indexes together—to make it easier to spot nonconfirmations at key turning points. Institutional investors periodically run up the 30-stock Dow while they liquidate the broader Nasdaq or a list of technology stocks under cover of the Dow run-up. It's like a big poker game, with players hiding their hands, bluffing, and faking."*

Certain Psychological Market Indicators Might at Times Help Now that trading in put and call options is the get-rich-quick scheme for many speculators, you can plot and analyze the ratio of calls to puts for another valuable insight into crowd temperament. Options traders buy calls, which are options to buy common stock, or puts, which are options to sell common stock. A call buyer hopes prices will rise; a buyer of put options wishes prices to fall. If the volume of call options in a given period of time is greater than the volume of put options, a logical assumption is that option speculators as a group are expecting higher prices and are bullish on the market. If the volume of put options is greater than that of calls, speculators hold a bearish attitude. When option players buy more puts than calls, the put-to-call ratio index rises a little above 1.0. Such a reading coincided with general market bottoms in 1990, 1996, 1998, and April and September 2001, but you can't always expect this to occur. The percentage of investment advisors who are bearish is an interesting measure of investor sentiment. When bear markets are near the bottom, the great majority of advisory letters will usually be bearish. Near market tops, most will be bullish. The majority is usually wrong when it's most important to be right. However, you cannot blindly assume that because 65% of investment advisors were bearish the last time the general market hit bottom, a major market decline will be over the next time the investment advisors' index reaches the same point. The short-interest ratio is the amount of short selling on the New York Stock Exchange, expressed as a percentage of total NYSE volume. This ratio can reflect the degree of bearishness shown by speculators in the market. Along bear market bottoms, you will usually see two or three major peaks showing sharply increased short selling. There's no rule governing how high the index should go, but studying past market bottoms can give you an idea of what the ratio looked like at key market junctures. An index that is sometimes used to measure the degree of speculative activity is the Nasdaq volume as a percentage of NYSE volume. This measure provided a helpful tip-off of impending trouble during the summer of 1983, when Nasdaq volume increased significantly relative to the Big Board's (NYSE). When a trend persists and accelerates, indicating wild, rampant speculation, you're close to a general market correction. The volume of Nasdaq trading has grown larger than that on the NYSE in recent years because so many new entrepreneurial companies are listed on the Nasdaq, so this index must be viewed differently now. Interpret the Overrated Advance-Decline Line Some technical analysts religiously follow advance-decline (A-D) data. These technicians take the number of stocks advancing each day versus the number that are declining, and then plot that ratio on a graph. Advance-decline lines are far from precise because they frequently veer sharply lower long before a bull market finally tops. In other words, the market keeps advancing toward higher ground, but it is being led by fewer but better stocks. The advance-decline line is simply not as accurate as the key general market indexes because analyzing the market's direction is not a simple total numbers game. Not all stocks are created equal; it's better to know where the real leadership is and how it's acting than to know how many more mediocre stocks are advancing and declining. The NYSE A-D line peaked in April 1998 and trended lower during the new bull market that broke out six months later in October. The A-D line continued to fall from October 1999 to March 2000, missing one of the market's most powerful rallies in decades. An advance-decline line can sometimes be helpful when a clear-cut bear market attempts a short-term rally. If the A-D line lags the market averages and can't rally, it's giving an internal indication that, despite the strength of the rally in the Dow or S&P, the broader market remains frail. In such instances, the rally usually fizzles. In other words, it takes more than just a few leaders to make a new bull market. At best, the advance-decline line is a secondary indicator of limited value. If you hear commentators or TV market strategists extolling its virtues bullishly or bearishly, they probably haven't done their homework. No secondary measurements can be as accurate as the major market indexes, so you don't want to get confused and overemphasize the vast array of other technical measures that most people use, usually with lackluster results. Watch Federal Reserve Board Rate Changes Among fundamental general market indicators, changes in the Federal Reserve Board's discount rate (the interest rate the FRB charges member banks for loans), the fed funds rate (the interest rate banks with fund reserves charge for loans to banks without fund reserves), and occasionally stock margin levels are valuable indicators to watch. As a rule, interest rates provide the best confirmation of basic economic conditions, and changes in the discount rate and the fed funds rate are by far the most reliable. In the past, three successive significant hikes in Fed interest rates have generally marked the beginning of bear markets and impending recessions. Bear markets have usually, but not always, ended when the rate was finally lowered. On the downside, the discount rate increase to 6% in September 1987, just after Alan Greenspan became chairman, led to the severe market break that October. Money market indicators mirror general economic activity. At times I have followed selected government and Federal Reserve Board measurements, including 10 indicators of the supply and demand for money and indicators of interest-rate levels. History proves that the direction of the general market, and also that of several industry groups, is often affected by changes in interest rates because the level of interest rates is usually tied to tight or easy Fed monetary policy. For the investor, the simplest and most relevant monetary indicators to follow and understand are the changes in the discount rate and fed funds rate. With the advent of program trading and various hedging devices, some funds now hedge portions of their portfolio in an attempt to provide some downside protection during risky markets. The degree to which these hedges are successful again depends greatly on skill and timing, but one possible effect for some managers may be to lessen the pressure to dump portfolio securities on the market. Most funds operate with a policy of being widely diversified and fully or nearly fully invested at all times. This is because most fund managers, given the great size of today's funds (billions of dollars), have difficulty getting out of the market and into cash at the right time and, most importantly, then getting back into the market fast enough to participate in the initial powerful rebound off the ultimate bottom. So they may try to shift their emphasis to big-cap, semidefensive groups. The Fed Crushes the 1981 Economy. The bear market and the costly, protracted recession that began in 1981, for example, came about solely because the Fed increased the discount rate in rapid succession on September 26, November 17, and December 5 of 1980. Its fourth increase, on May 8, 1981, thrust the discount rate to an all-time high of 14%. That finished off the U.S. economy, our basic industries, and the stock market for the time being. Fed rate changes, however, should not be your primary market indicator because the stock market itself is always your best barometer. Our analysis of market cycles turned up three key market turns that the discount rate did not help predict. Independent Fed actions are typically very constructive, as the Fed tries to counteract overheated excesses or sharp contractions in our economy. However, its actions and results clearly demonstrate how much our overall federal government, not our stock markets reacting to all events, can and does at times significantly influence our economic future, for good or bad. In fact, the subprime real estate mortgage meltdown and the financial credit crisis that led to the highly unusual market collapse of 2008 can be easily traced to moves in 1995 by the then-current administration to substantially beef up the Community Reinvestment Act (CRA) of 1977. These actions required banks to make more higher-risk loans in lower-income areas than they would otherwise have made. Failure to comply meant stiff penalties, lawsuits, and limits on getting approvals for mergers and branch expansion. Our government, in effect, encouraged and coerced major banks to lower their long-proven safe-lending standards. Most of the more than $1 trillion of new subprime CRA loans had adjustable rates. Many such loans eventually came to require no documentation of the borrower's income and in some cases little or no down payment. In addition, for the first time, new regulatory rules not only allowed but encouraged lenders to bundle the new, riskier subprime loans with prime loans and sell these assumed government-sponsored loan packages to other institutions and countries that thought they were buying safe AAA bonds. The first of these bundled loans hit the investment market in 1997. That action allowed loan originators and big banks to make profits faster and eliminate future risk and responsibility for many of those lower-quality loans. It let the banks turn around and make even more CRA-type loans, then sell them off in packages again, with little future risk or responsibility. In time, the unintended result was a gigantic government-sponsored pyramiding mechanism, with Fannie Mae and Freddie Mac providing the implied government backing by buying vast quantities of the more risky subprimes; this led to their facing bankruptcy and needing enormous government bailouts. Freddie and Fannie's management had also received huge bonuses and were donors to certain members of Congress, who repeatedly defended the highly leveraged, extremely risky lending against any sound reforms. Bottom line: this was a Big Government program that was started with absolutely good, worthy social intentions, but with little insight and absolutely zero foresight that over time resulted in severe damage and enormous unintended consequences that affected almost everything and everyone, including, sadly, the very lower-income people that this rather inept government operation was supposed to be helping. It put our whole financial system in jeopardy. Big Wall Street firms got involved after the rescinding of the GlassSteagall Act in 1998, and both political parties, Congress, and the public all played key parts in creating the great financial fiasco. The 1962 Stock Market Break. Another notable stock market break occurred in 1962. In the spring, nothing was wrong with the economy, but the market got skittish after the government announced an investigation of the stock market and then got on the steel companies for raising prices. IBM dropped 50%. That fall, after the Cuban missile showdown with the Russians, a new bull market sprang to life. All of this happened with no change in the discount rate. There have also been situations in which the discount rate was lowered six months after the market bottom was reached. In such cases, you would be late getting into the game if you waited for the discount rate to drop. In a few instances, after Fed rate cuts occurred, the markets continued lower or whipsawed for several months. This also occurred dramatically in 2000 and 2001. The Hourly Market Index and Volume Changes At key turning points, an active market operator can watch the market indexes and volume changes hour by hour and compare them to volume in the same hour of the day before. A good time to watch hourly volume figures is during the first attempted rally following the initial decline off the market peak. You should be able to see if volume is dull or dries up on the rally. You can also see if the rally starts to fade late in the day, with volume picking up as it does, a sign that the rally is weak and will probably fail. Hourly volume data also come in handy when the market averages reach an important prior low point and start breaking that "support" area. (A support area is a previous price level below which investors hope that an index will not fall.) What you want to know is whether selling picks up dramatically or by just a small amount as the market collapses into new low ground. If selling picks up dramatically, it represents significant downward pressure on the market. After the market has undercut previous lows for a few days, but on only slightly higher volume, look for either a volume dry-up day or one or two days of increased volume without the general market index going lower. If you see this, you may be in a "shakeout" area (when the market pressures many traders to sell, often at a loss), ready for an upturn after scaring out weak holders. Overbought and Oversold: Two Risky Words The short-term overbought/oversold indicator has an avid following among some individual technicians and investors. It's a 10-day moving average of advances and declines in the market. But be careful. At the start of a new bull market, the overbought/oversold index can become substantially "over-bought." This should not be taken as a sign to sell stocks. A big problem with indexes that move counter to the trend is that you always have the question of how bad things can get before everything finally turns. Many amateurs follow and believe in overbought/oversold indicators. Something similar can happen in the early stage or first leg of a major bear market, when the index can become unusually oversold. This is really telling you that a bear market may be imminent. The market was "oversold" all the way down during the brutal market implosion of 2000. I once hired a well-respected professional who relied on such technical indicators. During the 1969 market break, at the very point when everything told me the market was getting into serious trouble, and I was aggressively trying to get several portfolio managers to liquidate stocks and raise large amounts of cash, he was telling them that it was too late to sell because his overbought/oversold indicator said that the market was already very oversold. You guessed it: the market then split wide open. Needless to say, I rarely pay attention to overbought/oversold indicators. What you learn from years of experience is usually more important than the opinions and theories of experts using their many different favorite indicators. Other General Market Indicators Upside/downside volume is a short-term index that relates trading volume in stocks that close up in price for the day to trading volume in stocks that close down. This index, plotted as a 10-week moving average, may show divergence at some intermediate turning points in the market. For example, after a 10% to 12% dip, the general market averages may continue to penetrate into new low ground for a week or two. Yet the upside/downside volume may suddenly shift and show steadily increasing upside volume, with downside volume easing. This switch usually signals an intermediate-term upturn in the market. But you'll pick up the same signals if you watch the changes in the daily Dow, Nasdaq, or S&P 500 and the market volume. Some services measure the percentage of new money flowing into corporate pension funds that is invested in common stocks and the percentage that is invested in cash equivalents or bonds. This opens another window into institutional investor psychology. However, majority—or crowd—thinking is seldom right, even when it's done by professionals. Every year or two, Wall Street seems to be of one mind, with everyone following each other like a herd of cattle. Either they all pile in or they all pile out. An index of "defensive" stocks—more stable and supposedly safer issues, such as utilities, tobaccos, foods, and soaps—may often show strength after a couple of years of bull market conditions. This may indicate the "smart money" is slipping into defensive positions and that a weaker general market lies ahead. But this doesn't always work. None of these secondary market indicators is anywhere near as reliable as the key general market indexes. Another indicator that is helpful at times in evaluating the stage of a market cycle is the percentage of stocks in defensive or laggard categories that are making new price highs. In pre-1983 cycles, some technicians rationalized their lack of concern with market weakness by citing the number of stocks that were still making new highs. But analysis of new-high lists shows that a large percentage of preferred or defensive stocks signals bear market conditions. Superficial knowledge can hurt you in the stock market. To summarize this complex but vitally important chapter: learn to interpret the daily price and volume changes of the general market indexes and the action of individual market leaders. Once you know how to do this correctly, you can stop listening to all the costly, uninformed, personal market opinions of amateurs and professionals alike. As you can see, the key to staying on top of the stock market is not predicting or knowing what the market is going to do. It's knowing and understanding what the market has actually done in the past several weeks and what it is currently doing now. We don't want to give personal opinions or predictions; we carefully observe market supply and demand as it changes day by day. One of the great values of this system of interpreting the price and volume changes in the market averages is not just the ability to better recognize market top and bottom areas, but also the ability to track each rally attempt when the market is on its way down. In most instances, waiting for powerful followthrough days keeps you from being drawn prematurely into rally attempts that ultimately end in failure. In other words, you have rules that will continue to keep you from getting sucked into phony rallies. This is how we were able to stay out of the market and in money market funds for most of 2000 through 2002, preserve the majority of the gains we had made in 1998 and 1999, and help those who read and followed our many basic rules. There is a fortune for you in this paragraph. Part I Review: How to Remember and Use What You've Read So Far It isn't enough just to read. You need to remember and apply all of what you've read. The CAN SLIM system will help you remember what you've read so far. Each letter in the CAN SLIM system stands for one of the seven basic fundamentals of selecting outstanding stocks. Most successful stocks have these seven common characteristics at emerging growth stages, so they are worth committing to memory. Repeat this formula until you can recall and use it easily: C = Current Quarterly Earnings per Share. Quarterly earnings per share must be up at least 18% or 20%, but preferably up 40% to 100% or 200% or more—the higher, the better. They should also be accelerating at some point in recent quarters. Quarterly sales should also be accelerating or up 25%. A = Annual Earnings Increases. There must be significant (25% or more) growth in each of the last three years and a return on equity of 17% or more (with 25% to 50% preferred). If return on equity is too low, pretax profit margin must be strong. N = New Products, New Management, New Highs. Look for new products or services, new management, or significant new changes in industry conditions. And most important, buy stocks as they emerge from sound, properly formed chart bases and begin to make new highs in price. S = Supply and Demand—Shares Outstanding plus Big Volume Demand. Any size capitalization is acceptable in today's new economy as long as a company fits all the other CAN SLIM rules. Look for big volume increases when a stock begins to move out of its basing area. L = Leader or Laggard.

Buy market leaders and avoid laggards. Buy the number one company in its field or space. Most leaders will have Relative Price Strength Ratings of 80 to 90 or higher and composite ratings of 90 or more in bull markets. I = Institutional Sponsorship. Buy stocks with increasing sponsorship and at least one or two mutual fund owners with top-notch recent performance records. Also look for companies with management ownership. M = Market Direction. Learn to determine the overall market direction by accurately interpreting the daily market indexes' price and volume movements and the action of individual market leaders. This can determine whether you win big or lose. You need to stay in gear with the market. It doesn't pay to be out of phase with the market. Is CAN SLIM Momentum Investing? I'm not even sure what "momentum investing" is. Some analysts and reporters who don't understand anything about how we invest have given that name to what we talk about and do. They say it's "buying the stocks that have gone up the most in price" and that have the strongest relative price strength. No one in her right mind invests that way. What we do is identify companies with strong fundamentals—large sales and earnings increases resulting from unique new products or services—and then buy their stocks when they emerge from properly formed price consolidation periods and before they run up dramatically in price during bull markets. When bear markets are beginning, we want people to protect themselves and nail down their gains by knowing when to sell and start raising cash. We are not investment advisors. We do not write and disseminate any research reports. We do not call or visit companies. We do not make markets in stocks, deal in derivatives, do underwritings, or arrange mergers. We don't manage any public or institutional money. We are historians, studying and discovering how stocks and markets actually work and teaching and training people everywhere who want to make money investing intelligently and realistically. These are ordinary people from all walks of life, including professionals. We do not give them fish. We teach them how to fish for their whole future so that they too can capitalize on the American Dream. Experts, Education, and Egos On Wall Street, wise men can be drawn into booby traps just as easily as fools. From what I've seen over many years, the length and quality of one's education and the level of one's IQ have very little to do with making money investing in the market. The more intelligent people are—particularly men—the more they think they really know what they're doing, and the more they may have to learn the hard way how little they really know about outsmarting the markets. We've all now witnessed firsthand the severe damage that supposedly bright, intelligent, and highly educated people in New York and Washington, D.C., caused this country in 2008. U.S. senators, heads of congressional committees, political types working for government-sponsored entities such as Fannie Mae and Freddie Mac, plus heads of top New York-based brokerage firms, lending banks, and mortgage brokers all thought they knew what they were doing, with many of them using absurd leverage of 50 to 1 to invest in subprime real estate loans. They created sophisticated derivatives and insurance programs to justify such incredible risks. No one group was solely to blame, since both Democrats and Republicans were involved. However, it all began as a well-intended Big Government program that was accelerated in 1995, 1997, and 1998, when the Glass-Steagall Act was rescinded, and things continued to escalate out of control. So maybe it's time for you to take more control of your investing and make up your mind that you're going to learn how to save and invest your hard-earned money more safely and wisely than Washington and Wall Street have done since the late 1990s. If you really want to do it, you certainly can. Anyone can. The few people I've known over the years who've been unquestionably successful investing in America were decisive individuals without huge egos. The market has a simple way of whittling all excessive pride and overblown egos down to size. After all, the whole idea is to be completely objective and recognize what the marketplace is telling you, rather than trying to prove that what you said or did yesterday or six weeks ago was right. The fastest way to take a bath in the stock market is to try to prove that you are right and the market is wrong. Humility and common sense provide essential balance. Sometimes, listening to quoted and accepted experts can get you into trouble. In the spring and summer of 1982, a well-known expert insisted that government borrowing was going to crowd out the private sector and that interest rates and inflation would soar back to new highs. Things turned out exactly the opposite: inflation broke and interest rates came crashing down. Another expert's bear market call in the summer of 1996 came only one day before the market bottom. Week after week during the 2000 bear market, one expert after another kept saying on CNBC that it was time to buy high-tech stocks—only to watch the techs continue to plummet further. Many high-profile analysts and strategists kept telling investors to capitalize on these once-in-a-lifetime "buying opportunities" on the way down! Buying on the way down can be a very dangerous pastime. Conventional wisdom or consensus thinking in the market is seldom right. I never pay any attention to the parade of experts voicing their personal opinions on the market in print or on TV. It creates entirely too much confusion and can cost you a great deal of money. In 2000, some strategists were telling people to buy the dips (short-term declines in price) because the cash position of mutual funds had increased greatly and all this money was sitting on the sidelines waiting to be invested. To prove this wrong, all anyone had to do was look at the General Markets & Sectors page in Investor's Business Daily. It showed that while mutual fund cash positions had indeed risen, they were still significantly below their historical highs and even below their historical averages. The only thing that works well is to let the market indexes tell you when it's time to enter and exit. Never fight the market—it's bigger than you are.

18

When You Must Sell and Cut Every Loss

Now that you've learned how and when to buy nothing but the best stocks, it's time for you to learn how and when to sell them. You've probably heard the sports cliché: "The best offense is a strong defense." The funny thing about clichés is they are usually true: a team that's all offense and no defense seldom wins the game. In fact, a strong defense can often propel a team to great heights. During their heyday, when Branch Rickey was president and general manager, the Brooklyn Dodgers typically had good pitching. In the game of baseball, the combination of pitching and fielding represents the defensive side of a team and probably 70% of the game. It's almost impossible to win without them. The same holds true in the stock market. Unless you have a strong defense to protect yourself against large losses, you absolutely can't win big in the game of investing. Bernard Baruch's Secret Market Method of Making Millions Bernard Baruch, a famous market operator on Wall Street and a trusted advisor to U.S. presidents, said it best: "If a speculator is correct half of the time, he is hitting a good average. Even being right 3 or 4 times out of 10 should yield a person a fortune if he has the sense to cut his losses quickly on the ventures where he has been wrong." As you can see, even the most successful investors make many mistakes. These poor decisions will lead to losses, some of which can become quite awful if you're not disciplined and careful. No matter how smart you are, how high your IQ, how advanced your education, how good your information, or how sound your analysis, you're simply not going to be right all the time. In fact, you'll probably be right less than half the time! You positively must understand and accept that the first rule for the highly successful individual investor is ... always cut short and limit every single loss. To do this takes never-ending discipline and courage. Marc Mandell of Winning on Wall Street has been reading Investor's Business Daily since 1987. He likes it for its many moneymaking ideas and its emphasis on risk-management strategies. "Lose small and win big," he believes, "is the holy grail of investing." Baruch's point about cutting losses was driven home to me by an account that I managed back in 1962. The general market had taken a 29% nosedive, and we were right on only one of every three commitments we had made in this account. Yet at the end of the year, the account was ahead. The reason was that the average profit on the 33% of decisions that were correct was more than twice the average of the small losses we took when we were off-target. I like to follow a 3-to-1 ratio between where to sell and take profits and where to cut losses. If you take some 20% to 25% gains, cut your losses at 7% or 8%. If you're in a bear market like 2008 and you buy any stocks at all, you might get only a few 10% or 15% gains, so I'd move quickly to cut every single loss automatically at 3%, with no exceptions. The whole secret to winning big in the stock market is not to be right all the time, but to lose the least amount possible when you're wrong. You've got to recognize when you may be wrong and sell without hesitation to cut short every one of your losses. It's your job to get in phase with the market and not try to get the market to be in phase with you. How can you tell when you may be wrong? That's easy: the price of the stock drops below the price you paid for it! Each point that your favorite brainchild falls below your cost increases both the chance that you're wrong and the price that you're going to pay for being wrong. Are Successful People Lucky or Always Right? People think that in order to be successful, you have to be either lucky or right most of the time. Not so. Successful people make many mistakes, and their success is due to hard work, not luck. They just try harder and more often than the average person. There aren't many overnight successes; success takes time. In search of a filament for his electric lamp, Thomas Edison carbonized and tested 6,000 specimens of bamboo. Three of them worked. Before that, he had tried thousands of other materials, from cotton thread to chicken feathers. Babe Ruth worked so hard for his home run record that he also held the lifetime record for strikeouts. Irving Berlin wrote more than 600 songs, but no more than 50 were hits. The Beatles were turned down by every record company in England before they made it big. Michael Jordan was once cut from his high school basketball team, and Albert Einstein made an F in math. (It also took him many years to develop and prove his theory of relativity.) It takes a lot of trial and error before you can nail down substantial gains in stocks like Brunswick and Great Western Financial when they doubled in 1961, Chrysler and Syntex in 1963, Fairchild Camera and Polaroid in 1965, Control Data in 1967, Levitz Furniture in 1970–1972, Prime Computer and Humana in 1977–1981, MCI Communications in 1981–1982, Price Company in 1982–1983, Microsoft in 1986–1992, Amgen in 1990–1991, International Game Technology in 1991–1993, Cisco Systems from 1995 to 2000, America Online and Charles Schwab in 1998–1999, and Qualcomm in 1999. These stocks dazzled the market with gains ranging from 100% to more than 1,000%. Over the years, I've found that only one or two out of ten stocks that I've bought turned out to be truly outstanding and capable of making this kind of substantial profits. In other words, to get the one or two stocks that make big money, you have to look for and buy ten. Which begs the question, what do you do with the other eight? Do you sit with them and hope, the way most people do? Or do you sell them and keep trying until you come up with even bigger successes? When Does a Loss Become a Loss? When you say, "I can't sell my stock because I don't want to take a loss," you assume that what you want has some bearing on the situation. But the stock doesn't know who you are, and it couldn't care less what you hope or want. Besides, selling doesn't give you the loss; you already have the loss. If you think you haven't incurred a loss until you sell the stock, you're kidding yourself. The larger the paper loss, the more real it will become. If you paid $40 per share for 100 shares of Can't Miss Chemical, and it's now worth $28 per share, you have $2,800 worth of stock that cost you $4,000. You have a $1,200 loss. Whether you convert the stock to cash or hold it, it's still worth only $2,800. Even though you didn't sell, you took your loss when the stock dropped in price. You'd be better off selling and going back to a cash position where you can think far more objectively. When you're holding on to a big loss, you're rarely able to think straight. You get emotional. You rationalize and say, "It can't go any lower." However, keep in mind that there are many other stocks to choose from where your chance of recouping your loss could be greater. Here's another suggestion that may help you decide whether to sell: pretend that you don't own the stock and you have $2,800 in the bank. Then ask yourself, "Do I really want to buy this stock now?" If your answer is no, then why are you holding onto it? Always, without Exception, Limit Losses to 7% or 8% of Your Cost Individual investors should definitely set firm rules limiting the loss on the initial capital they have invested in each stock to an absolute maximum of 7% or 8%. Institutional investors who lessen their overall risk by taking large positions and diversifying broadly are unable to move into and out of stocks quickly enough to follow such a loss-cutting plan. This is a terrific advantage that you, the nimble and decisive individual investor, have over the institutions. So use it. When the late Gerald M. Loeb of E. F. Hutton was writing his last book on the stock market, he came down to visit me, and I had the pleasure of discussing this idea with him. In his first work, The Battle for Investment Survival, Loeb advocated cutting all losses at 10%. I was curious and asked him if he always followed the 10% loss policy himself. "I would hope," he replied, "to be out long before they ever reach 10%." Loeb made millions in the market. Bill Astrop, president of Astrop Advisory Corp. in Atlanta, Georgia, suggests a minor revision of the 10% loss-cutting plan. He thinks that individual investors should sell half of their position in a stock if it is down 5% from their cost and the other half once it's down 10%. This is sound advice. To preserve your hard-earned money, I think a 7% or 8% loss should be the limit. The average of all your losses should be less, perhaps 5% or 6%, if you're strictly disciplined and fast on your feet. If you can keep the average of all your mistakes and losses to 5% or 6%, you'll be like the football team on which opponents can never move the ball. If you don't give up many first downs, how can anyone ever beat you? Now here's a valuable secret: if you use charts to time your buys precisely off sound bases (price consolidation areas), your stocks will rarely drop 8% from a correct buy point. So when they do, either you've made a mistake in your selection or a general market decline may be starting. This is a big key to your future success. Barbara James, an IBD subscriber who has attended several of our workshops, didn't know anything about stocks when she started investing after 20 years in the real estate business. She first traded on paper using the IBD rules. This worked so well that she finally had the confidence to try it with real money. That was in the late 1990s, when the market seemed to have only one direction—up. The first stock she bought using the IBD rules was EMC. When she sold it in 2000, she had a 1,300% gain. She also had a gain of over 200% in Gap. Ten years after her start, with the profits she made using IBD, she was able to pay off her house and her car. And thanks to the 7% rule, Barbara can take advantage of the market once it improves. Before the market started to correct in the fall of 2007, she had bought three CAN SLIM stocks—Monolithic Power, China Medical, and St. Jude Medical. "I bought them all at exactly the right pivot point, and I got forced out of all three as the market started to correct in July and August," she says. "I am happy to lose money when it's only 7% or 8%. If it hadn't been for the sell rules, I would have lost my shirt. And I wouldn't have resources for the next bull market." Here's what another IBD subscriber, Herb Mitchell, told us in February 2009: "Over and over again, the buy and sell rules—especially the sell rules—have been proven to work. It took me a couple of years to finally get it through my head, but then the results started to show. I spent most of 2008 on the sidelines, and I now get compliments from friends who say that they lost thousands—50% or more—in their IRA accounts while I had a 5% gain for the year. I think I should have done better, but you live and learn." Also, there's no rule that says you have to wait until every single loss reaches 7% to 8% before you take it. On occasion, you'll sense the general market index is under distribution (selling) or your stock isn't acting right and you are starting off amiss. In such cases, you can cut your loss sooner, when the stock may be down only one or two points. Before the market broke wide open in October 1987, for example, there was ample time to sell and cut losses short. That correction actually began on August 26. If you're foolish enough to try bucking the market by buying stocks in bearish conditions, at least move your absolute loss-cutting point up to 3% or 4%. After years of experience with this technique, your average losses should become less as your stock selection and timing improve and you learn to make small "follow-up buys" in your best stocks. It takes a lot of time to learn to make follow-up buys safely when a stock is up, but this method of money management forces you to move your money from slower-performing stocks into your stronger ones. I call this force-feeding.

You'll end up selling stocks that are not yet down 7% or 8% because you are raising money to add to your best winners during clearly strong bull markets. Remember: 7% to 8% is your absolute loss limit. You must sell without hesitation—no waiting a few days to see what might happen; no hoping that the stock will rally back; no need to wait for the day's market close. Nothing but the fact that you're down 7% or 8% below your cost should have a bearing on the situation at this point. Once you're significantly ahead and have a good profit, you can afford to give the stock a good bit more room for normal fluctuations off its price peak. Do not sell a stock just because it's off 7% to 8% from its peak price. It's important that you definitely understand the difference. In one case, you probably started off wrong. The stock is not acting the way you expected it to, and it is down below your purchase price. You're starting to lose your hard-earned money, and you may be about to lose a lot more. In the other case, you have begun correctly. The stock has acted better, and you have a significant gain. Now you're working on a profit, so in a bull market, you can afford to give the stock more room to fluctuate so that you don't get shaken out on a normal 10% to 15% correction. Don't chase your stock up too far when you're buying it, however. The key is timing your stock purchases exactly at breakout points to minimize the chance that a stock will drop 8%.

All Common Stocks Are Speculative and Risky There is considerable risk in all common stocks, regardless of their name, quality, purported blue-chip status, previous performance record, or current good earnings. Keep in mind that growth stocks can top at a time when their earnings are excellent and analysts' estimates are still rosy. There are no sure things or safe stocks. Any stock can go down at any time ... and you never know how far it can go down. Every 50% loss began as a 10% or 20% loss. Having the raw courage to sell and take your loss cheerfully is the only way you can protect yourself against the possibility of much greater losses. Decision and action should be instantaneous and simultaneous. To be a big winner, you have to learn to make decisions. I've known at least a dozen educated and otherwise intelligent people who were completely wiped out solely because they would not sell and cut a loss. What should you do if a stock gets away from you and the loss becomes greater than 10%? This can happen to anyone, and it's an even more critical sign that the stock positively must be sold. The stock was in more trouble than normal, so it fell faster and further than normal. In the market collapse of 2000, many new investors lost heavily, and some of them lost it all. If they had just followed the simple sell rule discussed earlier, they would have protected most of their capital. In my experience, the stocks that get away from you and produce larger-thannormal losses are the truly awful selections that absolutely must be sold. Something is really going wrong with either the stock or the whole market, and it's even more urgent that the stock be sold to avoid a later catastrophe. Keep in mind that if you let a stock drop 50%, you must make 100% on your next stock just to break even! And how often do you buy stocks that double? You simply can't afford to sit with a stock where the loss keeps getting worse. It is a dangerous fallacy to assume that because a stock goes down, it has to come back up. Many don't. Others take years to recover. AT&T hit a high of $75 in 1964 and took 20 years to come back. Also, when the S&P 500 or Dow declines 20% to 25% in a bear market, many stocks will plummet 60% to 75%. If the S&P dives 52%, as it did in 2008, some stocks can fall 80% to 90%. Who would have projected that General Motors would sell for $2 a share, down from $94? The auto industry is important to the United States, but it will require a serious, top-to-bottom restructuring and will possibly have to go through bankruptcy if it is to survive and compete effectively in the highly competitive world market. For 14 years, from 1994 to 2008, GM stock's relative price strength line declined steadily. What will GM do in the future if India or China sells cars in the United States that get 50 miles per gallon and have a much lower price? The only way to prevent bad stock market losses is to cut them without hesitation while they're still small. Always protect your account so that you can live to invest successfully another day. In 2000, many new investors incorrectly believed that all you had to do was buy high-tech stocks on every dip in price because they would always go back up and there was easy money to be made. This is an amateur's strategy, and it almost always leads to heavy losses. Semiconductor and other technology stocks are two to three times as volatile and risky as others. So if you're in these stocks, moving rapidly to cut short every loss is even more essential. If your portfolio is in nothing but high-tech stocks, or if you're heavily margined in tech stocks, you are asking for serious trouble if you don't cut your losses quickly. You should never invest on margin unless you're willing to cut all your losses quickly. Otherwise, you could go belly-up in no time. If you get a margin call from your broker (when you're faced with the decision to either sell stock or add money to your account to cover the lost equity in a falling stock), don't throw good money after bad. Sell some stock, and recognize what the market and your margin clerk are trying to tell you. Cutting Losses Is Like Buying an Insurance Policy This policy of limiting losses is similar to paying insurance premiums. You're reducing your risk to precisely the level you're comfortable with. Yes, the stock you sell will often turn right around and go back up. And yes, this can be frustrating. But when this happens, don't conclude that you were wrong to sell it. That is exceedingly dangerous thinking that will eventually get you into big trouble. Think about it this way: If you bought insurance on your car last year and you didn't have an accident, was your money wasted? Will you buy the same insurance this year? Of course you will! Did you take out fire insurance on your home or your business? If your home or business hasn't burned down, are you upset because you feel that you made a bad financial decision? No. You don't buy fire insurance because you know your house is going to burn down. You buy insurance just in case, to protect yourself against the remote possibility of a serious loss. It's exactly the same for the winning investor who cuts all losses quickly. It's the only way to protect against the possible or probable chance of a much larger loss from which it may not be possible to recover. If you hesitate and allow a loss to increase to 20%, you will need a 25% gain just to break even. Wait longer until the stock is down 25%, and you'll have to make 33% to get even. Wait still longer until the loss is 33%, and you'll have to make 50% to get back to the starting gate. The longer you wait, the more the math works against you, so don't vacillate. Move immediately to cut out possible bad decisions. Develop the strict discipline to act and to always follow your selling rules. Some people have gone so far as to let losing stocks damage their health. In this situation, it's best to sell and stop worrying. I know a stockbroker who in 1961 bought Brunswick at $60 on the way down in price. It had been the market's super leader since 1957, increasing more than 20 times. When it dropped to $50, he bought more, and when it dropped to $40, he added again. When it dropped to $30, he dropped dead on the golf course. History and human nature keep repeating themselves in the stock market. In the fall of 2000, many investors made the identical mistake: they bought the prior bull market's leader, Cisco Systems, on the way down at $70, $60, $50, and lower, after it had topped at $87. Seven months later it had sunk to $13, an 80% decline for those who bought at $70. The moral of the story is: never argue with the market. Your health and peace of mind are always more important than any stock. Small losses are cheap insurance, and they're the only insurance you can buy on your investments. Even if a stock moves up after you sell it, as many surely will, you will have accomplished your critical objective of keeping all your losses small, and you'll still have money to try again for a winner in another stock. Take Your Losses Quickly and Your Profits Slowly There's an old investment saying that the first loss in the market is the smallest. In my view, the way to make investment decisions is to always (with no exceptions) take your losses quickly and your profits slowly. Yet most investors get emotionally confused and take their profits quickly and their losses slowly. What is your real risk in any stock you buy when you use the method we've discussed? It's 8%, no matter what you buy, if you follow this rule religiously. Still, most investors stubbornly ask, "Shouldn't we sit with stocks rather than selling and taking a loss?" Or, "How about unusual situations where some bad news hits suddenly and causes a price decline?" Or, "Does this loss-cutting procedure apply all the time, or are there exceptions, like when a company has a good new product?" The answer: there are no exceptions. None of these things changes the situation one bit. You must always protect your hard-earned pool of capital. Letting your losses run is the most serious mistake that almost all investors make. You must accept the fact that mistakes in stock selection and timing are going to be made frequently, even by the most experienced of professional investors. I'd go so far as to say that if you aren't willing to cut short and limit your losses, you probably shouldn't buy stocks. Would you drive your car down the street without brakes? If you were a fighter pilot, would you go into battle without a parachute? Should You Average Down in Price? One of the most unprofessional things a stockbroker can do is hesitate or fail to call customers whose stocks are down in price. That's when the customer needs help the most. Shirking this duty in difficult periods shows a lack of courage under pressure. About the only thing that's worse is for brokers to take themselves off the hook by advising customers to "average down" (buy more of a stock that is already showing a loss). If I were advised to do this, I'd close my account and look for a smarter broker. Everyone loves to buy stocks; no one loves to sell them. As long as you hold a stock, you can still hope it might come back up enough to at least get you out even. Once you sell, you abandon all hope and accept the cold reality of temporary defeat. Investors are always hoping rather than being realistic. Knowing and acting is better than hoping or guessing. The fact that you want a stock to go up so you can at least get out even has nothing to do with the action and brutal reality of the market. The market obeys only the law of supply and demand. A great trader once noted there are only two emotions in the market: hope and fear. "The only problem," he added, "is we hope when we should fear, and we fear when we should hope." This is just as true in 2009 as it was in 1909. The Turkey Story Many years ago, I heard a story by Fred C. Kelly, the author of Why You Win or Lose, that illustrates perfectly how the conventional investor thinks when the time comes to make a selling decision: A little boy was walking down the road when he came upon an old man trying to catch wild turkeys. The man had a turkey trap, a crude device consisting of a big box with the door hinged at the top. This door was kept open by a prop, to which was tied a piece of twine leading back a hundred feet or more to the operator. A thin trail of corn scattered along a path lured turkeys to the box. Once they were inside, the turkeys found an even more plentiful supply of corn. When enough turkeys had wandered into the box, the old man would jerk away the prop and let the door fall shut. Having once shut the door, he couldn't open it again without going up to the box, and this would scare away any turkeys that were lurking outside. The time to pull away the prop was when as many turkeys as one could reasonably expect were inside. One day he had a dozen turkeys in his box. Then one sauntered out, leaving 11. "Gosh, I wish I had pulled the string when all 12 were there," said the old man. "I'll wait a minute and maybe the other one will go back." While he waited for the twelfth turkey to return, two more walked out on him. "I should have been satisfied with 11," the trapper said. "Just as soon as I get one more back, I'll pull the string." Three more walked out, and still the man waited. Having once had 12 turkeys, he disliked going home with less than 8. He couldn't give up the idea that some of the original turkeys would return. When finally there was only one turkey left in the trap, he said, "I'll wait until he walks out or another goes in, and then I'll quit." The solitary turkey went to join the others, and the man returned empty-handed. The psychology of normal investors is not much different. They hope more turkeys will return to the box when they should fear that all the turkeys could walk out and they'll be left with nothing. How the Typical Investor Thinks If you're a typical investor, you probably keep records of your transactions. When you think about selling a stock, you probably look at your records to see what price you paid for it. If you have a profit, you may sell, but if you have a loss, you tend to wait. After all, you didn't invest in the market to lose money. However, what you should be doing is selling your worst-performing stock first. Keep your flower patch free of weeds. You may decide to sell your shares in Myriad Genetics, for example, because it shows a nice profit, but you'll keep your General Electric because it still has a ways to go before it's back to the price you paid for it. If this is the way you think, you're suffering from the "price-paid bias" that afflicts 95% of all investors. Suppose you bought a stock two years ago at $30, and it's now worth $34. Most investors would sell it because they have a profit. But what does the price you paid two years ago have to do with what the stock is worth now? And what does it have to do with whether you should hold or sell the stock? The key is the relative performance of this stock versus others you either own or could potentially own. Analyzing Your Activities To help you avoid the price-paid bias, particularly if you are a longer-term investor, I suggest you use a different method of analyzing your results. At the end of each month or quarter, compute the percentage change in the price of each stock from the last date you did this type of analysis. Now list your investments in order of their relative price performance since your previous evaluation period. Let's say Caterpillar is down 6%, ITT is up 10%, and General Electric is down 10%. Your list would start with ITT on top, then Caterpillar, then GE. At the end of the next month or quarter, do the same thing. After a few reviews, you will easily recognize the stocks that are not doing well. They'll be at the bottom of the list; those that did best will be at or near the top. This method isn't foolproof, but it does force you to focus your attention not on what you paid for your stocks, but on the relative performance of your investments in the market. It will help you maintain a clearer perspective. Of course, you have to keep records of your costs for tax reasons, but you should use this more realistic method in the longer-term management of your portfolio. Doing this more often than once a quarter can only help you. Eliminating the price-paid bias can be profitable and rewarding. Any time you make a commitment to a security, you should also determine the potential profit and possible loss. This is only logical. You wouldn't buy a stock if there were a potential profit of 20% and a potential loss of 80%, would you? But if you don't try to define these factors and operate by well-thought-out rules, how do you know this isn't the situation when you make your stock purchase? Do you have specific selling rules you've written down and follow, or are you flying blind? I suggest you write down the price at which you expect to sell if you have a loss (8% or less below your purchase price) along with the expected profit potential of all the securities you purchase. For instance, you might consider selling your growth stock when its P/E ratio increases 100% or more from the time the stock originally began its big move out of its initial base pattern. If you write these numbers down, you'll more easily see when the stock has reached one of these levels. It's bad business to base your sell decisions on your cost and hold stocks down in price simply because you can't accept the fact you made an imprudent selection and lost money. In fact, you're making the exact opposite decisions from those you would make if you were running your own business. The Red Dress Story Investing in the stock market is really no different from running your own business. Investing is a business and should be operated as such. Assume that you own a small store selling women's clothing. You've bought and stocked women's dresses in three colors: yellow, green, and red. The red dresses go quickly, half the green ones sell, and the yellows don't sell at all. What do you do about it? Do you go to your buyer and say, "The red dresses are all sold out. The yellow ones don't seem to have any demand, but I still think they're good. Besides, yellow is my favorite color, so let's buy some more of them anyway"? Certainly not! The clever merchandiser who survives in the retail business looks at this predicament objectively and says, "We sure made a mistake. We'd better get rid of the yellow dresses. Let's have a sale. Mark them down 10%. If they don't sell at that price, mark them down 20%. Let's get our money out of those 'old dogs' no one wants, and put it into more of the hot-moving red dresses that are in demand." This is common sense in any retail business. Do you do this with your investments? Why not? Everyone makes buying errors. The buyers for department stores are pros, but even they make mistakes. If you do slip up, recognize it, sell, and go on to the next thing. You don't have to be correct on all your investment decisions to make a good net profit. Now you know the real secret to reducing your risk and selecting the best stocks: stop counting your turkeys and get rid of your yellow dresses! Are You a Speculator or an Investor? There are two often-misunderstood words that are used to describe the kinds of people who participate in the stock market: speculator and investor. When you think of the word speculator, you might think of someone who takes big risks, gambling on the future success of a stock. Conversely, when you think of the word investor, you might think of someone who approaches the stock market in a sensible and rational manner. According to these conventional definitions, you may think it's smarter to be an investor. Baruch, however, defined speculator as follows: "The word speculator comes from the Latin 'speculari,' which means to spy and observe. A speculator, therefore, is a person who observes and acts before [the future] occurs." This is precisely what you should be doing: watching the market and individual stocks to determine what they're doing now, and then acting on that information. Jesse Livermore, another stock market legend, defined investor this way: "Investors are the big gamblers. They make a bet, stay with it, and if it goes wrong, they lose it all." After reading this far, you should already know this is not the proper way to invest. There's no such thing as a long-term investment once a stock drops into the loss column and you're down 8% below your cost. These definitions are a bit different from those you'll read in Webster's Dictionary, but they are far more accurate. Keep in mind that Baruch and Livermore at many times made millions of dollars in the stock market. I'm not sure about lexicographers. One of my goals is to get you to question many of the faulty investment ideas, beliefs, and methods that you've heard about or used in the past. One of these is the very notion of what it means to invest. It's unbelievable how much erroneous information about the stock market, how it works, and how to succeed at it is out there. Learn to objectively analyze all the relevant facts about a stock and about how the market is behaving. Stop listening to and being influenced by friends, associates, and the continuous array of experts' personal opinions on daily TV shows.

> *"For Safety, Why Not Diversify Widely? Wide diversification is a substitute for lack of knowledge. It sounds good, and it's what most people advise. But in a bad bear market, almost all of your stocks will go down, and you could lose 50% percent or more in some stocks that will never come back. So diversification is a poor substitute for a sound defensive plan with rules to protect your account. Also, if you have 20 or 30 stocks and you sell 3 or 4, it won't help you when you lose heavily on the rest."*

"I'm Not Worried; I'm a Long-Term Investor, and I'm Still Getting My Dividends" It's also risky and possibly foolish to say to yourself, "I'm not worried about my stocks being down because they are good stocks, and I'm still getting my dividends." Good stocks bought at the wrong time can go down as much as poor stocks, and it's possible they might not be such good stocks in the first place. It may just be your personal opinion they're good. Furthermore, if a stock is down 35% in value, isn't it rather absurd to say you're all right because you are getting a 4% dividend yield? A 35% loss plus a 4% income gain equals a whopping 31% net loss. To be a successful investor, you must face facts and stop rationalizing and hoping. No one emotionally wants to take losses, but to increase your chances of success in the stock market, you have to do many things you don't want to do. Develop precise rules and hard-nosed selling disciplines, and you'll gain a major advantage. Never Lose Your Confidence There's one last critical reason for you to take losses before they have a chance to really hurt you: never lose your courage to make decisions in the future. If you don't sell to cut your losses when you begin to get into trouble, you can easily lose the confidence you'll need to make buy and sell decisions in the future. Or, far worse, you can get so discouraged that you finally throw in the towel and get out of the market, never realizing what you did wrong, never correcting your faulty procedures, and giving up all the future potential the stock market—one of the most outstanding opportunities in America—has to offer. Wall Street is human nature on daily display. Buying and selling stocks properly and making a net profit are always a complicated affair. Human nature being what it is, 90% of people in the stock market—professionals and amateurs alike—simply haven't done much homework. They haven't really studied to learn whether what they're doing is right or wrong. They haven't studied in enough detail what makes a successful stock go up and down. Luck has nothing to do with it, and it's not a total mystery. And it certainly isn't a "random walk" or an efficient market, as some inexperienced university professors formerly believed. It takes some work to become really good at stock selection, and still more to know how and when to sell. Selling a stock correctly is a tougher job and the one that is least understood by everyone. To do it right, you need a plan to cut losses and the discipline to do this quickly without wavering.

> "*Forget your ego, swallow your pride, stop trying to argue with the market, and don't get emotionally attached to any stock that's losing you money. Remember: there are no good stocks; they're all bad ... unless they go up in price. Learn from the 2000 and 2008 experience. Those who followed our selling rules protected their capital and nailed down gains. Those who did not have or follow any selling rules got hurt.*"

19

When to Sell and Take Your Worthwhile Profits

This is one of the most vital chapters in this book, covering an essential subject few investors handle well. So study it very carefully. Common stock is just like any other merchandise. You, as the merchant, must sell your stock if you're to realize a profit, and the best way to sell a stock is when it's on the way up, while it's still advancing and looking strong to everyone else. This may be contrary to your human nature, because it means selling when your stock is strong, is up a lot in price, and looks like it could make even more profit for you. But if you do this, you won't get caught in the heartrending 20% to 40% corrections that can hit market leaders and put downside pressure on your portfolio. You'll never sell at the exact top, so don't kick yourself if a stock goes still higher after you sell. If you don't sell early, you'll be late. The object is to make and take significant gains and not get excited, optimistic, greedy, or emotionally carried away as your stock's advance gets stronger. Keep in mind the old saying: "Bulls make money and bears make money, but pigs get slaughtered." The basic objective of every account should be to show a net profit. To retain worthwhile profits, you must sell and take them. The key is knowing when to do just that. Bernard Baruch, the financier who built a fortune in the stock market, said, "Repeatedly, I have sold a stock while it was still rising—and that has been one reason why I have held on to my fortune. Many a time, I might have made a good deal more by holding a stock, but I would also have been caught in the fall when the price of the stock collapsed." When asked if there was a technique for making money on the stock exchange, Nathan Rothschild, the highly successful international banker, said, "There certainly is. I never buy at the bottom, and I always sell too soon." Joe Kennedy, one-time Wall Street speculator and father of former President John F. Kennedy, believed "only a fool holds out for the top dollar." "The object," he said, "is to get out while a stock is up before it has a chance to break and turn down." And Gerald M. Loeb, a highly successful financier, stressed "once the price has risen into estimated normal or overvaluation areas, the amount held should be reduced steadily as quotations advance." What all these Wall Street legends believed was this: you simply must get out while the getting is good. The secret is to hop off the elevator on one of the floors on the way up and not ride it back down again. You Must Develop a Profit-and-Loss Plan To be a big success in the stock market, you need definite rules and a profitand-loss plan. I developed many of the buy and sell rules described in this book in the early 1960s, when I was a young stockbroker with Hayden, Stone. These rules helped me buy a seat on the New York Stock Exchange and start my own firm shortly thereafter. When I started out, though, I concentrated on developing a set of buy rules that would locate the very best stocks. But as you'll see, I had only half of the puzzle figured out. My buy rules were first developed in January 1960, when I analyzed the three best-performing mutual funds of the prior two years. The standout was the thensmall Dreyfus Fund, which racked up gains twice as large as those of many of its competitors. I sent away for copies of every Dreyfus quarterly report and prospectus from 1957 to 1959. Then I calculated the average cost of each new stock the fund had purchased. Next, I got a book of stock charts and marked in red the average price Dreyfus had paid for its new holdings each quarter. After looking at more than a hundred new Dreyfus purchases, I made a stunning discovery: every stock had been bought at the highest price it had sold for in the past year. In other words, if a stock had bounced between $40 and $50 for many months, Dreyfus bought it as soon as it made a new high in price and traded between $50 and $51. The stocks had also formed certain chart price patterns before leaping into new high ground. This gave me two vitally important clues: buying on new highs was important, and certain chart patterns spelled big profit potential. Jack Dreyfus Was a Chartist Jack Dreyfus was a chartist and a tape reader. He bought all his stocks based on market action, and only when the price broke to new highs off sound chart patterns. He was also beating the pants off every competitor who ignored the real-world facts of market behavior (supply and demand) and depended only on fundamental, analytical personal opinions. Jack's research department in those early, big-performance days consisted of three young Turks who posted the day's price and volume action of hundreds of listed stocks to very oversized charts. I saw these charts one day when I visited Dreyfus's headquarters in New York. Shortly thereafter, two small funds run by Fidelity in Boston started doing the same thing. They, too, produced superior results. One was managed by Ned Johnson, Jr., and the other by Jerry Tsai. Almost all the stocks that the Dreyfus and Fidelity funds bought also had strong increases in their quarterly earnings reports. So the first buy rules I made in 1960 were as follows: 1. Concentrate on listed stocks that sell for more than $20 a share with at least some institutional acceptance. 2. Insist that the company show increases in earnings per share in each of the past five years and that the current quarterly earnings are up at least 20%. 3. Buy when the stock is making or about to make a new high in price after emerging from a sound correction and price consolidation period. This breakout should be accompanied by a volume increase to at least 50% above the stock's average daily volume. The first stock I bought under my new set of buy rules was Universal Match in February 1960. It doubled in 16 weeks, but I failed to make much money because I didn't have much money to invest. I was just getting started as a stockbroker, and I didn't have many customers. I also got nervous and sold it too quickly. Later that year, sticking with my well-defined game plan, I selected Procter & Gamble, Reynolds Tobacco, and MGM. They, too, made outstanding price moves, but I still didn't make much money because the money I had to invest was limited. About this time, I was accepted to Harvard Business School's first Program for Management Development (PMD). In what little extra time I had at Harvard, I read a number of business and investment books in the library. The best was How to Trade in Stocks, by Jesse Livermore. From this book, I learned that your objective in the market was not to be right, but to make big money when you were right. Jesse Livermore and Pyramiding After reading his book, I adopted Livermore's method of pyramiding, or averaging up, when a stock advanced after I purchased it. "Averaging up" is a technique where, after your initial stock purchase, you buy additional shares of the stock when it moves up in price. This is usually warranted when the first purchase of a stock is made precisely at a correct pivot, or buy, point and the price has increased 2% or 3% from the original purchase price. Essentially, I followed up what was working with additional but always smaller purchases, allowing me to concentrate my buying when I seemed to be right. If I was wrong and the stock dropped a certain amount below my cost, I sold the stock to cut short every loss. This is very different from how the majority of people invest. Most of them average down, meaning they buy additional shares as a stock declines in price in order to lower their cost per share. But why add more of your hard-earned money to stocks that aren't working? Learning by Analysis of My Failures In the first half of 1961, my rules and plan worked great. Some of the top winners I bought that year were Great Western Financial, Brunswick, KerrMcGee, Crown Cork & Seal, AMF, and Certain-teed. But by summer, all was not well. I had bought the right stocks at exactly the right time and I had pyramided with several additional buys, so I had good positions and profits. But when the stocks finally topped, I held on too long and watched my profits vanish. If you've been investing for a while, I'll bet you know exactly what I'm talking about. It's a problem you must tackle and solve if you want real results. When you snooze, you lose. It was hard to swallow. I'd been dead right on my stock selections for more than a year, but I had just broken even. I was so upset that I spent the last six months of 1961 carefully analyzing every transaction I had made during the prior year. Much like doctors do postmortem operations and the Civil Aeronautics Board conducts postcrash investigations, I took a red pen and marked on charts exactly where each buy and sell decision was made. Then I overlaid the general market averages. Eventually my problem became crystal clear: I knew how to select the best leading stocks, but I had no plan for when to sell them and take profits. I had been completely clueless, a real dummy. I was so unaware that I had never even thought about when should a stock be sold and a profit taken. My stocks went up and then down like yo-yos, and my paper profits were wiped out. For example, the way I handled Certain-teed, a building materials company that made shell homes, was especially poor. I bought the stock in the low $20s, but during a weak moment in the market, I got scared and sold it for only a twoor three-point gain. Certain-teed went on to triple in price. I was in at the right time, but I didn't recognize what I had and failed to capitalize on a phenomenal opportunity. My analysis of Certain-teed and other such personal failures proved to be the critical key to my seeing what I had been doing wrong that I had to correct if I was to get on the right track to future success. Have you ever analyzed every one of your failures so you can learn from them? Few people do. What a tragic mistake you'll make if you don't look carefully at yourself and the decisions you've made in the stock market that did not work. You get better only when you learn what you've done wrong. This is the difference between winners and losers, whether in the market or in life. If you got hurt in the 2000 or 2008 bear market, don't get discouraged and quit. Plot out your mistakes on charts, study them, and write some additional new rules that, if you follow them, will correct your mistakes and let you avoid the actions that cost you a lot of time and money. You'll be that much closer to fully capitalizing on the next bull market. And in America, there will be many future bull markets. You're never a loser until you quit and give up or start blaming other people, like most politicians do. If you do what I've suggested here, it could just change your whole life. "There are no secrets to success," said General Colin Powell, former secretary of state. "It is the result of preparation, hard work, and learning from failure." My Revised Profit-and-Loss Plan As a result of my analysis, I discovered that successful stocks, after breaking out of a proper base, tend to move up 20% to 25%. Then they usually decline, build new bases, and in some cases resume their advances. With this new knowledge in mind, I made a rule that I'd buy each stock exactly at the pivot buy point and have the discipline not to pyramid or add to my position at more than 5% past that point. Then I'd sell each stock when it was up 20%, while it was still advancing. In the case of Certain-teed, however, the stock ran up 20% in just two weeks. This was the type of super winner I was hoping to find and capitalize on the next time around. So, I made an absolutely important exception to the "sell at +20% rule": if the stock was so powerful that it vaulted 20% in only one, two, or three weeks, it had to be held for at least eight weeks. Then it would be analyzed to see if it should be held for a possible sixmonth long-term capital gain. (Six months was the long-term capital gains period at that time.) If a stock fell below its purchase price by 8%, I would sell it and take the loss. So, here was the revised profit-and-loss plan: take 20% profits when you have them (except with the most powerful of all stocks) and cut your losses at a maximum of 8% below your purchase price. The plan had several big advantages. You could be wrong twice and right once and still not get into financial trouble. When you were right and you wanted to follow up with another, somewhat smaller buy in the same stock a few points higher, you were frequently forced into a decision to sell one of your more laggard or weakest performers. The money in your slower-performing stock positions was continually force-fed into your best performers. Over a period of years, I came to almost always make my first follow-up purchase automatically as soon as my initial buy was up 2% or 2½% in price. This lessened the chance that I might hesitate and wind up making the additional buy when the stock was up 5% to 10%. When you appear to be right, you should always follow up. When a boxer in the ring finally has an opening and lands a powerful punch, he must always follow up his advantage ... if he wants to win. By selling your laggards and putting the proceeds into your winners, you are putting your money to far more efficient use. You could make two or three 20% plays in a good year, and you wouldn't have to sit through so many long, unproductive corrections while a stock built a whole new base. A 20% gain in three to six months is substantially more productive than a 20% gain that takes 12 months to achieve. Two 20% gains compounded in one year equals a 44% annual rate of return. When you're more experienced, you can use full margin (buying power in a margin account), and increase your compounded return to nearly 100%. How I Discovered the General Market System Another exceedingly profitable observation I made from analyzing every one of my money-losing, out-of-ignorance mistakes was that most of my marketleading stocks that topped had done so because the general market started into a decline of 10% or more. This conclusion finally led to my discovering and developing our system of interpreting the daily general market averages' price and volume chart. It gave us the critical ability to establish the true trend and major changes of direction in the overall market. Three months later, by April 1, 1962, following all of my selling rules had automatically forced me out of every stock. I was 100% in cash, with no idea the market was headed for a real crash that spring. This is the fascinating thing: the rules will force you out, but you don't know how bad it can really get. You just know it's going down and you're out, which sooner or later will be worth its weight in gold to you. That's what happened in 2008. Our rules forced us out, and we had no idea the market was headed for a major breakdown. Most institutional investors were affected because their investment policy was to be fully invested (95% to 100%). In early 1962, I had finished reading Reminiscences of a Stock Operator, by Edwin LeFevre. I was struck by the parallels between the stock market panic of 1907, which LeFevre discussed in detail, and what seemed to be happening in April 1962. Since I was 100% in cash and my daily Dow analysis said the market was weak at that point, I began to sell short stocks such as Certain-teed and Alside (an earlier sympathy play to Certain-teed). For this, I got into trouble with Hayden, Stone's home office on Wall Street. The firm had just recommended Certain-teed as a buy, and here I was going around telling everyone it was a short sale. Later in the year, I sold Korvette short at over $40. The profits from both of these short sales were good. By October 1962, during the Cuban missile crisis, I was again in cash. A day or two after the Soviet Union backed down from President Kennedy's wise naval blockade, a rally attempt in the Dow Jones Industrial Average followed through, signaling a major upturn according to my new system. I then bought the first stock of the new bull market, Chrysler, at 58 5⁄8. It had a classic cup-with-handle base. Throughout 1963, I simply followed my rules to the letter. They worked so well that the "worst"-performing account I managed that year was up 115%. It was a cash account. Other accounts that used margin were up several hundred percent. There were many individual stock losses, but they were usually small, averaging 5% to 6%. Profits, on the other hand, were awesome because of the concentrated positions we built by careful, disciplined pyramiding when we were right. Starting with only $4,000 or $5,000 that I had saved from my salary, plus some borrowed money and the use of full margin, I had three back-to-back big winners: Korvette on the short side in late 1962, Chrysler on the buy side, and Syntex, which was bought at $100 per share with the Chrysler profit in June 1963. After eight weeks, Syntex was up 40%, and I decided to play this powerful stock out for six months. By the fall of 1963, the profit had topped $200,000, and I decided to buy a seat on the New York Stock Exchange. So don't ever let anyone tell you it can't be done! You can learn to invest wisely as long as you're willing to study all of your mistakes, learn from them, and write new selfcorrecting rules. This can be the greatest opportunity of a lifetime, if you are determined, not easily discouraged, and willing to work hard and prepare yourself. Anyone can make it happen. For me, many long evenings of study led to precise rules, disciplines, and a plan that finally worked. Luck had nothing to do with it; it was persistence and hard work. You can't expect to watch television, drink beer, or party with your friends every night and still find the answers to something as complicated as the stock market or the U.S. economy. In America, anyone can do anything by working at it. There are no limits placed on you. It all depends on your desire and your attitude. It makes no difference where you're from, what you look like, or where you went to school. You can improve your life and your future and capture the American Dream. And you don't have to have a lot of money to start. If you get discouraged at times, don't ever give up. Go back and put in some detailed extra effort. It's always the study and learning time that you put in after nine to five, Monday through Friday, that ultimately makes the difference between winning and reaching your goals, and missing out on truly great opportunities that really can change your whole life. Two Things to Remember about Selling Before we examine the key selling rules one by one, keep these two key points in mind. First, buying precisely right solves most of your selling problems. If you buy at exactly the right time off a proper daily or weekly chart base in the first place, and you do not chase or pyramid a stock when it's extended in price more than 5% past a correct pivot buy point, you will be in a position to sit through most normal corrections. Winning stocks very rarely drop 8% below a correct pivot buy point. In fact, most big winners don't close below their pivot point. Buying as close to the pivot point as possible is therefore absolutely essential and may let you cut the smaller number of resulting losses more quickly than 8%. A stock might have to drop only 4% or 5% before you know something could be wrong. Second, beware of the big-block selling you might see on a ticker tape or your PC just after you buy a stock during a bull market. The selling might be emotional, uninformed, temporary, or not as large (relative to past volume) as it appears. The best stocks can have sharp sell-offs for a few days or a week. Consult a weekly basis stock chart for an overall perspective to avoid getting scared or shaken out in what may just be a normal pullback. In fact, 40% to 60% of the time, a winning stock may pull back to its exact buy point or slightly below and try to shake you out. But it should not be down 8% unless you chased it too high in price when you bought it. If you're making too many mistakes and nothing seems to be working for you, check and make sure you're not making a number of your buys 10%, 15%, or 20% above the precise, correct buy point. Chasing stocks rarely works. You can't buy when you get more excited. Technical Sell Signs By studying how the greatest stock market winners, as well as the market itself, all topped, I came up with the following list of factors that occur when a stock tops and rolls over. Perhaps you've noticed that few of the selling rules involve changes in the fundamentals of a stock. Many big investors get out of a stock before trouble appears on the income statement. If the smart money is selling, so should you. Individual investors don't stand much chance when institutions begin liquidating large positions. You buy with heavy emphasis on the fundamentals, such as earnings, sales, profit margins, return on equity, and new products, but many stocks peak when earnings are up 100% and analysts are projecting continued growth and higher price targets. On the same day in 1999 that I sold Charles Schwab stock on a climax top run-up and an exhaustion gap, one of the largest brokerage firms in America projected that the stock would go up 50 points more. Virtually all of my successful stocks were sold on the way up, while they were advancing and the market was not affected. A bird in the hand is worth two imaginary ones in the bush. Therefore, you must frequently sell based on unusual market action (price and volume movement), not personal opinions from Wall Street. You must wean yourself from listening to personal opinions. Since I never worked on Wall Street, I never got distracted by these diversions. There are many signals to look for when you're trying to recognize when a stock could be in a topping process. These include the price movement surrounding climax tops, adverse volume, and other weak action. A lot of this will become clearer to you as you continue to study this information and apply it to your daily decision making. These rules and principles have been responsible for most of my better decisions in the market, but they can seem a bit complicated at first. I suggest that you reread Chapter 2 on chart reading, then read these selling rules again. In fact, most of the IBD subscribers I've met at our hundreds of workshops who have enjoyed real success with their investments have told me that they read this entire book two or three times, or even more. You probably aren't going to get it all in one reading. Some who have been distracted by all the outside noise say that they read it periodically to help them get back on the right track. Climax Tops Many leading stocks top in an explosive fashion. They make climax runs— suddenly advancing at a much faster rate for one or two weeks after an advance of many months. In addition, they often end in exhaustion gaps—when a stock's price opens up on a gap from the prior day's close, on heavy volume. These and related bull market climax signals are discussed in detail here. 1. Largest daily price run-up. If a stock's price is extended—that is, if it's had a significant run-up for many months from its buy point off a sound and proper base—and it closes for the day with a larger price increase than on any previous up day since the beginning of the whole move up, watch out! This usually occurs very close to a stock's peak. 2. Heaviest daily volume. The ultimate top might occur on the heaviest volume day since the beginning of the advance. 3. Exhaustion gap. If a stock that's been advancing rapidly is greatly extended from its original base many months ago (usually at least 18 weeks out of a first- or second-stage base and 12 weeks or more if it's out of a later-stage base) and then opens on a gap up in price from the previous day's close, the advance is near its peak. For example, a twopoint gap in a stock's price after a long run-up would occur if it closed at its high of $50 for the day, then opened the next morning at $52 and held above $52 during the day. This is called an exhaustion gap. 4. Climax top activity. Sell if a stock's advance gets so active that it has a rapid price run-up for two or three weeks on a weekly chart, or for seven of eight days in a row or eight of ten days on a daily chart. This is called a climax top. The price spread from the stock's low to its high for the week will almost always be greater than that for any prior week since the beginning of the original move many months ago. In a few cases, around the top of a climax run, a stock may retrace the prior week's large price spread from the prior week's low to its high point and close the week up a little, with volume remaining very high. I call this "railroad tracks" because on a weekly chart, you'll see two parallel vertical lines. This is a sign of continued heavy volume distribution without real additional price progress for the week. 5. Signs of distribution. After a long advance, heavy daily volume without further upside price progress signals distribution. Sell your stock before unsuspecting buyers are overwhelmed. Also know when savvy investors are due to have a long-term capital gain. 6. Stock splits. Sell if a stock runs up 25% to 50% for one or two weeks on a stock split. In a few rare cases, such as Qualcomm at the end of 1999, it could be 100%. Stocks tend to top around excessive stock splits. If a stock's price is extended from its base and a stock split is announced, in many cases the stock could be sold. 7. Increase in consecutive down days. For most stocks, the number of consecutive down days in price relative to up days in price will probably increase when the stock starts down from its top. You may see four or five days down, followed by two or three days up, whereas before you would have seen four days up and then two or three down. 8. Upper channel line. You should sell if a stock goes through its upper channel line after a huge run-up. (On a stock chart, channel lines are somewhat parallel lines drawn by connecting the lows of the price pattern with one straight line and then connecting three high points made over the past four to five months with another straight line.) Studies show that stocks that surge above their properly drawn upper channel lines should be sold. 9. 200-day moving average line. Some stocks may be sold when they are 70% to 100% or more above their 200-day moving average price line, although I have rarely used this one. 10. Selling on the way down from the top. If you didn't sell early while the stock was still advancing, sell on the way down from the peak. After the first breakdown, some stocks may pull back up in price once.

> *"Low Volume and Other Weak Action 1. New highs on low volume. Some stocks will make new highs on lower or poor volume. As the stock goes higher, volume trends lower, suggesting that big investors have lost their appetite for the stock. 2. Closing at or near the day's price low.*

Tops can also be seen on a stock's daily chart in the form of "arrows" pointing down. That is, for several days, the stock will close at or near the low of the daily price range, fully retracing the day's advance. 3. Third- or fourth-stage bases. Sell when your stock makes a new high in price off a third- or fourth-stage base. The third time is seldom a charm in the market. By then, an advancing stock has become too obvious, and almost everyone sees it. These late-stage base patterns are often faulty, appearing wider and looser. As much as 80% of fourth-stage bases should fail, but you have to be right in determining that this is a fourth-stage base. 4. Signs of a poor rally. When you see initial heavy selling near the top, the next recovery will follow through weaker in volume, show poor price recovery, or last fewer days. Sell on the second or third day of a poor rally; it may be the last good chance to sell before trend lines and support areas are broken. 5. Decline from the peak. After a stock declines 8% or so from its peak, in some cases examination of the previous run-up, the top, and the decline may help you determine whether the advance is over or whether a normal 8% to 15% correction is in progress. You may occasionally want to sell if a decline from the peak exceeds 12% or 15%. 6. Poor relative strength. Poor relative price strength can be another reason for selling. Consider selling when a stock's IBD's Relative Price Strength Rating drops below 70. 7. Lone Ranger. Consider selling if there is no confirming price strength by any other important member of the same industry group. Breaking Support Breaking support occurs when stocks close for the week below established major trend lines. 1. Long-term uptrend line is broken. Sell if a stock closes at the end of the week below a major long-term uptrend line or breaks a key price support area on overwhelming volume. An uptrend line should connect at least three intraday or intraweek price lows occurring over a number of months. Trend lines drawn over too short a time period aren't valid. 2. Greatest one-day price drop. If a stock has already made an extended advance and suddenly makes its greatest one-day price drop since the beginning of the move, consider selling if the move is confirmed by other signals. 3. Falling price on heavy weekly volume. In some cases, sell if a stock breaks down on the largest weekly volume in its prior several years. 4. 200-day moving average line turns down. After a prolonged upswing, if a stock's 200-day moving average price line turns down, consider selling the stock. Also, sell on new highs if a stock has a weak base with much of the price work in the lower half of the base or below the 200-day moving average price line. 5. Living below the 10-week moving average. Consider selling if a stock has a long advance, then closes below its 10-week moving average and lives below that average for eight or nine consecutive weeks, unable to rally and close the week above the line. Other Prime Selling Pointers 1. If you cut all your losses at 7% or 8%, take a few profits when you're up 20%, 25%, or 30%. Compounding three gains like this could give you an overall gain of 100% or more. However, don't sell and take a 25% or 30% gain in any market leader with institutional support that's run up 20% in only one, two, or three weeks from the pivot buy point on a proper base. Those could be your big leaders and should be held for a potentially greater profit. 2. If you're in a bear market, get off margin, raise more cash, and don't buy very many stocks. If you do buy, maybe you should take 15% profits and cut all your losses at 3%. 3. In order to sell, big investors must have buyers to absorb their stock. Therefore, consider selling if a stock runs up and then good news or major publicity (a cover article in BusinessWeek, for example) is released. 4. Sell when there's a great deal of excitement about a stock and it's obvious to everyone that the stock is going higher. By then it's too late. Jack Dreyfus said, "Sell when there is an overabundance of optimism. When everyone is bubbling over with optimism and running around trying to get everyone else to buy, they are fully invested. At this point, all they can do is talk. They can't push the market up anymore. It takes buying power to do that." Buy when you're scared to death and others are unsure. Wait until you're happy and tickled to death to sell. 5. In most cases, sell when the percentage increases in quarterly earnings slow materially (or by two-thirds from the prior rate of increase) for two consecutive quarters. 6. Be careful of selling on bad news or rumors; they may be of temporary influence. Rumors are sometimes started to scare individual investors—the little fish—out of their holdings. 7. Always learn from all your past selling mistakes. Do your own postanalysis by plotting your past buy and sell points on charts. Study your mistakes carefully, and write down additional rules to avoid past mistakes that caused excessive losses or big missed opportunities. That's how you become a savvy investor. When to Be Patient and Hold a Stock Closely related to the decision on when to sell is when to sit tight. Here are some suggestions for doing just that. Buy growth stocks where you can project a potential price target based on earnings estimates for the next year or two and possible P/E expansion from the stock's original base breakout. Your objective is to buy the best stock with the best earnings at exactly the right time and to have the patience to hold it until you have been proven right or wrong. In a few cases, you may have to allow 13 weeks after your first purchase before you conclude that a stock that hasn't moved is a dull, faulty selection. This, of course, applies only if the stock did not reach your defensive, losscutting sell price first. In a fast-paced market, like the one in 1999, tech stocks that didn't move after several weeks while the general market was rallying could have been sold earlier, and the money moved into other stocks that were breaking out of sound bases with top fundamentals. When your hard-earned money is on the line, it's more important than ever to pay attention to the general market and check IBD's "The Big Picture" column, which analyzes the market averages. In both the 2000 top and the top in the 2007–2008 market, "The Big Picture" column and our sell rules got many subscribers out of the market and helped them dodge devastating declines. If you make new purchases when the market averages are under distribution, topping, and starting to reverse direction, you'll have trouble holding the stocks you've bought. (Most breakouts will fail, and most stocks will go down, so stay in phase with the general market. Don't argue with a declining market.) After a new purchase, draw a defensive sell line in red on a daily or weekly graph at the precise price level at which you will sell and cut your loss (8% or less below your buy point). In the first one to two years of a new bull market, you may want to give stocks this much room on the downside and hold them until the price touches the sell line before selling. In some instances, the sell line may be raised but kept below the low of the first normal correction after your initial purchase. If you raise your loss-cutting sell point, don't move it up too close to the current price. This will keep you from being shaken out during any normal weakness. You definitely shouldn't continue to follow a stock up by raising stop-loss orders because you will be forced out near the low of an inevitable, natural correction. Once your stock is 15% or more above your purchase price, you can begin to concentrate on the price where or under what rules you will sell it on the way up to nail down your profit. Any stock that rises close to 20% should never be allowed to drop back into *the loss column. If you buy a stock at $50 and it shoots up to $60 (+20%) or more, even if you don't take the profit when you have it, there's no intelligent reason to ever let the stock drop all the way back to $50 or below and create a loss. You may feel embarrassed, ridiculous, and not too bright if you buy at $50, watch the stock hit $60, and then sell at $50 to $51. But you've already made the mistake of not taking your profit. Now avoid making a second mistake by letting it develop into a loss. Remember, one important objective is to keep all your losses as small as possible. Also, major advances require time to complete. Don't take profits during the first eight weeks of a move unless the stock gets into serious trouble or is having a two- or three-week "climax" run-up on a stock split in a late-stage base. Stocks that show a 20% profit in less than eight weeks should be held through the eight weeks unless they are of poor quality without institutional sponsorship or strong group action. In many cases, stocks that advance dramatically by 20% or more in only one to four weeks are the most powerful stocks of all—capable of doubling, tripling, or more. If you own one of these true CAN SLIM market leaders, try to hold it through the first couple of times it pulls back in price to, or slightly below, its 10-week moving average price line. Once you have a decent profit, you could also try to hold the stock through its first short-term correction of 10% to 20%. When a stock breaks out of a proper base, after its first move up, 80% of the time it will pull back somewhere between its second and its sixth week out of the base. Holding for eight weeks, of course, gets you through this first selling squall and into a resumed uptrend, and you'll then have a better profit cushion. Remember, your objective is not just to be right but to make big money when you are right. "It never is your thinking that makes big money," said Livermore. "It's the sitting." Investors who can be right and sit tight are rare. It takes time for a stock to make a large gain. The first two years of a new bull market typically provide your best and safest period, but they require courage, patience, and profitable sitting. If you really know and understand a company thoroughly and its products well, you'll have the crucial additional confidence required to sit tight through several inevitable but normal corrections. Achieving giant profits in a stock takes time and patience and following rules. You've just read one of the most valuable chapters in this book. If you review it several times and adopt a disciplined profit-and-loss plan for* *your own investments, it could be worth several thousand times what you paid for this book. You might even make a point of rereading this chapter once every year. You can't become a big winner in the market until you learn to be a good seller as well as a good buyer. The readers who followed these historically proven sell rules during 2000 nailed down most of the substantial gains they had made in 1998 and 1999. A few serious students made 500% to 1,000% or more during that fast-moving period. Again in 2008, an even greater percentage of IBD readers, although not every one, after much work and study were able to implement proper selling rules to protect and preserve their hard-earned capital rather than succumb to the dramatic declines in the year's third and fourth quarters.*"

20

How Many Stocks Should You Really Own?

"Once you have decided to participate in the stock market, you are faced with more decisions than just which stock to purchase. You have to decide how you will handle your portfolio, how many stocks you should buy, what types of actions you will take, and what types of investments are better left alone. This and the following chapter will introduce you to the many options and alluring diversions you have at your disposal. Some of them are beneficial and worthy of your attention, but many others are overly risky, extremely complicated, or unnecessarily distracting and less rewarding. Regardless, it helps to be informed and to know as much about the investing business as possible—if for no other reason than to know all the things you should avoid. I say don't make it too complicated; keep it simple."

identified on intraday charts of five-minute intervals can reveal a stock that is breaking out from an intraday pattern. If this is done with real skill in a positive market, it might work for some people, but it requires lots of time, study, and experience. Should You Use Margin? In the first year or two, while you're still learning to invest, it's much safer to invest on a cash basis. It usually takes most new investors at least two to three years before they gain enough market experience (by making several bad decisions, wasting time trying to reinvent the wheel, and experimenting with unsound beliefs) to be able to make and keep significant profits. Once you have a few years' experience, a sound plan, and a strict set of both buy and sell rules, you might consider buying on margin (using borrowed money from your brokerage firm in order to purchase more stock). Generally, margin buying should be done by younger investors who are still working. Their risk is somewhat less because they have more time to prepare for retirement. The best time to use margin is generally during the first two years of a new bull market. Once you recognize a new bear market, you should get off margin immediately and raise as much cash as possible. You must understand that when the general market declines and your stocks start sinking, you will lose your initial capital twice as fast if you're fully margined than you would if you were invested on a cash basis. This dictates that you absolutely must cut all losses quickly and get off margin when a major general market deterioration begins. If you speculate in small-capitalization or high-tech stocks fully margined, a 50% correction can cause a total loss. This happened to some new investors in 2000 and early 2001. You don't have to be fully margined all the time. Sometimes you'll have large cash reserves and no margin. At other times, you'll be invested on a cash basis. At still other points, you'll be using a small part of your margin buying power. And in a few instances, when you're making genuine progress in a bull market, you may be fully invested on margin. All of this depends on the current market situation and your level of experience. I've always used margin, and I believe it offers a real advantage to an experienced investor who knows how to confine his buying to high-quality market leaders and has the discipline and common sense to always cut his losses short with no exceptions. Your margin interest expense, depending on laws that change constantly, might be tax-deductible. However, in certain periods, margin interest rates can become so high that the probability of substantial success may be limited. To buy on margin, you'll also need to sign a margin agreement with your broker. Never Answer a Margin Call If a stock in your margin account collapses in value to the point where your stockbroker asks you to either put up money or sell stock, don't put up money; think about selling stock. Nine times out of ten, you'll be better off. The marketplace is telling you that you're on the wrong path, you're getting hurt, and things aren't working. So sell and cut back your risk level. Again, why throw good money after bad? What will you do if you put up good money and the stock continues to decline and you get more margin calls? Go broke backing a loser? Should You Sell Short? I did some research and wrote a booklet on short selling in 1976. It's now out of print, but not much has changed on the subject since then. In 2005, the booklet was the basis for a book titled How to Make Money Selling Short. The book was written with Gil Morales, who rewrote, revised, and updated my earlier work. Short selling is still a topic few investors understand and an endeavor at which even fewer succeed, so consider carefully whether it's right for you. More active and seasoned investors might consider limited short selling. But I would want to keep the limit to 10% or 15% of available money, and most people probably shouldn't do even that much. Furthermore, short selling is far more complicated than simply buying stocks, and most short sellers are run in and lose money. What is short selling? Think of it as reversing the normal buy and sell process. In short selling, you sell a stock (instead of buying it)—even though you don't own it and therefore must borrow it from your broker—in the hope that it will go down in price instead of up. If the stock falls in price as you expect, you can "cover your short position" by buying the stock in the open market at a lower price and pocket the difference as your profit. You would sell short if you think the market is going to drop substantially or a certain stock is ready to cave in. You sell the stock first, hoping to buy it back later at a lower price. Sounds easy, right? Wrong. Short selling rarely works out well. Usually the stock that you sell short, expecting a colossal price decrease, will do the unexpected and begin to creep up in price. When it goes up, you lose money. Effective short selling is usually done at the beginning of a new general market decline. This means you have to short based on the behavior of the daily market averages.

In selling short, you also have to minimize your risk by cutting your losses at 8%. Otherwise, the sky's the limit, as your stock could have an unlimited price increase. My first rule in short selling: don't sell short during a bull market. Why fight the overall tide? But sooner or later you may disregard the advice in this book, try it for yourself, and find out the same hard way—just as you learn that "wet paint" signs usually mean what they say. In general, you should save the short selling for bear markets. Your odds will be a little better. The second rule is: never sell short a stock with a small number of shares outstanding. It's too easy for market makers and professionals to run up a thinly capitalized stock on you. This is called a "short squeeze" (meaning you could find yourself with a loss and be forced to cover by buying the stock back at a higher price), and when you're in one, it doesn't feel very good. It's safer to short stocks that are trading an average daily volume of 5 to 10 million shares or more. The two best chart price patterns for selling short are shown on the two graphs on page 288. 1.

The "head-and-shoulders" top. The "right shoulder" of the price pattern on the stock chart must be slightly lower than the left. The correct time to short is when the third or fourth pullback up in price during the right shoulder is about over. (Note the four upward pullbacks in the right shoulder of the Lucent Technologies head-andshoulders top.) One of these upward price pullbacks will reach slightly above the peak of a rally a few weeks back. This serves to run in the premature short sellers. Former big market leaders that have broken badly can have several upward price pullbacks of 20% to 40% from the stock's low point in the right shoulder. The stock's last run-up should cross over its moving average line. The right time to short is when the volume picks up as the stock reverses lower and breaks below its 10-week moving average line on volume but hasn't yet broken to new low ground, at which point it is too late and then becomes too obvious and apparent to most traders. In some, but not all, cases, either there will be a deceleration in quarterly earnings growth or earnings will have actually turned down. The stock's relative strength line should also be in a clear downtrend for at least 20 weeks up to 34 weeks. In fact, we found through research on model stocks over 50 years that almost all outstanding short-selling patterns occurred five to seven months after a formerly huge market leader has clearly topped. John Wooden, the great UCLA basketball coach, used to tell his players, "It's what you learn after you know it all that counts." Well, one know-it-all investor wrote and told us that we obviously didn't know what we were talking about, that no knowledgeable person would ever sell a stock short seven months after it had topped. Few people understand this, and most short sellers lose money because of premature, faulty, or overly obvious timing. Lucent at point 4 was in its eighth month and fell 89%. Yahoo! was in its eighth month after it had clearly topped, and it then fell 87%. Big egos in the stock market are very dangerous ... because they lead you to think you know what you're doing. The smarter you are, the more losses ego can create. Humility and respect for the market are more valuable traits. 2. Third- or fourth-stage cup-with-handle or other patterns that have definitely failed after attempted breakouts. The stock should be picking up trading volume and starting to break down below the "handle" area.

For years, short selling had to be executed on an "uptick" from the previous trade. An uptick is any trade that is higher than the previous trade by at least a penny. (It used to be ⅛ or ¼ point or more up.) Therefore, orders should normally be entered either at the market or at a maximum, with a limit of $0.25 or so below the last price. A weak stock could trade down a point or more without having an uptick. After a careful study, the SEC recently rescinded the uptick rule. It should and probably will be reinstated at some point, with more than a penny price increase being required—perhaps a 10- or 20-cent rally. This should reduce volatility in some equities, especially in bad, panicky markets. The uptick rule was originally created in early 1937 after the market had broken seriously in the prior year. Its purpose was to require a ⅛ or ¼ of 1 point uptick, which would be 12½ or 25 cents, to slow down the uninterrupted hammering that a stock would be subject to during severe market breaks. One alternative to selling short is buying put options, which don't need an uptick to receive an executed trade. You could also short tracking indexes like the QQQs (Nasdaq 100), SMHs (semiconductors), or BBHs (biotech). These also do not require an uptick. Shorting must be done in a margin account, so check with your broker to see if you can borrow the stock you want to sell short. Also, if the stock pays a dividend while you are short, you'll have to pay the dividend to the person who owned the stock you borrowed and sold. Lesson: don't short big dividend-paying stocks. Short selling is treacherous even for professionals, and only the more able and daring should give it a try. One last warning: don't short an advancing stock just because its price or the P/E ratio seems too high. You could be taken to the cleaners. What Are Options, and Should You Invest in Them? Options are an investment vehicle where you purchase rights (contracts) to buy ("call") or sell ("put") a stock, stock index, or commodity at a specified price before a specified future time, known as the option expiration date. Options are very speculative and involve substantially greater risks and price volatility than common stocks. Therefore, most investors should not buy or sell options. Winning investors should first learn how to minimize the investment risks they take, not increase them. After a person has proved that she is able to make money in common stocks and has sufficient investment understanding and actual experience, then the limited use of options could be intelligently considered. Options are like making "all or nothing" bets. If you buy a three-month call option on McDonald's, the premium you pay gives you the right to purchase 100 shares of MCD at a certain price at any time during the next three months. When you purchase calls, you expect the price of the stock to go up, so if a stock is currently trading at $120, you might buy a call at $125. If the stock rises to $150 after three months (and you have not sold your call option), you can exercise it and pocket the $25 profit less the premium you paid. Conversely, if three months go by and your stock is down and didn't perform as expected, you would not exercise the option; it expires worthless, and you lose the premium you paid. As you might expect, puts are handled in a similar manner, except that you're making a bet that the price of the stock will decrease instead of increase. Limiting Your Risk when It Comes to Options If you do consider options, you should definitely limit the percentage of your total portfolio committed to them. A prudent limit might be no more than 10% to 15%. You should also adopt a rule about where you intend to cut and limit all of your losses. The percentage will naturally have to be more than 8%, since options are much more volatile than stocks. If an option fluctuates three times as rapidly as the underlying stock, then perhaps 20% or 25% might be a possible absolute limit. On the profit side, you might consider adopting a rule that you'll take many of your gains when they hit 50% to 75%. Some aspects of options present challenges. Buying options whose price can be significantly influenced by supply and demand changes as a result of a thin or illiquid market for that particular option is problematic. Also problematic is the fact that options can be artificially and temporarily overpriced simply because of a short-lived increase in price volatility in the underlying stock or the general market. Buy Only the Best When I buy options, which is rarely, I prefer to buy them for the most aggressive and outstanding stocks with the biggest earnings estimates, those where the premium you have to pay for the option is higher. Once again, you want options on the best stocks, not the cheapest. The secret to making money in options doesn't have much to do with options. You have to analyze and be right on the selection and timing of the underlying stock. Therefore, you should apply your CAN SLIM system and select the best possible stock at the best possible time. If you do this and you are right, the option will go up along with the stock, except that the option should move up much faster because of the leverage. By buying only options on the best stocks, you also minimize slippage caused by illiquidity. (Slippage is the difference between the price you wanted to pay and the price you actually paid at the time the order was executed. The more liquid the stock, the less slippage you should experience.) With illiquid (smallcapitalization) stocks, the slippage can be more severe, and this ultimately could cost you money. Buying options on lower-priced, illiquid stocks is similar to the carnival game where you're trying to knock down all the milk bottles. The game may be rigged. Selling your options can be equally tricky in a thin (smallcapitalization) stock. In a major bear market, you might consider buying put options on certain individual stocks or on a major stock index like the S&P, along with selling shares of common stock short. The inability of your broker to borrow a stock may make selling short more difficult than buying a put. It is generally not wise to buy puts during a bull market. Why be a fish trying to swim upstream? If you think a stock is going up and it's the right time to buy, then buy it, or purchase a long-term option and place your order at the market. If it's time to sell, sell at the market. Option markets are usually thinner and not as liquid as the markets for the underlying stock itself. Many amateur option traders constantly place price limits on their orders. Once they get into the habit of placing limits, they are forever changing their price restraints as prices edge away from their limits. It is difficult to maintain sound judgment and perspective when you are worrying about changing your limits. In the end, you'll get some executions after tremendous excess effort and frustration. When you finally pick the big winner for the year, the one that will triple in price, you'll lose out because you placed your order with a ¼-point limit below the actual market price. You never make big money in the stock market by eighths and quarters. You could also lose your shirt if your security is in trouble and you fail to sell and get out because you put a price limit on your sell order. Your objective is to be right on the big moves, not on the minor fluctuations. Short-Term Options Are More Risky If you buy options, you're better off with longer time periods, say, six months or so. This will minimize the chance your option will run out of time before your stock has had a chance to perform. Now that I've told you this, what do you think most investors do? Of course, they buy shorter-term option—30 to 90 days —because these options are cheaper and move faster in both directions, up and down! The problem with short-term options is that you could be right on your stock, but the general market may slip into an intermediate correction, with the result that all stocks are down at the end of the short time period. You will then lose on all your options because of the general market. This is also why you should spread your option buying and option expiration dates over several different months. Keep Option Trading Simple One thing to keep in mind is that you should always keep your investments as simple as possible. Don't let someone talk you into speculating in such seemingly sophisticated packages as strips, straddles, and spreads. A strip is a form of conventional option that couples one call and two puts on the same security at the same exercise price with the same expiration date. The premium is less than it would be if the options were purchased separately. A straddle can be either long or short. A long straddle is a long call and a long put on the same underlying security at the same exercise price and with the same expiration month. A short straddle is a short call and a short put on the same security at the same exercise price and with the same expiration month. A spread is a purchase and sale of options with the same expiration dates. It's difficult enough to just pick a stock or an option that is going up. If you confuse the issue and start hedging (being both long and short at the same time), you could, believe it or not, wind up losing on both sides. For instance, if a stock goes up, you might be tempted to sell your put early to minimize the loss, and later find that the stock has turned downward and you're losing money on your call. The reverse could also happen. It's a dangerous psychological game that you should avoid. Should You Write Options? Writing options is a completely different story from buying options. I am not overly impressed with the strategy of writing options on stocks. A person who writes a call option receives a small fee or premium in return for giving someone else (the buyer) the right to "call" away and buy the stock from the writer at a specified price, up to a certain date. In a bull market, I would rather be a buyer of calls than a writer (seller) of calls. In bad markets, just stay out or go short. The writer of calls pockets a small fee and is, in effect, usually locked in for the time period of the call. What if the stock you own and wrote the call against gets into trouble and plummets? The small fee won't cover your loss. Of course, there are maneuvers the writer can take, such as buying a put to hedge and cover himself, but then situation gets too complicated and the writer could get whipsawed back and forth. What happens if the stock doubles? The writer gets the stock called away, and for a relatively small fee loses all chance for a major profit. Why take risks in stocks for only meager gains with no chance for large gains? This is not the reasoning you will hear from most people, but then again, what most people are saying and doing in the stock market isn't usually worth knowing. Writing "naked calls" is even more foolish, in my opinion. Naked call writers receive a fee for writing a call on a stock they do not own, so they are unprotected if the stock moves against them. It's possible that large investors who have trouble making decent returns on their portfolio may find some minor added value in writing short-term options on stocks that they own and feel are overpriced. However, I am always somewhat skeptical of new methods of making money that seem so easy. There are few free lunches in the stock market or in real estate. Great Opportunities in Nasdaq Stocks Nasdaq stocks are not traded on a listed stock exchange, but instead are traded through over-the-counter dealers. The over-the-counter dealer market has been enhanced in recent years by a wide range of ECNs (electronic communication networks), such as Instinet, SelectNet, Redibook, and Archipelago, which bring buyers and sellers together within each network, and through which orders can be routed and executed. The Nasdaq is a specialized field, and in many cases the stocks traded are those of newer, less-established companies. But now even NYSE firms have large Nasdaq operations. In addition, reforms during the 1990s have removed any lingering stigma that once dogged the Nasdaq. There are usually hundreds of intriguing new growth stocks on the Nasdaq. It's also the home of some of the biggest companies in the United States. You should definitely consider buying better-quality Nasdaq stocks that have institutional sponsorship and fit the CAN SLIM rules. For maximum flexibility and safety, it's vital that you maintain marketability in all your investments, regardless of whether they're traded on the NYSE or on the Nasdaq. An institutional-quality common stock with larger average daily volume is one defense against an unruly market. Should You Buy Initial Public Offerings (IPOs)? An initial public offering is a company's first offering of stock to the public. I usually don't recommend that investors purchase IPOs. There are several reasons for this. Among the numerous IPOs that occur each year, there are a few outstanding ones. However, those that are outstanding are going to be in such hot demand by institutions (who get first crack at them) that if you are able to buy them at all, you may receive only a tiny allotment. Logic dictates that if you, as an individual investor, can acquire all the shares you want, they are possibly not worth having. The Internet and some discount brokerages have made IPOs more accessible to individual investors, although some brokers place limits on your ability to sell soon after a company comes public. This is a dangerous position to be in, since you may not be able to get out when you want to. You may recall that during the IPO craze of 1999 and early 2000, there were some new stocks that rocketed on their first day or two of trading, only to collapse and never recover. Many IPOs are deliberately underpriced and therefore shoot up on the first day of trading, but more than a few could be overpriced and drop. Because IPOs have no trading history, you can't be sure whether they're overpriced. In most cases, this speculative area should be left to experienced institutional investors who have access to the necessary in-depth research and who are able to spread their new issue risks among many different equities. This is not to say that you can't purchase a new issue after the IPO when the stock is up in its infancy. Google should have been bought in mid-September 2004, in the fifth week after its new issue, when it made a new high at 114. The safest time to buy an IPO is on the breakout from its first correction and basebuilding area. Once a new issue has been trading in the market for one, two, or three months or more, you have valuable price and volume data that you can use to better judge the situation. Within the broad list of new issues of the previous three months to three years, there are always standout companies with superior new products and excellent current and recent quarterly earnings and sales that you should consider. (Investor's Business Daily's "The New America" page explores most of them. Past articles on a company may be available.) CB Richard Ellis formed a perfect flat base after its IPO in the summer of 2004 and then rose 500%. Experienced investors who understand correct selection and timing techniques should definitely consider buying new issues that show good positive earnings and exceptional sales growth, and also have formed sound price bases. They can be a great source of new ideas if they are dealt with in this fashion. Most big stock winners in recent years had an IPO at some point in the prior one to eight or ten years. Even so, new issues can be more volatile and occasionally suffer massive corrections during difficult bear markets. This usually happens after a period of wild excess in the IPO market, where any and every offering seems to be a "hot issue." For example, the new issue booms that developed in the early 1960s and the beginning of 1983, as well as that in late 1999 and early 2000, were almost always followed by a bear market period. Congress, at this writing in early 2009, should consider lowering the capital gains tax to create a powerful incentive for thousands of new entrepreneurs to start up innovative new companies. Our historical research proved that 80% of the stocks that had outstanding price performance and job creation in the 1980s and 1990s had been brought public in the prior eight to ten years, as mentioned earlier. America now badly needs a renewed flow of new companies to spark new inventions and new industries ... and a stronger economy, millions more jobs, and millions more taxpayers. It has always paid for Washington to lower capital gains taxes. This will be needed to reignite the IPO market and the American economy after the economic collapse that the subprime real estate program and the credit crisis caused in 2008. I learned many years ago that if rates are raised, many investors will simply not sell their stock because they don't want to pay the tax and then have significantly less money to reinvest. Washington can't seem to understand this simple fact. Fewer people will sell their stocks, and the government will always get less revenue, not more.

I've had many older, retired people tell me they will keep their stock until they die so they won't have to pay the tax. What Are Convertible Bonds, and Should You Invest in Them? A convertible bond is one that you can exchange (convert) for another investment category, typically common stock, at a predetermined price. Convertible bonds provide a little higher income to the owner than the common stock typically does, along with the potential for some possible profits. The theory goes that a convertible bond will rise almost as fast as the common stock rises, but will decline less during downturns. As so often happens with theories, the reality can be different. There is also a liquidity question to consider, since convertible bond markets may dry up during extremely difficult periods. Sometimes investors are attracted to this medium because they can borrow heavily and leverage their commitment (obtain more buying power). This simply increases your risk. Excessive leverage can be dangerous, as Wall Street and Washington learned in 2008. It is for these several reasons that I do not recommend that most investors buy convertible bonds. I have also never bought a corporate bond. They are poor inflation hedges, and, ironically, you can also lose a lot of money in the bond market if you make what ultimately turns out to be a higher-risk investment in stretching for a higher yield. Should You Invest in Tax-Free Securities and Tax Shelters? The typical investor should not use these investment vehicles (IRAs, 401(k) plans, and Keoghs excepted), the most common of which are municipal bonds. Overconcern about taxes can confuse and cloud investors' normally sound judgment. Common sense should also tell you that if you invest in tax shelters, there is a much greater chance the IRS may decide to audit your tax return. Don't kid yourself. You can lose money in munis if you buy them at the wrong time or if the local or state government makes bad management decisions and gets into real financial trouble, which some of them have done in the past. People who seek too many tax benefits or tax dodges frequently end up investing in questionable or risky ventures. The investment decision should always be considered first, with tax considerations a distant second. This is America, where anyone who really works at it can become successful at saving and investing. Learn how to make a net profit and, when you do, be happy about it rather than complaining about having to pay taxes because you made a profit. Would you rather hold on until you have a loss so you have no tax to pay? Recognize at the start that Uncle Sam will always be your partner, and he will receive his normal share of your wages and investment gains. I have never bought a tax-free security or a tax shelter. This has left me free to concentrate on finding the best investments possible. When these investments work out, I pay my taxes just like everybody else. Always remember ... the U.S. system of freedom and opportunity is the greatest in the world. Learn to use, protect, and appreciate it. Should You Invest in Income Stocks? Income stocks are stocks that have high and regular dividend yields, providing taxable income to the owner. These stocks are typically found in supposedly more conservative industries, such as utilities and banks. Most people should not buy common stocks for their dividends or income, yet many people do. People think that income stocks are conservative and that you can just sit and hold them because you are getting your dividends. Talk to any investor who lost big on Continental Illinois Bank in 1984 when the stock plunged from $25 to $2, or on Bank of America when it crashed from $55 to $5 as of the beginning of 2009, or on the electric utilities caught up in the past with nuclear power plants. (Ironically, 17 major nations now get or for years have gotten more of their electricity from nuclear power plants than the United States does. France gets 78% of its electricity from nuclear power.) Investors also got hurt when electric utilities nosedived in 1994, and the same was true when certain California utilities collapsed in 2001. In theory, income stocks should be safer, but don't be lulled into believing that they can't decline sharply. In 1999–2000, AT&T dropped from over $60 to below $20. And how about the aforementioned Citigroup, the New York City bank that so many institutional investors owned? I don't care how much it paid in dividends; if you owned Citigroup at $50 and watched it nosedive to $2, when it was in the process of going bankrupt until the government bailed it out, you lost an enormous amount of money. Incidentally, even if you do invest in income stocks, you should use charts. In October of 2007, Citigroup stock broke wide open on the largest volume month that it ever traded, so that even an amateur chartist could have recognized this and easily sold it in the $40s, avoiding a serious loss. If you do buy income stocks, never strain to buy the highest dividend yield available. That will typically entail much greater risk and lower quality. Trying to get an extra 2% or 3% yield can significantly expose your capital to larger losses. That's what a lot of Wall Street firms did in the real estate bubble, and look what happened to their investments. A company can also cut its dividends if its earnings per share are not adequately covering those payouts, leaving you without the income you expected to receive. This too has happened. If you need income, my advice is to concentrate on the very best-quality stocks and simply withdraw 6% of your investments each year for living expenses. You could sell off a few shares and withdraw 1½% per quarter. Higher rates of withdrawal are not usually advisable, since in time they might lead to some depletion of your principal. What Are Warrants, and Are They Safe Investments? Warrants are an investment vehicle that allows you to purchase a specific amount of stock at a specific price. Sometimes warrants are good for a certain period of time, but it's common for them not to have time limits. Many of them are cheap in price and therefore seem appealing. However, most investors should shy away from low-priced warrants. This is another complex, specialized field that sounds fine in concept but that few investors truly understand. The real question comes down to whether the common stock is correct to buy. Most investors will be better off if they forget the field of warrants. Should You Invest in Merger Candidates? Merger candidates can often behave erratically, so I don't recommend investing in them. Some merger candidates run up substantially in price on rumors of a possible sale, only to have the price drop suddenly when a potential deal falls through or other unforeseen circumstances occur. In other words, this can be a risky, volatile business, and it should generally be left to experienced professionals who specialize in this field. It is usually better to buy sound companies, based on your basic CAN SLIM evaluation, than to try to guess whether a company will be sold or merged with another. Should You Buy Foreign Stocks? A few foreign stocks have excellent potential if they are bought at the right time and the right place, but I don't suggest that people spend too much time getting substantially invested in them. The potential profit from a foreign stock should be a good bit more than that from a standout U.S. company to justify the potential additional risk. For example, investors in foreign securities must understand and closely follow the general market of the particular country involved. Sudden changes in that country's interest rates, currency, or government policy could, through one unexpected action, make your investment less attractive. It isn't necessary for you to search out a lot of foreign stocks when there are more than 10,000 securities to select from in the United States. Many worthy foreign stocks also trade in the United States, and a number had excellent success in the past, including Research in Motion, China Mobile, and America Movil. I owned two of them in the last bull market. All of these stocks benefited from the worldwide wireless boom, but corrected 60% or more in the bear market that followed this bull move. There are also some mutual funds that excel in foreign securities. As weak as our stock market was in 2008, many foreign markets declined even more.

Baidu, a Chinese stock leader, dropped from $429 to $100. And the Russian market plummeted straight down from 16,291 to 3,237 once Putin invaded and intimidated the nation of Georgia. Avoid Penny Stocks and Low-Priced Securities The Canadian and Denver markets list many stocks that you can buy for only a few cents a share. I strongly advise that you avoid gambling in such cheap merchandise, because everything sells for what it's worth. You get what you pay for. These seemingly cheap securities are unduly speculative and extremely low in quality. The risk is much higher with them than with better-quality, higher-priced investments. The opportunity for questionable or unscrupulous promotional practices is also greater with penny stocks. I prefer not to buy any common stock that sells for below $15 per share, and so should you. Our extensive historical studies of 125 years of America's super winners show that most of them broke out of chart bases between $30 and $50 a share. What Are Futures, and Should You Invest in Them? Futures involve buying or selling a specific amount of a commodity, financial issue, or stock index at a specific price on a specific future date. Most futures fall into the categories of grains, precious metals, industrial metals, foods, meats, oils, woods, and fibers (known collectively as commodities); financial issues; and stock indexes. The financial group includes government T-bills and bonds, plus foreign currencies. One of the more active stock indexes traded is the S&P 100, better known by its ticker symbol OEX. Large commercial concerns, such as Hershey, use the commodity market for "hedging." For example, Hershey might lock in a current price by temporarily purchasing cocoa beans in May for December delivery, while arranging for a deal in the cash market. It is probably best for most individual investors not to participate in the futures markets. Commodity futures are extremely volatile and much more speculative than most common stocks. It is not an arena for the inexperienced or small investor unless you want to gamble or lose money quickly. However, once an investor has four or five years of experience and has unquestionably proven her ability to make money in common stocks, if she is strong of heart, she might consider investing in futures on a limited basis. With futures, it is even more important that you be able to read and interpret charts. The chart price patterns in commodity prices are similar to those in individual stocks. Being aware of futures charts can also help stock investors evaluate changes in basic economic conditions in the country. There are a relatively small number of futures that you can trade. Therefore, astute speculators can concentrate their analysis. The rules and terminology of futures trading are different, and the risk is far greater, so investors should definitely limit the proportion of their investment funds that they commit to futures. There are worrisome events involved in futures trading, such as "limit down" days, where a trader is not allowed to sell and cut a loss. Risk management (i.e., position size and cutting losses quickly) is never more important than when trading futures. You should also never risk more than 5% of your capital in any one futures position. There is an outside chance of getting stuck in a position that has a series of limit up or limit down days. Futures can be treacherous and devastating; you could definitely lose it all. I have never bought commodity futures. I do not believe you can be a jack-ofall-trades. Learn just one field as completely as possible. There are thousands of stocks to choose from. Should You Buy Gold, Silver, or Diamonds? As you might surmise, I do not normally recommend investing in metals or precious stones. Many of these investments have erratic histories. They were once promoted in an extremely aggressive fashion, with little protection afforded to the small investor. In addition, the dealer's profit markup on these investments may be excessive. Furthermore, these investments do not pay interest or dividends. There will always be periodic, significant run-ups in gold stocks caused by fears or panics brought about by potential problems in certain foreign countries. A few gold companies may also be in their own cycle, like Barrick Gold was in the late 1980s and early 1990s. This type of commodity-oriented trading can be an emotional and unstable game, so I suggest care and caution. Small investments in such equities, however, can be timely and reasonable at certain points. Should You Invest in Real Estate? Yes, at the right time and in the right place. I am convinced that most people should work toward being able to own a home by building a savings account and investing in common stocks or a growth-stock mutual fund. Home ownership has been a goal for most Americans. The ability over the years to obtain longterm borrowed money with only a small or reasonable down payment has created the leverage necessary to eventually make real estate investments possible for most Americans. Real estate is a popular investment vehicle because it is fairly easy to understand and in certain areas can be highly profitable. About two-thirds of American families currently own their own homes. Time and leverage usually pay off. However, this is not always the case. People can and do lose money in real estate under many of the following realistic unfavorable conditions: 1. They make a poor initial selection by buying in an area that is slowly deteriorating or is not growing, or the area in which they've owned property for some time deteriorates. 2. They buy at inflated prices after several boom years and just before severe setbacks in the economy or in the particular geographic area in which they own real estate. This might occur if there are major industry layoffs or if an aircraft, auto, or steel plant that is an important mainstay of a local community closes. 3. They get themselves personally overextended, with real estate payments and other debts that are beyond their means, or they get into inviting but unwise variable-rate loans that could create difficult problems later, or they take out and live off of home equity— borrowing, rather than paying down their mortgage over time. 4. Their source of income is suddenly reduced by the loss of a job, or by an increase in rental vacancies should they own rental property. 5. They are hit by fires, floods, tornadoes, earthquakes, or other acts of nature. People can also be hurt by well-meaning government policies and social programs that were not soundly thought through before being implemented, promoted, managed, operated, and overseen by the government. The subprime fiasco from 1995 to 2008 was caused by a good, well-intended government program that over time got completely out of control, with totally unexpected consequences that caused many of the very people the government hoped to help to lose their homes. It also caused huge job losses as business contracted. In the greater Los Angeles area alone, many minority owners in San Bernardino, Riverside, and Santa Ana were dramatically hurt by foreclosures. Basically, no one should ever buy a home unless he can come up with a down payment of at least 5%, 10%, or 20% on his own and has a relatively secure job. You need to earn and save toward your home-buying goal. And avoid variablerate loans and smooth-talking salespeople who talk you into buying homes to “flip,” which exposes you to far more risk. And finally, don’t take out home equity loans that can put your home in a greater risk position. Also beware of getting into the terrible habit of using credit cards to run up big debts. That’s a bad habit that will hurt you for years. You can make money and develop skill by learning about and concentrating on the correct buying and selling of high-quality growth-oriented equities rather than scattering your efforts among the myriad high-risk investment alternatives. As with all investments, do the necessary research before you make your decision. Remember, there’s no such thing as a risk-free investment. Don’t let anyone tell you there is. If something sounds too easy and good to be true, watch out! To summarize so far, diversification is good, but don’t overdiversify. Concentrate on a smaller list of well-selected stocks, and let the market help you determine how long each of them should be held. Using margin may be okay if you're experienced, but it involves significant extra risk. Don't sell short unless you know exactly what you're doing. Be sure to learn to use charts to help with your selection and timing. Nasdaq is a good market for newer entrepreneurial companies, but options and futures have considerable risk and should be used only if you're very experienced, and then they should be limited to a small percentage of your overall investments. Also be careful when investing in tax shelters and foreign stocks

> *"It's best to keep your investing simple and basic–high-quality, growthoriented stocks, mutual funds, or real estate. But each is a specialty, and you need to educate yourself so that you're not dependent solely on someone else for sound advice and investments"*

www.ingramcontent.com/pod-product-compliance
Ingram Content Group UK Ltd.
Pitfield, Milton Keynes, MK11 3LW, UK
UKHW021908190726
13853UKWH00002B/576